GET BACK UP

(once more)

OTHER BOOKS
BY LYNNE ZOTALIS

Hippie at Heart (What I Used To Be, I Still Am)
Saying Goodbye to Chuck
Mysterious Existence

GET BACK UP

(once more)

Lynne Zotalis

PREFACE

After writing *Hippie at Heart (What I Used To Be, I Still Am)* I felt as if I'd crossed a threshold. Relating the saga, putting ten years of my journey in black and white was cathartic, to say the least. As is fairly common with writers, it isn't long before the muse comes beckoning. That is how *Get Back Up* came to be. Not exactly a sequel, the work stands on its own but definitely follows my life into the subsequent decade. I am not finished with either writing or evolving so it makes perfect sense to embark on this next phase of my existence on this complicated planet as the next years unfold.

Get Back Up (once more) is a work of creative nonfiction. Some of the events described happened as related, others were expanded and changed. Some of the individuals portrayed are composites of more than one person, and many names and identifying characteristics have been changed as well.

This is dedicated to all those I love
who will remain unnamed
because if I forget someone,
I'll never forgive myself.

1   A Life in Process

Still so much fragility in me,
      hidden by bravado.

The tears pour over a welling
      of my lower lid
      to cheeks
      that anticipate anointing.
I lick my lip and it's salty,
      and I miss the taste of my sweet love.

Sitting on this faded plum, nylon chair
      you bought,
      I don't remember where or when,
but you scoured the back roads along the Mississippi
      before you discovered it,
      paying twenty dollars.

      Better than that was the wrong turn onto gravel,
"I found this clearing enclosed by walnuts and red oak,"
you'd tell me,
      knowing I'd fix a picnic basket
      and we'd spend a sun-bathed fall afternoon there
      immersed in the nature
      of each other.

      I can still close my eyes
            and feel your soft breath
            in my ear
            six years after the ocean
            called your name

Have you ever heard of salt water asphyxia? Me neither. My husband, Nick, and I had moved from a miniscule Norwegian community in southern Minnesota to a slightly less stunted 'metropolis' in Wisconsin called Dendrobia, population 9,657 six months before his tragic death. Yes, DEATH! On the third day of our extravagant holiday to Tulum, Mexico to celebrate our 31st anniversary Nick aspirated salt water and died in my arms. He what, you ask? When a person inhales salt water, the salt concentration increases so much that water from your own blood rushes into the lungs to dilute it blocking all oxygen causing cardiac arrest in minutes. Immediate, irreversible trauma. Death. Also, I'll bet you didn't know this: nearly 80% of people who die from drowning are male! Who knew?

Our idyllic empty nest turned into my personal hell, our four grown children having flown to their own lives. No friends, family or connection close enough to gravitate to but I did, at least, feel safe in my four bedroom Victorian residence, built in 1896, in the heart of town surrounded by mostly decent, staid, law-abiding neighbors. On the surface. Nodding, smiling cordial and courteous folks, solitary strolls were pleasant enough but the challenges, although varied and bountiful, were now going to be met with this toughened and wizened heart. Never one to whine or complain, Mother Dearest drummed that out of me, I knew in my deepest recesses that life *did* go on, it could always be worse and I had to make the choice to carve out a new existence.

Healthy lifestyle options include walking or biking to the local grocery store doing my level best to avoid eighty- year-old drivers. They drive as if they're steering the trusty Allis Chalmers WD45 on the back forty. Wide turns, no turn signals, not a clue how to negotiate a four way stop. They look at you like 'who's ready?' hesitate, then politely wave you on, then edge out, then stop, smile, wave you again. I've gotten close to hopping out, marching to the middle of the damn intersection and personally directing the whole shit show. Pedestrians and bicyclists are prudent to keep a wary eye on elders behind the wheel. Either they don't see you or do but haven't grasped the concept of right of way. With pristine façade and ugly underbelly Dendrobia possessed layers of delicious decadence that I, of course, wanted to learn about but would be eighteen years in the discovery phase. Slow learner much?

When one resides in a small town it's acutely and quite soon apparent the overlapping relationships. There are only so many options so you get a lot of recycling of partners. I was not, in any way, ready to date being that it had been over three decades since I'd been with anyone other than Nick. Two starter boyfriends gave me a glimpse of what I was in for but they weren't boys or friends, better classified as manfuckers but that's kinda crass, don'tcha think? Anyway, both train wrecks. So yah, if it ain't Prince Charming, I'm not hasslin' with it. Not perfect, but I know in my heart, soul, and spirit a certain type, most likely a widower— deep— we'd have a sense, almost like kismet — looking into each other's eyes, a spark, connection. We'd both get it. Totally pie in the sky. Like that happens! Cinderella syndrome. If not a widower, then fully divorced, with papers signed, sealed and delivered. None of this, 'I'm in the process' bullshit. We've all heard that one, 'it's too complicated right now and it would drain my assets, so I have to wait until the timing is right.' Like hell, you say! Anyway, *my* Mr. Possibility is ideally an old hippie. I'm not looking, like I said, not seeking.

Resolved. Even content. I know myself. I don't need anyone else. Yes, it's lonesome at times, to have that deepest itch scratched, but what I had for thirty-one years can't be replicated by just *any* man, which brings me back to my point.

What I came to understand in Dendrobia is that eventually it feels like everyone has been *with* everyone else. Envision a population map, names of long-time residents across the top of the page; then you have plastic overlays that you flip down, say about ten, one on top of the previous one until you have this network of interwoven connections involving virtually the entire population. I know stepchildren that have married so that their children connect the divorced grandparents ad infinitum. It gets difficult to follow and isn't worth the effort but seriously bizarre. There was the happily married duo from California, (the west coast always freaks out Midwesterners), that divorced, he 'came out,' and with the divorce settlement she built the trendy Etoile Cuisine in town. There are the local herpes-laden sluts, sharing the wealth, sabotaging wedding vows, bragging about how many amours they've chalked up. One woman found her groom grinding away in a back room with one said skank, just hours after the ceremony and figured, well hell, she'd just keep the guy anyway! About once a year there's a woman who breezes into town from God knows where, as if popped out of the sky on a broomstick with that unmistakable magnetism like being mesmerized by a fatal car crash. The first time I met Geneva I was dining at Etoile Cuisine when she floated in, sashaying right up to the bar, sweet as you please, ordering a glass of champagne.

The bartender said, "We don't sell it by the glass. You have to buy a bottle."

So she says, "Fine, I'll have my glass and treat your guests to the rest."

With a performance befitting a prima ballerina spouting the most distinctive French accent she proceeded to flit from one table to the next offering a quaff to all. I naturally assumed she was foreign, with her charmingly floppy toque perched amid shoulder length chestnut waves, filmy skirt, and tank top defining pert, unharnessed breasts. Sitting down at my table she conversed sprinkling in floridly French phrases to solidify the mystique. The charade was exposed when I learned of her humble beginnings, which hailed from one tiny armpit town to the east, which she'd fled post senior high and did reside in France maybe all of two months. A few weeks later, at the same establishment, she slyly donned an expensive looking winter coat, not hers, and sidled out. When said owner realized her coat was missing, more than one patron immediately suspected Geneva. The sheriff was dispatched, the coat recovered and it eludes me what the punishment was that time. Regaled with stories of infamy she earned her living by suing soon to be ex-husbands, supporting her always outlandish life style and garishly revealing fashion. My favorite Geneva anecdote went like this, driving along a country road she happened upon a fresh deer roadkill. Her passenger helped her load it atop her vehicle and they proceeded to her second floor apartment on Main Street. Hauling the carcass up the back stairs, adroitly butchering it, they discarded the hide and innards in the dumpster out back unequivocally corroborating the tale. A month later, just about the time she'd been incognito long enough for folks to be grateful for her departure while continuing to dread her return, she showed up uninvited to an outdoor wedding wearing a gauzy dress sans underwear. Geneva was escorted

5

off the premises after a brief chase across the lawn. Always the show stealer, the youngsters were enthralled or more likely traumatized by the anatomy lesson. Geneva eventually was banned from so many businesses that soon enough we didn't have to worry about her unwelcome appearance along with antics sabotaging each and every event.

With exes and potential hook-ups, heart breaks and rebounds, it was remarkable there weren't more blows leveled as the evenings wore on. Or murder! It reminded me of a population locked in virtual teen years. Sisters taking cast offs, the ex now Auntie Caroline, confusing children as well as in-laws.

We can't fail to recognize the hippie/co-op/commune crowd (granola munchers), that used to scare me when I patronized the local health food store. They deemed me not natural enough to shop there. I wore make-up and dyed my hair. Which seriously? Hippies are the most in need of a make-over of any sector besides the homeless, who actually have an excuse. Hippies are touting this wholesome lifestyle, but look so unhealthy, right? Like, please, slather on some lipstick already! I should know. I looked like that for about a decade.

Then there are the *arteests*. A few bona fide talents and the myriad of wanna-bes. The country club haves, lawyers, doctors, professionals but one of the best stories is about the prominent, hot shot attorney whose wife 'accidentally' died, he remarried posthaste to his secretary and a few years later 'accidentally' ran off a cliff while jogging, in his bare feet, wearing pajamas in January! No investigation ensued, tight lipped and over-all denial kept the status quo intact. And as far as my understanding goes that was the only lawyer worth his salt in the entire town.

The well-respected pharmacist threw wild naked hot tub parties (invitation only) that if the highfalutin' Lutherans and Catholics had gotten wind of I'll bet they'd have stopped allowing his slimy fingers to fill their scrips. The religious community so polite, (to your face) so proud of their Western European heritage, so passively aggressive, your best friend if you patronize their businesses and attend services regularly but ignore you with not so much as a nod in passing, if you don't. What a remarkably frayed texture woven into the local tapestry.

More beauty shops than any town I've lived in, for good reason, but without more than a handful of decent stylists! The cuts I'd get were nothing like the picture I proffered, not a whit like my description. When finished I wanted to yell, "I'll give you a ten second head start!"

Or the stylist seemed good enough for as much as a year and then it was like they'd completely forgotten how to cut hair or had forgotten I'd ever been in their chair. Hairdressers would actually argue with me, explaining why this or that wouldn't work with my texture, starting to hack away ignoring my protests, me ending up with scary hairy.

Lawn chair night, which I figured a better nomenclature would have been wheel-chair night, was every Thursday throughout the summer months. The hoi polloi would bring a folding chair to set up on the courthouse lawn and listen to local musicians perform. It drew a devoted number of oldsters. Quaint and generally tame. But you've got to love the cracks that occasionally expose the fissures. I wish I would have been witness to the local drunk riding in on his full-dress Harley parting the crowd like the Red Sea. He bumped up onto the sidewalk and proceeded up the courthouse steps. Three tiers of twelve each, making it to the

7

first landing before several do-gooders rushed the offender, rescuing lawn chair night from calamity.

This same individual had the water in his apartment terminated by the city after he refused to pay his bill. Bathing took place, once a week at best, in the Montello River that meandered through town. He'd trot down to the water, and completely clothed, squirt himself with dish washing liquid, rub it around and proceed into the drink. I encountered him one such night on my bike ride, slamming into him at the corner of Main and Broadway, almost running him over. He smacked right into me, splashing as we struck. Luckily, I only sustained a moist splat. Surprised, but not overly, we both got a goofy laugh as I peddled on.

Using every means available to drag myself out of the morass of Nick's untimely death it didn't take much to upset my tentative equilibrium. Wary of the bizarre local society I consciously kept my circle extremely narrow in order to maintain stability. But there were still moments, those events totally out of my control. It was only seven arduous months later I was once again shaken to my core. On that devastating day, September 11, 2001, awakening to a changed landscape, the TV shattered my world. With morning quaff in hand, strong dark roast doctored with equal parts cream and sugar, I stood frozen, the cup tilting just enough to spill onto my recliner. Sinking down, legs buckling the second plane sliced through the tower, Katy Couric trying to keep her voice steady and professional as if this wasn't the most lurid sight she'd ever witnessed, stating, 'the tower is collapsing' and all I could mutter was oh no, oh no, oh no. After downing a quarter Xanax, gripping my coffee cup, stain ignored I sat transfixed, so utterly alone, paralyzed with fear as I dialed each of my four kids. I had to hear them say hello, a single word to connect them, to reassure myself that I still had them.

My oldest son, Aaron, at work in downtown Chicago, I advised, "Don't take the subway, it's vulnerable."

"It's already suspended," he told me, opting to walk the seven miles from DePaul University to his apartment. He promised to call me as soon as he arrived safely home. I'd depended on his take charge attitude after Nick's death. He must have been the one who retrieved my luggage that horrible day. It took three days but I'd finally gotten clearance to bring Nick's body home from Mexico after his tragic death, reuniting with our family in the Minneapolis airport. As I deplaned I glanced back catching sight of Nick's coffin being offloaded onto the tarmac. Did Aaron find the Swiss army knife Nick inadvertently neglected to remove from his pocket before we'd arrived at the airport? How did that resolve? Out of control, life happening independently of one's will.

The feeling was so familiar watching the scene unfold in New York. I had been so completely oblivious in Mexico to details like that, me in shock, post-traumatic stress, every minute spiraling down into the vortex. The force of nature kept sanity intact. God knows how. Aaron even confessed his hope *my* plane would crash so I wouldn't have to deal with death. I didn't tell him the entire flight home I prayed my breath *would* stop.

The mask I wore the first year after Nick died gave little reprieve from my condition. I went to work anyway that September 11th, to the tiny gift shop on Main Street, superfluous beyond imagination. Only one customer ventured in the entire day who tentatively apologized, offering, 'I didn't know where else to go.'

9

Panic attacks, PTSD, the emotional upheaval triggered by the horror of that day kept me in a familiar limbo, wanting to recover but paralyzed by flashbacks. I couldn't get out of it, some would call it wallowing but one has to experience the *now* feelings in order to process, in whatever time frame. The tendrils of memory are welded to my psyche. Now I understand how deeply we were and still are connected, Nick's love, my security, his care implicit. Did he ever let me down? It wasn't perfect, humanity so flawed, but I never questioned his loyalty or faithfulness, holding my heart as if it was his own. If it takes one year, two or five, I shouldn't have to make excuses or try to justify my grief.

One year hence, I'm muddling through, having had to give up my laid back part time gig at the gift shop to work as a medical records clerk in the local clinic, secured solely for the health insurance benefits. Pay is meager, co-workers are MEAN girls, making life a chore trudging through winter months thinking if I can hang on until spring, I'll survive. I mean the worst assholes you don't ever want to meet, let alone encounter every damn day.

That's when I miss my close girlfriends in the worst way. Having a confidante, someone to bare my soul to, drink and laugh with. Since my grade school best friend, who died when she was only nine, I've always formed deep connections. Like one of the elements, air and water, girlfriends have been my life-giving sustenance. I hadn't had time or inclination to cultivate relationships in my grieving period and I suffered for it.

It's taken me weeks to master the confusing computer system with post-its covering absolutely every inch of the counter surrounding my station. The ringleader of the department, (one reason she has it in for me, I surmise, is due to my svelte figure and her rotund one), thwarted my painstaking efforts by 'cleaning up' my notes. The bitch just threw them away. I stuck it out for close to two years, dreading each day as if heading to the guillotine. Jane, blasting through our department like a raging bull, forfeited her breaks, even lunch hour at times, in order to be ahead of everyone else, with a competitive streak bordering on Olympic fervor. There is a type of person, we've all encountered such, whatever it is, chemistry, personality conflict, where there's an instant dislike, mostly unexplainable but nonetheless palpable. Jane was that individual who emitted a soul crushing nastiness emanating from her very pores. In my present emotional turmoil I was particularly sensitive to her demeaning behavior, whether it was comments about my age, my melancholy or some imagined infraction concerning my 'incompetence' she waged war against my presence. I believe her goal was to either get me fired or have me quit out of frustration.

"Jane, you've heard of OSHA rules, right?" I queried, feeling particularly piqued that morning, watching her blast around, top speed, huffing past the rest of us.

Obviously clueless, exasperated at having been interrupted by me, she managed a response, "What are you talking about now?" (wasting my time with?)

It's abundantly clear she sees me as a total slacker as well as way too old to be performing this job efficiently. Which actually I'm sure she applies that particular indictment to each and every member of the office pool. No one can measure up to her ridiculously maniacal standard.

Sitting leisurely at my station, sipping coffee and munching a shortbread cookie I'd made from scratch, my fave, as I began my explanation, "OSHA rules are labor department laws that concern health and safety on the job. We are entitled to a fifteen minute break for four and a half hours of work and thirty minutes if you work more than six hours. There's nothing lazy about me having a cup of coffee. I know you think we should all be killing ourselves for six dollars an hour but your alacrity does not impress me."

I threw alacrity in there being sure she didn't know what it meant. Well, and also to provoke her.

"How else are we going to get all of the charts done? Have you seen the stacks for tomorrow?"

Before electronic records every individual medical chart was processed for the following day's appointments assuring every doctor's notes and tests were updated. Some patient's charts were three to four inches thick requiring painstaking attention to each section.

"You know, if we can't perform the tasks in an eight hour day, then I guess they need to hire another person or two. We all work hard. This break is standard and if you want to kill yourself to satisfy some … "

She stomped off, unwilling to continue the debate and waste another minute slowing her production. My other coworkers took their breaks and were in agreement with me but somehow they didn't garner the same contempt Jane had for me. How lucky was I? On some level I enjoyed the ire I was able to elicit from the twit. Just chill the fuck out! The number of HR meetings prompted by our department's inability to comport ourselves was a blot, admittedly, but I had to hold my ground against inequity. I didn't burn my bra for nothing, didn't participate in sit-ins on my university campus to acquiesce now. What were the 60s for? Instead of peace I was now consumed with animosity having to tamp down my angst to keep the goddamn job. Life is all about fairness, right? Hah.

I can't tell you how many times I had this specific dream during that season. I'd be driving up an incline, getting steeper and steeper, my foot pressing the gas pedal with increasing force, finally the car was vertical to the ground, me fearing a tumble backwards. I looked it up, the interpretation. "To dream of a hill represents an obstacle in your life, a struggle to achieve a goal, the steepness of hill reflects how big the challenge is that you're facing ... feeling the difficulty of a situation or that something is getting harder, that a problem is too much for you. You may also be experiencing an enormous challenge or lots of pressure to meet a deadline. Fighting against the odds. A sign that you need to tough it out. Patience and dedication will benefit you." [DUH!]

OH MY GOD! I thought. But there was no way out. No way to remedy the situation. At least, not at that juncture.

Stress dreams. That occupied way too much of my current and past life, including one from high school and college. You know the one, where you haven't attended class for an entire semester and now it's the day of the final or this variation where you can't find where the class is and you lost your schedule that gives the room numbers and time so you're in the office trying to get a duplicate. I must have had that one well into my thirties.

If I could just be coming home to him. That strange feeling of no one there, no one to rehash my day with, about the stupid people I work with that piss me off or the nice ones that are genuinely decent. He'd know what I meant, together in thought, aligned in ideology. He got it. He used to pick me up from the gift shop, waiting in the warm truck, ready to connect, give me that gentle smile with love and understanding, his eyes reflecting the unspoken bond. It was nice. I miss him. I'll always miss him. Love him. All that first year, I would wrap myself in his green velour robe, still able to detect the faint scent of his deodorant, his flesh, still able to transport myself into security. For that moment. Encircled, protected. Dreams and visitations kept me on the precipice of insanity the first year, me clinging to mélange that I could somehow have him stay, on a spirit, fantasy level. Maybe that's where I was driving.

2

So here I sit. The fresh four inch snowfall suffocates me, now the end of March, caging me indoors. People see a strong person, me camouflaging a desperate need to be taken care of. Sipping my French roast brew, perfectly doctored, I'm comfy enough, not cold but not exactly toasty, looking out the frost spackled window, the thermometer reads a mere thirty-seven degrees and frankly, in the Midwest, anything above freezing is moderate enough to consider an outing. As the snow melts, thoughts meander along freshly drifted snow disturbed only by squirrel tracks and I'm reminded of wild northern winters where snow covered my dad's 1953 Studebaker. The neighborhood gang hung out in tunneled forts, bread-tin igloos, reveling outdoors trudging to the hill above the creek, pronounced crik, careening through stately oaks, precariously halting at the water's edge, oblivious to danger or icy toes. Daddy drove across the frozen river! A short cut into town, only after old lady Pearson hazarded that maiden run. We'd skate for hours, the rink at the end of our block littered with children bothered not one whit or even aware snotty icicles dangling off noses. Finally, reluctantly filing into the warming shack, hand knit woolen mittens tossed on the wood stove to sizzle and dry out. We'd squash together on smoothly worn wooden benches, until we caught our breath and then raced back out anxious for squandering precious minutes of fun.

Now this is as close as I care to be, simply watching the snow through paned glass— diamonds in the sun, bright, clean, tranquil. Pine boughs plunge under the heavy white blanket and I'm thankful I don't *have* to go out, except to walk to the garage, get into my car, from car to store or the clinic. Sledding? Skating? Being flung into snow banks, 'crack the whip' and there are moments in my daydream where wistful memories stir such a longing for that simple joy of a child's winter, this child, that I could almost brave the elements. Almost. I do wish I had that drive or energy and maybe if I was independently wealthy I could make it happen. It always comes back to the budget, invariable necessities. Now my capabilities have to extend to bills, taxes, maintenance, house, car, everything. Alone. I can't ask for help. Well, I can but won't. I want people to offer. Aren't there people like that anymore? The ones that just know or see a need and extend themselves. Philanthropists. Remember 'The Millionaire' TV show with that character John Beresford Tipton? Keep dreaming.

The following day, snow a memory, in my slushy back yard retreat I'm enveloped by a six foot privacy fence where I can isolate and relax with sunshine baking color into my pale flesh. So much better than anti-depressants. I've tried two such medications with no success. It's like my head is on someone else's body, my heart pounding to freak-out intensity. Why do we all have to be better? Happy? Why can't I be left in my funk, on the brink, in this tough place, with heartache? Without? Without the love of my life, comfort of my soulmate? Processing Nick's death I chronicled every dream I could recall finding comfort in such nebulous visitations whether real or fabricated. I even convinced myself if I was in the right head or heart space I could facilitate his contacts. This one particular occurrence was so tangible when he laid down next to me, palpable, feeling the pressure curling up my legs, around my back, pressing, touching, contact. It woke me up. *He* did. Lying down next to me, on top of the fluffy down comforter, the familiar gentleness there, existent. It was shocking but so intimate, so welcome. My soul groaned, 'stay, stay through the night.' Maybe he'd been with me, lying next to me for hours, soothing, reassuring but I didn't become cognizant until. Until what? Until he let me, allowed me to… see… feel him? No one could ever convince me it didn't happen. That singular sense has not been extinguished, ablaze, still, now two years later. Someone said or I read that as long as you were together, that is how long their absence is felt. Even forever. Or how 'bout takotsubo cardiomyopathy, where one dies of a broken heart? A thirty-one year connection, woven together in everything will require many more years to figure out how to live without Nick. All we get to keep are our precious memories.

Whether classic insomnia or those mind-bending dreams, sleep is continually elusive. When I take my clothes off— well, no, downstairs, first I fill up a water glass and then fill the Brita pitcher. Done. Bring the water up with me and I forget my phone, so have to go back downstairs and get it. Now, in my room I take my pants off so I can rub my progesterone cream into my thighs. I leave my shirt on because at night it's so frikkin' cold still or maybe it's just this house. While the cream soaks in I look through three closets (I have a major problem) for a shirt to wear with my jeans tomorrow. I'm going to the last day of a much coveted writer's conference so I have to figure this out. Because how can you be taken seriously if your outfit doesn't at least hint competence, creativity, and productive life? Maybe I'm expecting too much from a shirt. I get that settled, until morning, at which time I'll hear the fashion demon scream, 'ABORT, ABORT!' Then I'll throw something on haphazardly and say, "I don't give a shit, I'm fine, I'm together." The writer's scarf draped around my neck will at least signify my belonging. I laughed out loud reading Nora Ephron's book, *I Feel Bad About My Neck* when she described noticing her lady friends attired in black turtlenecks, every one of them, in that aha! moment of awareness over the collective saggy under-chin, (turkey neck wattle) also found on the under arm unaffectionately referred to as the hammock. The worst is the errant chin and neck hairs that are difficult to detect until they're an inch long. Tweezers don practically every flat surface of my house, but the most useful is having one in my car. As I idle at a red light, in the bright sunshine I cock my mirror examining the chin and neck and every time, I swear, there's one I missed.

I can't recall which Woody Allen film it is where his lady seated at her vanity is mouthing vowels stretching her neck and jaw muscles and he tells her to knock it off because it looks like she's having an epileptic seizure. Hey, a girl's gotta do, right? At a certain point of aging, I noticed troubling signs. Dried up syndrome. Skin, fingernails, hair, VaJ.J. My hair is mostly grey-white and I'm deciding whether to let it go or dye it. I do love the drama of a stark snowy shock, sort of like swirling smoke.

I was getting ready for bed, right? Brushing my teeth with the Sonicare, instead of the two minute quota, I spend two top and two more bottom because I had gum surgery a few years back and I'm freaked as hell. It was a nightmare. A dentist told me I'd lose my teeth if I didn't have the surgery and like an idiot I didn't think to ask him 'When?' I'll never do it again. Brush, brush, brush, then floss, then I do gum sticks or this rubber tipped gum massager or those teeny brushes that go between your teeth. Take a breath... put in a period already. Anyway, I've forgotten to rinse and gargle with mouthwash because I ran out and seriously, do I need to?! I told the periodontist I had to quit my job in order to have time to maintain my oral health.

Now I'm in bed. I put on my toe separators. This is supposed to alleviate squashed nerve syndrome (Morton's neuroma). If you give a shit, look it up. Did I mention the layer of Oil of Olay that slathers me in youth, smoothing out my wrinkles as I sleep? God, I wish I had more time to break out the dildo, also wrinkle curative, but I'm way too tired by this time. I have to journal which I do longhand, pen and spiral notebook thank you very much. I read a few pages of my current book whereupon my eyes cross, I reach up and turn off the light, feel around my bed for all my paraphernalia and start getting settled. I have three magnets. Two go on back areas, where it aches, and one on my left sinus, which I keep in place with an eye pillow. Supposedly, magnets have energy that increase circulation, alleviating pain. I have four pillows. Two scrunched together under my head and one on either side, against my ears to block out noise. Ear plugs don't work. I can't, for the life of me, get them to stay in. My ears are not receptive hosts. Stuck-up bitches!

Is that all? So as I lay there my mind, the committee, begins its calisthenics. What shall we deduce, reconnoiter, rehash, imagine, envision, ad infinitum until I realize, damn me, fifteen minutes have elapsed. So I begin my latest sure-fire knock-out method, counting backwards from three hundred by threes. I learned it from Anne Lamott in her novel, *Crooked Little Heart*. It works every time bringing slumber before I reach one hundred. Once in a great while I have to do it twice but then I'm good until I wake up either at 1:00 or 2:00 to pee or just because my sinus is very plugged or my ear is aching where I'm putting pressure on it with all my pillows. And I'm tired becauuuuse …? GOOD NIGHT!

But after journaling now I have to pee—I *should* rub my feet with cream and put socks on as long as I'm up. God, would I be a catch for some guy! Anyone?

We are not meant to be alone—not meant to be solitary and as much as I reconcile myself to that status, my heart is always moved by love stories, by intimate letters, by observing the gentle touch of someone's hand upon a shoulder, imagining one finger gingerly running the length of my spine, whispered touch of lips on my earlobe, tasting, the hand like velvet sliding along my inner thigh, the small of my back. So many things, the smallest gesture signifying tenderness, eliciting a silent groan in my viscera, not to mention my groin. It's there, at each witnessed occurrence and yet even though I've felt it untold times, it still surprises me the depth to which I experience the pang, the heart on fire.

There must be something innate—survival of the species—that will not be extinguished. I can use all the logic I'm able to muster convincing myself that my life is complete, full and 'singly' fine until I read, see, or hear anything to do with the romantic, the arrow slicing effortlessly through my cool exterior, my façade, showing me the dominion of such sentimentality.

Loneliness is a powerful force. When asked recently if I was dating, not having given it much thought, I over-explained instead of being honest and simply saying, no.

Now I'm ready for the next time. It is bizarre to me that people think you need help in forming social connections. I didn't even have any kind of personal relationship with said set-up person which blows me away. I really don't have need of a man. Two years widowed is going along alright, making my way. I've come to terms with it, me, a single person. A singularly *angry* person.

Then in the midst of that late spring snow, which I don't have energy to shovel or even haul out the snow blower, I'm getting my period again. Goddammit! That's it for that birth control pill! Why? Everything had all but ceased when my doctor recommended taking it for the hormones due to my post-menopausal condition. What does that mean? My body says one thing, fini, and the doctor says, no, take the pill, so I have my period again. What the hell for? Don't our bodies know how to work, how to end it? Isn't there a natural reason, a biological sequence of events? Why circumvent all that to keep a uterus functioning like a thirty or forty year old? He also told me it would help my inner-bitch. Not his exact words but I know what he intimated. God, such cramping, such heavy bleeding after six months of blessed cessation. I debated whether to go to the ER, but I couldn't afford it. It's a brutal reality, these choices. Shocking, slapping me awake, profoundly hard truths to face. How long do you suffer, hemorrhage before knuckling under to the debt of medical expenses. This time I toughed it out and I quit the pill. Pondering the subject it occurred to me that possibly older men's universal prostate issue could be nature's balance for us women having to cope with periods a major portion of our lives. At any rate, it makes me think it's equitable.

21

Pulling myself up, I dress for work, summoning energy, strength, optimism, being pressed, stressed, till I'm spent, coming home to glorious peace in my yard, the sunset calming every trouble. The double lot with its privacy fence is partly why Nick and I settled on this property. Daffodils and tulips embroider the double lot dancing, mingling amidst our respite. Those fabulous seven months. That's all he got. And then it came crashing down. Moving from the country to the center of town after thirty-five years was a transition that still required a modicum of privacy. With twenty trees amid perennial gardens my sanctuary is my sanity, my solace. Forget about the worrisome circumstances, forget about the job I mostly hate, the people that grate. Remember the sweetness of love, the tenderness of Nick's shoulder, arm pressing against mine as we spotted the evening's first twinkling lights of stars and fireflies, silence, serenity, relishing the swish, swish of the majestic maple swaying in the summer breeze on idyllic summer nights. I could sleep outside. But I have to get up for work. Obligated. Compelled. I have to have that pay check. I think, God *I'd* make a good humanitarian, helping so many in need, spreading it around. I maintain a fantasy, a mental list of designees who have urgent financial problems that I would meet if I won the lottery. Why do some have such lavish, extravagant life styles, spending millions on homes, vehicles, whatever? And for what? Are they happy? Thoughts drift to causes I continually shake my head over. Lack of education funding, hungry, even starving children, the shrinking middle class vs. the 1%.

One of my best longtime friends finally found time to visit. Our plans having been waylaid for months. Martha and I go back decades, now sharing widow status after raising kids together. The infusion, spending the afternoon with girl talk is a lifeline.

"How could we let so much time elapse?" she queried.

I want to say, "Because you don't call me or understand how lonesome and desperate I've become." But instead, I hug her as we sit on the couch in the TV room where I'd served lunch. Tuna sandwiches, dill pickles, sparkling water, both of us agreeing it's too early for wine. And she has to drive.

Talking with our mouths full, not wasting a single minute, Martha said, "It's so good to be with you, see that you're doing okay. I so worry about you, your situation, too far from me."

"I know."

It's an hour and a half drive to Martha's, us both working full time and to carve out time together, well, this was our first in over a year.

I don't want to launch right into my failings, depression, job stress, so I wade in, "So how are the kids, where are they? I have a hard time keeping up with your five as well as my four, their spouses, work, it's exhausting."

"You don't have to tell me. They're all fine, busy, can't visit as much as I want or like."

"That's the thing, right? I want to see them so much more, want them to be involved in my life but I can't let them know how needy I am and to travel to see them is cost prohibitive with not enough time to do it. Oh God, I can barely hang on some days."

Martha sensed the frayed edge unraveling as my eyes welled. Hers filled at seeing it and we just let it go, me sobbing, "I don't know if I can do it. I *am* going on, moving on but it always has that heaviness, pervasive emptiness. I have thoughts of something seriously wrong with me, maybe

I won't wake up, there's this dizziness, a confusion, an ache all over with random pain, my chest hurts, my vision goes haywire and I can't tell if it's all imagination or a migraine coming on, or what if it's a stroke. I'm so goddamn tired. Exhausted, but then I lie down at night and can't nod off or wake after three hours."

"Is that all?" Martha quipped, trying to lighten it up, slightly.

"No, not half. I have this bitch boss that one of the others calls Satan. Her husband cheated on her so she's hurting, the boss, and betrayal engenders mistrust, hate. I like to say, 'I hate everyone. I googled that and this one site was Let Me Tell You Why I Hate Everyone.' I'm glad I'm not the only one! Anyway, the boss is such a cold individual and I don't want to trash her but what a target. I'm grateful to have this job but it sucks. It's so hard going there, being in that atmosphere of judgment, jealousy. Then I make mistakes because I'm paranoid and I think I have a tumor, and I'll have an aneurism."

"You know I'm a nurse, right? You know you're okay."

"Of course, how would I forget that? Help. Tell me what's going on."

"Well, it's mainly stress, the way I see it. Money, right? That's such a huge component and how do we function without that security? Is there anything else you can do? You were a floral designer in your other life. Isn't there a shop here that you could work for?"

"The thing is that I need health insurance and they don't offer that. I'd apply in a heartbeat and know they'd hire me but I'm afraid to take that risk."

"Right, I get it but on the other hand, this present situation is going to ruin your health. Rather absurd in the larger picture. You don't show this side of yourself often. I know it's there but you are such a good actress, putting out confidence, ability. Maybe you need to have more outlets of expression, where you can be real, vent. I am so sorry you are going through this."

She held me, heart to heart, soul sisters and it was exactly the tonic I needed to weather the weeks ahead. Sometimes all it takes is a friend. With my schedule I hadn't had any time or energy left over to cultivate that element and sorely missed quality female relationships. The older you get the harder it seems to make new friends. People pretty much have their circles delineated, aren't looking to extend, especially in a small community. Especially if you don't go to church. Their church. I rambled on about my massive conspiracy theory that I'd been mulling over since my switch to a new job as a pharmacy tech. The lateral move wasn't the fix I thought it would be, with equally MEAN girls and a near psychotic boss. The pharmacy industry acquainted me with inordinate percentages of children on Ritalin, controlling, dumbing down, compounding their ADHD with poor diets loaded with sugar, high fructose corn syrup, fat and caffeine. How can children be expected to sit still or concentrate on anything for any length of time? Constantly attached to their cell phone, hovered over by parents, never given the opportunity to figure out a dilemma, work their way out of trouble, losing or never even developing their sense of adventure or exploration. Where will our leaders and inventors come from? God, in the 60s we'd ride our bikes (bike hikes), in Minneapolis to the metro airport, twenty miles roundtrip. That was before the freeway was the only route. It took the entire Saturday. Our parents didn't have a clue where we were and they didn't give a shit. Adults, as well, on antidepressants without any coinciding therapy or counseling, just blanket prescriptions to mask the problem, a panacea. So everyone is numbed out. No more deep feelings, except the rage that must explode at some point, resulting in mass shootings. Whole schools, entire towns placid, uncaring. Is that how the war machine continues?

I was on a serious roll, waxing philosophical about how I call myself a peacemaker, confessing to Martha I haven't talked to my brother in years, not solely because he's a religious fanatic but being a recovering Jesus freak myself, I'm now passionate about liberal, democratic ideals which explains my guardedness toward my Repulsican sister. Or is it Repube lican?

Opining further thoughts on war, I asked, "What makes the human race fight, constantly contending with each other or resisting another's beliefs? What makes us think our way is the only way, better?"

Martha interrupted, "Ya, about that, I wanted to remember to ask whatever happened to your brother? I remember you telling me how you and Nick bailed him out, again and again, rescuing him from how many near death incidents?"

"Oh, God, that one time he got to the Twin Cities, I don't remember, probably hitchhiked from California or Montana or who knows where? He was supposed to be on the corner of 6th and Robert Street downtown St. Paul and we'd pick him up and take him to our house to give him yet another fresh start. Coming around the block for the second time I looked at this man and finally recognized my brother. Wearing grubby pants and a weird plaid short sleeved shirt he leaned up against a building holding a small paper sack. Nick pulled over as I waved him in wondering how this could be the same person. Too thin, glassy eyed, matted hair and one measly

26

sack to his name. It was one of the most pathetic experiences I'd had. Anyway, we tried so many times and finally gave up."

Martha offered, "Well, I think you did all you could. At some point you have to let fate play out, let the chips fall and hope for the best. You guys went above and beyond."

Continuing along the conversation we'd been having about my previous hypocritically fundamental beliefs, and as often happened, the church's rhetoric didn't align with practice because in essence God was really a lot more pissed off than anyone thought. Hence, the judgementalism, self-righteous intolerance. I *do* want peace in my life, in the world, but like God, I'm a lot more pissed off than I let on and also one degree away from being PPO, permanently pissed off!

Martha agreed, of course, particularly regarding the rabid dispensing of pharmaceuticals. As a medical professional she dealt with it firsthand. Her thoughts about food additives, high fructose corn syrup and the altered nature of food in the last forty years made perfect sense. I made a note to look up the connection between pervasive obesity and when diets changed so drastically with junk and fast food, wanting to determine how much high fructose corn syrup was contributing to the now epidemic obesity rates.

We went on and on, both of us needing that conversation, our values so aligned. Relationships, attachment dysfunction, the divorce rate, consumerism, plastic filled oceans, throw-away society destroying our economy with capitalist greed and one-upmanship, keeping up with the Joneses.

Picking up the Time magazine from the coffee table, I flipped to an article I'd read by Leonard Michaels, reading an excerpt:

"How many generations does it affect as children grow up in broken homes? Do they learn to value people in the expendable context? Even if it's for self-preservation or protection. The pain continuum: hurting people hurt people. It's difficult to have sympathy when someone wrongs you but the cycle has to be interrupted.

I read, "Adultery is not about sex or romance. Ultimately, it is about how little we mean to one another."

Martha added, "Even if it's for self-preservation or protection. I totally believe that. Not happy with work. Do the job, get the check to perpetuate the vicious cycle of more and better. Is that how we pacify the need, the emptiness? Are deep, long-term relationships and friendships replaced by things, the substitute for contentment on a personal level? Where does it end?"

"Why don't we care... more? Enough to protest the present system? Fear? Disconnection, dysfunction?"

Martha shook her head, taking a sip of tea.

"I shouldn't even say this but you wouldn't believe how many people are on medication for herpes in this town. Christ, it's a huge percentage. Good to know if I ever have sex again!"

That lightened the mood considerably both of us chuckling. Martha bolstered me, always encouraging, forever loyal, applauding my decision to vacate the clinic for my new pharmacy tech position but then, all too soon, it was time for her to get going, both of us promising to see each other more often. Her love was a powerful infusion of hope.

Unfortunately, hope was short lived. Sadly, I'd jumped from the frying pan into the fire. Most people take fifteen months to two years to be certified as a pharmacy tech. But the pharmacist had assured me they'd train me in all of the complicated aspects. HAH! Big mistake. The job market for me was a revolving door of frustration for approximately three years trying to stay afloat, toughing it out at several service positions. I had this analogy for the way my brain worked at this age of maturity. Likening it to an old juke box, I imagined trying to recall a certain fact or name or event, so, like the long arm retrieving the record it would slide back and forth until it found the proper slot, falling into place to play. The same thing applied as a thought bobbed around in my brain until it found the proper synapse, and BOOM! George Washington Carver, or whatever.

3

The first year after Nick died I contemplated suicide as a plausible option, a path out of agony. Thankfully, I could not saddle my kids with that trauma. They saved me. At that juncture of my life I became the child, relying on them to rescue me, to stand in the gap while I wallowed in grief unable to pull myself out of it. Intense grief breeds a terrible kind of madness. I needed them so desperately and they stepped up but subsequently their lives separated from me. Too far, in my opinion. 'Get back up, once more' was the mantra I adopted, looping my psyche around a vision of a straight spine, seeing footsteps trudging away from death. Questions constantly surfaced to challenge my resolve. Having them at home, their support was only a stopgap knowing they had to return to their own lives.

Life. What would it be like in this home by myself? Every moment unfathomable because this journey, completely new, had no gauge, no compass, no experience. Shaky. . . about everything. Hunger was a tease. Food smelled delicious but my stomach rebelled. More than a few bites caused indigestion, requiring antacid and gingerale.

They'd ask,"Can I get you anything, Mom, a sandwich, fruit, toast, soup?"

Nothing appealed. I only wanted Nick, wanted the emptiness filled. There is such a vacuum, unreality to sudden death. Shock is a blanket, wrapping itself around in a protective cloak.

I'd like to drink till I pass out. This was two weeks since he died, DIED, not 'passed away.' His death was so sudden, final and shocking that there was no passing, no drifting slowly. Now, I think how fortunate we are that Nick died instantly and not by inches. Harsh reality, hard, fast truth that won't go away, won't be altered, won't be softened.

My need embarrassed me so I faked it. Exhaustion left me with no reserve to uphold the status quo even though to the outward appearance I still functioned. At the grocery store, running into my old nemesis, Jane, from medical records, upset my mind with such murderous thoughts, I felt like a psycho. Could I get away with it? Who am I? Would it bring relief? I'd entertain various scenarios experiencing a bit of satisfaction fantasizing revenge. I heard this somewhere, 'that murder should be a misdemeanor.' Foolhardy, yes, but it makes a certain amount of sense. But then I'd ponder her children, the two of them, suffering the loss of their mom. Is it really worth all of this energy? These insane musings? Or wouldn't they be better off, the world improved, rid of Jane's toxicity? They're most likely destined to grow up to be assholes like her. Seriously, who am I? Jesus, get a grip, Anne!

Many friends and relatives wanted to swathe the pain pushing me into getting over, getting on with living. While medication is needful, helpful, even lifesaving I truly believed I had to walk through and experience the process of laying my soul bare in order to arrive on the pathway to health. One doctor told me if I wasn't back to my normal routine after three months, I needed medication. I envisioned jumping off the examining table and choking him. Again, murder, a misdemeanor. Where's a consigliere when you need one? The state of shock I existed in abated the second year but then the depression set in realizing how long it

31

would take to recover. I know Nick was imparting understanding about his journey through my dream-life. It sounds crazy but I took comfort in every revelation. I'm convinced he showed me how it was for him when he died, as if he'd been hovering above watching the scene.

(I really believed he told me this)

"For over an hour you worked on my lifeless body attempting, commanding, imploring my spirit to return, in those first critical minutes, waiting for the gasp, the sputter, the breath to return, pounding, pummeling my breast bone, cracking ribs to save me, blowing your will, your life, your essence, your force into collapsed lungs, seeing my chest rise and fall with herculean efforts. Then the scuba tank that spelled the resuscitating team, another failed endeavor to commute the sentence, fresh oxygen to coax a beat from my static heart. I know you could not see me hovering overhead, could not fathom where I'd gone, did not understand I would never return, even when they loaded my body into the ambulance, observing unmoved, I will tell you unequivocally, it is utter peace."

I sat straight up in bed, out of the dream but could still hear his voice. I know it was him speaking to me. I can't prove it happened but you'll never convince me it didn't. There is no getting over. It becomes the totality of experience shaping one's psyche, part and parcel of the individual forever.

Spring is so close, warming up, my inner core thawing out, my stiffness due to lack of exercise. I'm so ready to have long walks, bike the path adjacent to the river. I love (pronounced luuhhve) my bike. When I am not able to ride during the winter months it feels like a part of me is missing.

Already I've had two rides, hopping on my bike after work, the afternoon sun ushering in my favorite season. My typical ride along the Montello River is singularly invigorating, my salvation. The moment I head out, hauling the bike down the couple of stairs from my back porch, I experience the familiar release. Fresh air gently blows the day's not so pleasant happenings away leaving me with a clean slate to enjoy Mother Nature. Gliding through the staid, lush green carpeted neighborhood I smile at the orange tissue paper petaled poppies. Pedaling up three blocks, to the first climb, feeling the exertion on the sloping plane I push, filling my lungs with deep breaths. Then I fly down a steep pitch, braking and down-shifting to maneuver a sharp left at the bottom of the street. Five more blocks and I'm embarking on the entrance to the trail, a black-topped path winding along tree-lined bluffs to my left and the river to my right. A steady incline forces me to engage those lazy muscles more attuned to coasting. The older I get the more stubborn they become. I will not be bullied. This body always seems surprised at my resolve, tightening and stiffening in rebellion as if I hadn't ridden this circuit dozens of times.

Natural springs miraculously break through the craggy limestone wall, drops trickle, sparkling as they catch the penetrating rays of sun poking through leaf laden branches. Cardinals, jays, even the occasional eagle call their greetings capturing my attention as I wend higher. Here and there, I spy a delicate pink orchid hiding amidst fern fronds shadowed by cottonwoods that angle almost perpendicular toward the meandering current. The final hundred yards are the toughest as the steep rise challenges me. Before I got myself conditioned, I had to get off and walk in humility bowing to my pathetic muscles. No longer. Reaching the top is always an achievement I relish no matter how many times I've accomplished it. Simple. Rewarding. Even spiritual to have the ability, the good fortune of such an opportunity. Level and downhill the next few miles, reminded of the bounty I'm blessed with, my reflections force gratefulness to the surface as I take stock of the powers that be, that imbue the peace of nature into my life.

The city decided to tear up my street, needing to replace old lead pipes carrying water into my house. Naturally, it's impossible for me to fathom or justify the cost, getting involved and attending a council meeting to voice my concerns. It appeared everyone from my neighborhood had the same reaction, many speaking to that point, myself included. However, my impassioned objection was met with tsk, tsk attitudes. It's clearly unaccepted practice to become emotional. In public!

"I'm a widow on a fixed income, barely able to make ends meet," I offered, but my voice broke as I choked back tears. I really abhorred exposing myself so blatantly but there it was.

When I remember how parsimonious I had been raising four children on our meager income I knew I had the ability or chutzpah to eke out a living, somehow. I'd always done what needed to be done whether that was staying up all night canning vegetables or stretching one pound of ground beef to somehow feed six people. It could always have been worse, like Martha experienced, who'd grown up in rural Iowa, having an outhouse until she was fourteen years old. Yeesh.

Slinking back to my seat after my meltdown, I spotted this woman with such a beautiful aura about her, whom I'd noticed almost daily walking past my house. You know, how

34

there is something drawing you into someone's energy field, something even spiritual, undeniable as if you were connected in another life? Well, that evening I felt that sensation as I caught her eye. She sat with her partner who definitely lacked that quality. Almost anathema and I wondered 'what does she see in him?' When the meeting ended I made a point of introducing myself, certainly out of character but like I said ... aura.

"Hi, I live at the corner and have seen you walk by. My name's Anne."

"Nice to meet you. I'm Vera and this is Jerry," she offered, with this affable smile that confirmed my initial impression of her. "We live two doors down, with my teenage son and daughter."

The way she said it told me they were her kids and not theirs.

"I walk to and from work every day. Downtown, managing an office, rentals. Right on Main St. Where do you work?"

"Oh, I just switched to a retail position also on Main St. A small shop, Rayker's, recently opened, that sells jewelry and designer purses, scarves, things like that. I'm not sure what kind of market there is for that type of establishment but hopefully enough to keep me employed," I answered, in a light hearted tone, with a dose of sarcasm thrown in.

She nodded acknowledgement, "I saw that in the works. I'll have to stop in and see what you have."

"Hope to see you around," I said, as we proceeded down the hall.

They both agreed, smiling and we exited the building, me thinking, 'what luck.' Kismet.

Vera's tall, personifying chic. About two inches taller than me, which I admire, me always wearing shoes that bump me up that much even if they do kill my bunions. Her shape is that classic, even statuesque long legged, shorter waist and more than ample chest that every woman desires, not to mention men. Her elegant demeanor is gentle, natural. Not devoid of make-up but just enough, her brown eyes enhanced to a flawless allure. I would say her eyes, with long lashes are her best feature, although I'd kill for those thighs. Straight up, not one lump or suggestion of fat. I've always hated my thighs, not to mention the stomach poof from four pregnancies. Still, I do my due diligence to keep myself from ballooning out. When Nick died I lost thirty-five pounds. The grief diet. I wasn't able to digest anything my life was so stressed, which apparently, at least for me, is the only way to lose weight, short of cutting off an arm or something. God, it's such a vicious circle: you starve yourself for a week and lose maybe two pounds and eat for one day and it's all back!

Early the next morning Jerry is knocking at my back door, "You know you've got some branches hanging onto your garage roof?"

He had this long trimming tool in hand ready to deal with the offenders.

"Let me show you what I mean," motioning me toward the garage. "I can take care of them for you. You don't want them rubbing against the shingles. They'll wear right through them, even if just the leaves are touching. It wouldn't seem like it but your roof can sustain significant damage if you ignore the limbs."

Too abrupt for me, catching me off guard, he unwittingly provoked my immediate opposition to the offer. The way he said it, making me feel less than, that he knew how to take care of my property and I didn't.

And when I told him it wasn't necessary, he jumped in, "It's only the ones that hang way down. Don't you see where they're touching your roof? You need to get those off of there."

His reaction solidified my stance. I'm embarrassed by his insistence. Couldn't I see, didn't I know enough? I dig in. My yard. My garage. My tree. I'm deciding how and when it will be dealt with. He is seriously weird about it especially because he doesn't know me. Yes, it is an over-reaction but I have to trust my gut. Since Nick died I've become fiercely private and coupled with all of the assholes I've recently worked with it is paramount for me to stand my ground. Murder, right? It's like I can't lose control of one more thing, even if it is illogical.

Shaking his head in bewilderment, he had to acquiesce retreating back down the alley toward his house, notwithstanding this last warning, "Let me know if you change your mind."

Right then and there I figured I wouldn't pursue a friendship with Vera as long as she was with that asshole. The rebel, my defense, is a part of my character, at the ready to fend off just that type of pressure. Advances, offers to date are regular enough in the recent past developing in me a new sense of empowerment, one that I'm exploring. It isn't the easiest thing in one's life to have to come to grips with, this altered sense of self at age fifty-two. Or any age for that matter but being on my own after thirty-one years with Nick, mostly concerned with being wife and Mom, has left precious little time for *my* life.

A short, butchy haircut helps. Hair therapy, I call it. It's a good cut, miracle, spiked up with paste. Every time I pass the mirror I have to pause, like, oh ya, that's me.

Remember the Toni home permanents? At a tender seven years old Mom would wind me up, burning my head with that toxic potion that practically blinded you from the fumes. My fried locks were hideous. The coup de gras was a couple of horror-hairdos in those confusing puberty years. The first was a salon perm that was supposed to be 'body' only. There was no such thing in the 60s. I peddled home from the shop, tears drying on my cheeks, jumping into the shower immediately upon arrival trying to relax the frizz. The next day I dragged myself to junior high, with extreme dread, doomed to censure by my peers, with no less than half a dozen clippies doing battle with the kinks. The final fiasco, god, slow-witted much? was the trim Mother Dearest insisted I required. My silky blond coif resembled Mary's of Peter, Paul and Mary.

"I'll just trim up the back, it's so shaggy," she argued.

Nothing short of neat as a pin was acceptable to the beyond OCD arbiter. She sat me on a stool hacking away at the back, me thinking that sounds like a lot. When she grabbed the electric clipper I jumped up running for the mirror.

"What in the hell are you doing!" I screamed.

"Watch your language, young lady."

"You've cut it all off," tears spilling over. "You've ruined me. Why did you do this?"

I stomped upstairs to my room plotting murder. The next day, when my friends saw me they thought I had it all wound up in a French twist. I never let Mom touch my head again, my hair eventually reaching my ass, providentially just in time for my hippie epoch.

Lost in my reverie, gardening, one day, I noticed the familiar head bobbing above my fence, turning into my yard, coming towards me. Walking across the lawn to the flower bed, her long arms extended, Vera wrapped me up, penetrating my cordoned soul with the warmest embrace. True caring, the deepest kinship infusing me with strength and courage.

That was the beginning, a relationship that would prove to stand the test of truth and missteps, spanning decades of laughter and tears. Months later I'd have this thought, that possibly I could return the favor and one day save her life.

"I dumped his ass," Vera announced, with a sly grin. "He moved out. Thought you might want to know. I just knew he was too pushy with that tree trimming offer, the way he is. I could tell you wouldn't appreciate his attitude, especially when he told me how you reacted. And of course, he was condescending. Nuff said."

"Are you okay behind it?"

Nodding determinedly, "Oh yeah, it's long over-due."

"Can we get together some time? Coffee, wine, here in my back yard?"

"Any time. When?"

We set it up for the next day around 5:30. I'm almost giddy. A friend. Yesss. A real friend. Fresh potential. I know I read way too much into it but stultifying loneliness will do that to you.

I gave her a quick tour of my house. I think you can convey a lot about who you are by surroundings, taste, style. Personally, I like to see how people decorate, certain eras definitely speak volumes signifying importance, affinity for specifics whether it be modern, eclectic, antique, minimalist.

I'm obviously in the antique genre with my three story Victorian. It's not stuffy though. On the contrary, the front entrance opens into an inviting parquet floored foyer, so rich and pleasing, it virtually embraces with welcome. Nick and I felt that way the instant we stepped through the front door, as if the house was proffering a hug.

I wasn't mistaken. We talked and drank, laughed. It was fluid, easy and instantly bonding. We probably could have talked all night, both equally needy, parched for that intimacy.

"He never really connected with my kids, always on the periphery even though we were together nine years. And he made me feel like I never measured up to his standards. He'd critique my choice of outfits, hairstyle, and this really torqued me off, he thought if I got a tummy tuck I'd be about perfect!"

This, from a man so not in her league. Really nothing to gush about. Mediocre minus. I've told you about her stunning looks, the whole package. I was incredulous he had the gall. Good riddance.

"How will you divide your property?"

"I'll have to buy him out. It won't be easy, probably get a loan, tighten up, more, but it'll be worth it. Maybe you moving here had something to do with it. I see you in your yard, know you're alone, making it work, handling everything and it inspires me. I have to try."

"Oh, you can do it alright. I know you have it in you. We don't have to settle. Why? Right? As women we do that, either with children for all the years they're growing up, or partners or with work. Deferential, compromising, we tend to take a back seat because there's so much to handle every single day of our lives. That's just the way it shakes out. My late husband was always supportive, didn't subjugate me but the dynamic was implicit. You don't even realize it, or at least, I didn't and it was the times, how I was raised but even though we operated on equal footing when he died I found out how much I relied on him, how much I abdicated to his needs or wants. Maybe that's just how a relationship functions, the give and take. How do you explain thirty-one years together?"

"Who knows? What I do know is that I'm free and so goddamn glad to be single."

What a fabulous night. Vera. Great name. Old fashioned but classy. She was mutually inspiring telling me how she often had three jobs as well as creative pursuits, gardening, basket weaving, essentially having no help from Jerry. Not that the relationship was all bad but certainly could have been so much better.

I told her, "Nick and I were madly in love all of our years, growing together, adapting and finding our way through some extremely challenging times. When I consider most of the relationships I know of I have to say it's surprising to see one that is truly vibrant and fulfilling. For too many, they fall into the typical rut, hanging in there out of habit, staying for the kids. My parents were a glaring example of that."

"Not too many people get what you and Nick had. You're one of the lucky ones."

"Oh, I'm well aware of that. Even though he died tragically, in his prime, I have to say I consider myself one of the most fortunate people on earth."

"How did he die? If you don't mind me asking."

"You know, let's save that for another conversation. It's really a downer and I don't want us to end the night with that."

"Sure, sure, I understand. Another time," Vera offered, her gracious smile blanketing me with warmth.

It was like the threads of our connection were being woven together. The long hug on my front porch, tacit understanding that this was a unique beginning, solidified the initial attraction. I'm such a sucker for those kismet elements. Her kids were twelve and fourteen, Emma and Taylor, mine were grown, two graduated from college, two finishing up. Having enough autonomy to jump into the social scene full force, her son referred to me as 'your joined-at-the-hip friend.' Almost daily now after work we'd meet in my back yard for a beer or a cocktail taking up smoking, vanilla soaked cigarillos called Cojimar. Just puffing, not inhaling. It was more for the avant-garde feel, to be rebellious and wicked. Because we could.

"Tell me about your kids," Vera inquired.

We'd met for lunch, splitting a turkey sandwich, each with a cup of wild rice soup. Our tastes were so similar. Water, maybe coffee afterwards, but we only had an hour so we talked and chewed, along with the unintentional slurp.

"Zelda's twenty-seven, lives in Minneapolis, Aaron, twenty-five, also in Minneapolis, both married, Chloe, twenty-three and David, twenty-one are in college, Wisconsin and Minnesota. Fabulous individuals, all of them. I'm so lucky. All tall, the girls 5'10, Aaron 6'5, David 6'3. Zelda looks a lot like me, fair, blond but acts just like Nick. Chloe is darker, chestnut hair like Nick but acts more emotional like me. It's so interesting how the genes shake out. Aaron and David are very opposite each other, kind of a crap shoot all swirled together but sometimes I'll notice some mannerism or they'll say something and it's exactly like their dad. A posture or a hand gesture, the curve of the mouth. Those early years were so intense, me trying to manage and cope. I was mostly at home until they were in school. I couldn't earn enough money to justify daycare, so we budgeted, I grew tons of food, sewed clothes and somehow we survived on Nick's meager salary."

"It sounds tough. I'm sure I'll meet them soon enough. Do they visit often?"

"Fairly, you know their lives are so jammed, we try to all get together in the summer and then everyone comes at either Christmas or Thanksgiving. Not nearly enough. Sometimes I'm so lonesome for them it hurts. When they're all here it gets pretty crazy with everyone's partner in the mix, drinking, lots. Like they're over the top. Cases of alcohol. Seriously. They have to pitch in or I'd go broke. I don't drink cheap shit but they're into this designer, foo-foo booze. Infused Vodka, small batch Bourbon, craft beer."

"We're tame compared to that. I suppose I'll be dealing with issues like that soon enough," Vera said.

"You won't believe how fast the teen years go. I'm still shocked. It really ramps up with their activities, all of them going in different directions. We could barely keep up. But I loved it. Nick and I would say, do everything in your power to get them on their way, to support and bolster them so they can make it on their own, and NOT come back. Now I fantasize about having them ask for advice and then actually heeding it. I battle against resentment at times, wanting more attention from them but honestly, you ultimately, ideally want them to separate and go their own way. Someone said something like this: nothing is more debilitating than to care about something you can't do anything about. And you can't do anything about your adult children. You can want better for them, and maybe even provide something for them, sometimes, and distance makes that much more possible than being up close to them, like in the same town. What do you think, will that work, the advice part?"

"Don't hold your breath," Vera quipped, both of us laughing.

Vera was almost finished with her lunch and I'd barely taken a few bites, blabbing away. You can always tell who's doing more of the talking. Either I had to talk faster, even with food in my mouth or shut the hell up. Not my forte. The hour passed too quickly, me thinking, will we ever run out of things to talk about? Hah! I have sayings plastered all over my fridge with magnets, some funny, inspirational, or educational. I say, everything I ever needed to know is on my fridge, such as 'Life is too important to be taken seriously' by Oscar Wilde.

Speaking my thought, "Why is it spelled f-r-i-*d*-g-e when refrigerator doesn't have a d?"

Vera just rolled her eyes.

4

So many happenings in town and the surrounding area during the summer months, now having someone to go out with, someone safe with no agenda. Not that I even wanted a cadre of people around me but one or two bosom friends felt like I could function somewhat normally again. 'Friends are few' was one of my tenets. I don't recall where I heard or read it, possibly some poet like Dickinson, or I dreamed it but all my life I had girlfriends that I treasured, soul sisters, loyal and true blue. Like gold. It was a definite turning point, this Vera.

Martini parties, gatherings with music, food, dancing, outdoor venues, with a group or just the two of us. We considered ourselves better than average dancers and had no compunction about getting out on the dance floor together. There's never enough male partners. I liked to mock those that had less than stellar moves mimicking them with hilarious accuracy, cracking Vera up with shamelessly bawdy antics.

She introduced me to her crowd, which was practically the entire population, her having grown up in Dendrobia. I thought I had a dysfunctional family but hers seemed to define the term, with step dad, half and step siblings, a large contingency of the town being a cousin of some degree, all manner of cra-cra. Somehow she escaped the rotten family tree carving out healthy new branches and growth, able to distance herself from the fall-out. Overcoming the obstacles, possessing a solid core of confidence and intelligence, she extended her sphere of influence to include me.

Vera and I had been out for dinner, enhancing our décolletage in sleek summer wear, strolling the few blocks uptown, turning heads, if I say so myself. She sported a short skirt defining those svelte legs, strappy wedge sandals, arms wreathed in bangles, and a low-cut short sleeve top. We both loved rings usually adorning every finger. Just for fun. I kept up in a pink and white polka dot dress, flowing calf length with matching wide belt sort of in the style of that famous Marilyn Monroe pic of her over the sidewalk vent where the wind is billowing the skirt around her while she tries to tame it. Now back home in my yard watching twilight unfold, the evening, the weather, everything was perfect. Eighty degrees, fireflies dotting the lawn, we lounged with a light sparkling white. Firing up my cigarillo I handed her the lighter.

"Sorry I made you leave so abruptly. But I got freaked out by that dude. Jesus Christ, who does that?"

"Don't even think you have to apologize. He was way out of line. Fuck him," Vera reassured.

We'd gone to the back room of the restaurant to play a game of pool and lining up my shot I bent over the table. This guy came up behind me and just started grinding into me. Like right now, this is happening. I was so unnerved but not enough to stop me from reacting.

"Fuck off!" I said, loud enough to get the room's attention as I rammed my cue backward into his gut.

"Jesus, bitch," he snarled, backing off.

All eyes were on us. I walked around the table to where Vera stood, her eyes questioning.

"We have to go. Now," I stated, moving toward the exit.

"What just happened? Are you okay?"

"That guy just about mounted me right there. What the hell? He pushed into me from behind and was hard. I could feel his dick. Jesus H Christ. Is that how people act now?"

"Holy shit! I missed it. When I heard you say 'fuck off' I looked over and the goddamn asshole was already backing away."

Walking toward my house keeping a wary eye out for the perpetrator, I didn't know what to expect, feeling shaken, violated, wondering, did I give him that signal? I was envisioning the scene, my ass from his viewpoint, and was that somehow an invitation? Turning into my yard I was so relieved we lived on the same block, could debrief, mellow out and maybe make sense of the incident. Secure within my fenced yard, sipping away, we hashed over the evening.

Launching into the diatribe, "I haven't had any contact with the party scene for decades so this is a stretch, honestly. I need to *ease* back in, especially the dating aspect. I'm in no rush. God, I shoved my cue into him, like a reflex, and really let him have it. Possibly too, too. My temper surprises me these days. I've also sensed some residual guilt over my dead husband. Don't ask me why. Now what? I have to think about STDs, safe sex, being naked in front of a stranger. Jesus, that's horrifying. I notice these barnacles, on my body, blemishes sort of, but dry and kind of crusty. Gawd! I still have dreams about Nick. The love of my life. Vividly, wonderful and heart wrenching fantasies. Somnambulism, performing various acts while sleeping. I love words."

"Ya, I've noticed your vocabulary. Did you have to look that one up? Damn, I wish I could have seen you hit him. I'm glad you reacted with such force. Men … turns out, you *can* live without 'em! I watched the despicable Anita Hill

47

hearings however many years ago and thought, shit, she doesn't stand a chance against all of these old, asshole men."

"For sure," I said. "How 'bout we lighten up? Anyway, yeah, words. I have notes all over my office with ones I've heard and need to look up. Someday I'm going to buy an OED. I heard of this book, *Reading the OED* by Ammon Shea who took a year to read the entire 21,000 odd pages of the tome which you'd think would make you want to hang yourself but it's an extraordinary read. I gleaned a few choice eye poppers like sesquipedalian, and how apt? It means using long, pretentious words. Hah! Or antithalian, against fun. Kerfuffle. And the zinger phrases, 'immoderately verbose, overpoweringly dull.' Know anyone like that? Love it. I'll forever wonder how far I could have gone if my parents would have supported or encouraged me one iota. Anyway, back to Nick, he's still with me, woven through memories. I'm a fish out of water and scared to think about it. If I ease up and see things as an experiment, it might be less stressful. Might."

"So what did happen to him? You said it was traumatic, an accident?"

"Sort of. No one's ever heard of this or at least the people *I've* talked to haven't. We were in Mexico celebrating our anniversary. We went snorkeling, floating along, hand in hand watching fish swim with us, seeing the coral on the ocean floor, the most peaceful experience. After about twenty minutes, we stopped, able to stand about neck deep and were remarking on the wonder of the ocean when Nick said, 'do your lungs hurt?' He had a strange look. I said, 'no, but let's go in.' When we turned toward the shore I saw that the back of his neck and down to his shoulder blades it was gray. Dark gray."

Vera drained her glass and I motioned for us to get a refill. She had the most concerned demeanor, of course, and at this point I always felt the panic surge, the retelling drumming up PTSD. I was careful when and where and to whom I embarked upon this conversation. It was why I couldn't venture out of my house, out of my yard the first months after Nick died. In a small town there are too many people that know exactly who you are, know what's happened to you, looking at you, seeing with such doleful eyes, even approaching to offer condolences or ask questions. My reaction was to run, to escape feeling naked in their presence as if they bore deep into my soul. Raw and too vulnerable I avoided every milieu of that sort relying on friends or delivery to supply my needs. I knew Vera was safe, that she could handle it but as I filled our glasses I had my typical anxiety.

Walking back outside I asked, "Are you okay with this?"

"I am. Are you?"

"Ya, you need to know this part of me. The whole person, warts and all."

We turned our lawn chairs to see the full moon rising over my garage, up through the trees, a shimmering glow as I continued.

"Nick was able to keep moving forward, I hooked my arm through his, pulling with all my strength. He was gagging, yellowish foam oozing out of his mouth but his legs kept plodding. I screamed for help and two people ran out to us, now only ten feet from the shore. Nick's eyes were glazed like he wasn't cognizant as the others grabbed hold of him. Right at the water's edge he collapsed with such a sound, like a tremor, that went through me so powerfully I can still hear it. He was dead."

49

This is where I break down. It happens every time. Vera rose, wrapping her arms around me, crying with me.

"I'm so sorry, Anne, so sorry. How awful for you. I can't even imagine."

We stayed that way for several minutes, digging tissues out, then settling back into our chairs. I took a few deep breaths, now ready to wrap it up.

"There's so much more to the saga, it goes on and on. The official cause of death was salt water asphyxia. What I had to deal with in Mexico, their corrupt legal system, pay-offs, calling the kids to tell them their dad was dead, I mean, that was almost as bad as having him die in my arms. I'll never go back there, Mexico, and when I hear of someone talking about vacationing there I cringe. If anyone asks me, I am candid, wanting them to know that if you're in the tourist venue, you probably don't have too much to worry about but God forbid, if anything goes awry, the prejudice and hatred I encountered were beyond cruel. In a foreign country, the language barrier, corruption."

"Why don't more people know about this? I mean, I've never heard of it, with the salt water."

"I know. I had to look it up when I got back to the states but it's a real thing, hypoxia. Hang on a second."

I ran inside to my purse, digging out my little notebook. I'd carried this with me since discovering it, this explanation, to have it at the ready in case I wanted to explain, as if it would help in my process.

"Here's the 4-1-1," I said and began reading. "The steps to death progress from aspiration of fluid to pulmonary dysfunction to hypoxiemia to anoxic brain injury and cardiac decompensation to death. Quite a mouthful, huh?"

"Well, ya, it seems pretty straightforward, and yet also very confusing. So he got salt water in his lungs and that cut off oxygen?"

"Right. Your lungs try to neutralize it by flooding with fluid which blocks all oxygen so your esophagus spasms and your heart or brain explodes. The only other person that had any knowledge of it was a WWII veteran who told me when they stormed the beaches they were warned against inhaling or ingesting the salt water because of its toxicity."

I told Vera about my recurring dreams, trying to get to Nick across an expanse of water, driving, driving to nowhere uphill until the car fell over backwards, hiking up a steep embankment throwing my leg over the top using every ounce of strength to heft myself over, all so excruciatingly impossible. All symptomatic of PTSD.

Wanting to end on a lighter note, I offered, "But you know what? We made it. We are the persons we are now because of what we've gone through, and although I'd never wish to experience that again, I have to say the lessons learned are invaluable. We hear of those people who are actually relieved when they lose their spouse. I know in certain situations, where one has suffered a horrible, protracted disease, it is indeed a comfort to end it but I would never have guessed how destroyed I would be losing him in five minutes. Then after certain time passes, the recovery results in strength and empowerment processing all of that, the sum total of survival. It is life shattering and altering but here I am, sitting in this yard with you, and I have to say, I'm happy. Truly."

Shaking her head, sort of incredulously, "I don't know how that happens, how we recover from shit like that. But I know we do. People do it every day. My God, how anyone survives the murder of a loved one, or the death of a child. I think I'd curl up and never leave my house again, even contemplating checking out."

"Oh, I had many thoughts of leaving this planet. There's an actual condition called taktsubo cardiomyopathy, heartbreak syndrome that is defined as dying of a broken heart. I was close to that at points experiencing tightness in my chest, shortness of breath, feeling like I'd pass out. No doctor diagnosed it specifically but I know I had all of the symptoms and you've heard of a scenario where one spouse dies within days or even hours of the other and I truly believe it is that shattered heart giving out. Johnny Cash died just four months after June died. Theirs was one of those classic love stories. For all of a year I seriously couldn't say if I'd come around, come out of the shock. It literally hurt that much. I wanted answers, obsessing about what else we could have done, if we should have done toxicology testing, second guessing every detail. But the saving grace was my kids. They prevented me. They were here and he was gone. I needed to get back to life for them, so they could stop worrying about my mental state. And there were those few precious friends that I'm forever indebted to. And now I'm adding you to that equation."

There are friends you keep for life, others attach for a period of time, even years and then fade away. It goes so far beyond geography. Hundreds of miles separate us, months and years elapse but if a friend is the real deal you can get together and it's as if there's been no gap. You simply take up where you left off. Beyond physical into spiritual. Sometimes I imagine I was with certain people in another life. Certainly with Nick, maybe many lives with him. I can't prove it but neither can you disprove it. What is a friend?

Aristotle said, "A single soul dwelling in two bodies." I like to call it woo-woo.

Grabbing my phone to see who was calling, "Finally, Crystal, where have you been? What happened?"

"This isn't Crystal. This is her phone. I'm here at her house taking care of things. My name is Gayle. I saw that you left three messages so wanted to let you know Crystal had another stroke."

"Oh my God, no. Is she okay? Where is she?"

"She'd gone to her dad's, which was good because someone else was there, but she's in the hospital, in ICU and it's bad. She's lost almost all movement, speech. They don't know if she will get any of it back."

"Are her kids there?"

"They're on their way."

"Can I go see her?"

"Yes, it will be good for her to see you. Obviously, you're one of her good friends."

After getting the particulars I thanked her, choking up, and determined I'd drive the hour and a half to the hospital the next day after work. Crystal and I'd been friends for about five years. She lived in my former town and our kids were close friends, my younger ones. Chloe even had lived in Crystal's home with her daughter, Carrie, in her senior year. Chloe was out of control and Nick and I were at our wits end dealing with drugs, truancy and abject rebellion. Crystal stepped up and offered the arrangement and as is sometimes the strange case, Chloe comported herself like a model citizen. To our great relief, Chloe and Carrie were grateful enough with the arrangement to settle down and stay out of trouble or at least moderate enough to stay under the radar.

Crystal and I had planned dinner at my house the week before and if time permitted probably watch a video. When she didn't show, my inclination was to assume I got my dates mixed up.

I called Vera that same night, to get her take on it, "It's odd, like I have it on my calendar and I do that so this doesn't happen. I have to notate everything. I'm sure she wouldn't blow me off."

"Try her again or wait till tomorrow. I'm sure there's a logical explanation."

"Right. I'll talk to you later."

Doctors were waiting for swelling to subside to further diagnose Crystal's condition. But it was bad. Horrible. I was able to be alone with her upon my arrival, no one else was around in the ICU. Her eyes were closed so I quietly approached the bed observing the myriad of wires, tubes, connections and machines doing the work of a human. Steady rhythmic pulsing making her viable or that was my hope. Maybe she sensed me, I don't know, but her head turned slightly toward me, eyes opening and I thought I detected a movement on her lips. A smile? My imagination? I smiled at her, bending down to put my cheek next to hers. A tear slid down the side of her face and I knew she recognized me, I knew it. Her mouth began to move forming words but only guttural sounds came out, nothing legible. She tried, I tried but shook my head, frustrated I couldn't make anything of it. Her one hand could move and one foot moved, a tad.

"You're my true, honest friend," I told her. "One of the best people I know. One of the beautiful people. I love how you believe in your kids, how you're always proud of them, how you are a successful single parent. You never have disparaging words but expect the best from people with your love and positive energy."

I think I was trying to bolster her into some semblance of recovery, wholeness, trying to talk her into it. It was a desperate attempt.

"You're always so upbeat, an encouragement to me. Once I asked you if you got discouraged or felt like giving up and you said no, just no. I keep on keepin' on, you said. I know you are going to hang in there now."

I held her hand gently squeezing it. I pressed it to my heart keeping eye contact, "I love you," I whispered.

I drove the distance every day after work until they moved her to an acute care facility where she died. One week in all. Her kids were there, I was there. I heard that when someone is at death's door they will not let go if family members are present. It's like they can't be released. Crystal did not want to exist like that, without hope, without any possibility of recovery. She was breathing on her own now but it was a struggle, exhausting to inhale, exhale, and I had the prescience to discern the finality. So I told her son and daughter to take a break, get some lunch or something to drink.

After they left I told her, "It's okay, Crystal, you can go, they're going to be fine, they'll do great because of you."

She took two more breaths and quit, exhaling peacefully, gently letting go. No more struggle. FREE. Running, jumping dancing, FREE to move every finger, every limb, even flying across and to the spirit world doing all the things she couldn't do on earth, painting the amazing scenes that were in her mind. I felt such an inner peace envisioning her.

There was a period in my life when I was a Jesus freak, a fundamentalist, but gave up the God Squad for sanity. Too much of it didn't compute and this was a perfect example. Why do these stellar people suffer such awful misfortune? And early death? When Nick died I had to do some deep reevaluation of philosophies and beliefs coming to some pretty radical conclusions. If God allows suffering when he wouldn't have to he's either not all powerful or an asshole. Is he simply unwilling to prevent suffering and premature death? How is that love? Our father? You know what you'd do to save your child from hurting. So many Christians justify hate and prejudice, the epitome of hypocrisy, that I want no part of organized religion. The male deity tenet was another sticking point solidifying my persuasion that god is a spirit and god is love inhabiting everything in the universe. It takes a lifetime to evolve and solidify one's ideology, sometimes like shifting sand, trying to find our center, our truth. My beliefs continue to adjust as I learn and grow coming down to this tongue in cheek religion: DBAA, pronounced DeeBaah — Don't Be An Asshole.

Crystal was one of those women you meet and feel like you've known your entire life. You can have many acquaintances but very few deep relationships. I treasure each and every one of my friendships especially the girlfriends, the longest with my old friend Meryl, spanning fifty-seven years! I cherish, trust, depend on them in the simplicity of love.

What do I think of Facebook friends? Hah! It bastardizes the word. Do they really care about you, *know* you? I resisted joining for years having only recently succumbed to the phenomenon, the social network which I think is an oxymoron. Oh, you don't say!

"Everyone's on it," someone told me in an attempt to get me to sign up. "You connect with all these people you haven't seen or heard from in twenty years. It's so amazing."

"I'm connected to all the people I want to be connected with, thank you very much," I argued. "Why do I want every Tom, Dick and Harry contacting me? No way. It's too phony, smacks of Big Brother."

He thinks I'm a dinosaur, Luddite, which is true but again, I had to protect my boundaries, my privacy after Nick died.

Driving back from Crystal's facility I reflected on my newfound friendship with Vera, how lucky I was at this very juncture of my life, how synchronistic, even wondering if Nick had something to do with orchestrating it. Things like that floated into my psyche, the supernatural, in extraordinary ways keeping the idealist alive in me with childlike faith.

I slammed on the brakes. Jesus Christ, I was barely paying attention glimpsing a form as the sunlight blazoned across my windshield. Back in town, the jaywalker almost bit it. Right in front of me stood Jane, glaring at me. Of all the luck. Another second and I might have realized my wildest desire. Certainly, it would have been an accident. Truly. Most probably. On that delicious fantasy note, I don't think she even recognized me. Goddamn Jane!

Completely shifting gears, I thought, I have to remember to tell Vera the story of dog-sitting at a lake home. She'll get a good laugh. It was four dogs. How I consented to that, I'll never know. After the Jane encounter/near-death experience I was all over the map with my random thoughts.

The next evening, Vera and I, having polished off one bottle of wine and I'm opening another, I launched into the story, "I know you're a dog lover, me too, but this is beyond reality. No, it *should* be a reality show! Indulging 'dogren' (my new coined term for dog children) is not my M.O."

57

Heading out the side door to our chairs, Vera wanted the play by play so I complied.

"So, I'm down at the lake on the dock, the house where I'm dog sitting, I set my phone on the tethered boat and it slides off. I watch it in slo-mo as it hits the dock, the back and battery fly out, it bounces, I make a desperate lunge, oooh, too short. The phone splashes in between the dock and boat. I'm yelling, 'No, no, no, oh shit, no God. Aaaaaagh.' I can see it shining, hanging there on the algae, so I jam the chair against the boat to hold the space. Grabbing the rake, I gingerly slide it down but as soon as it touches the muck, the phone sinks out of sight. More, 'shit, shit, shit, noawa, c'mon, don't do this to me.' Futilely I dredge, pulling up black, brackish sludge. The phone is probably inches away, but I know I won't find it."

I call Zelda from the home phone, and after she stops laughing, I implore, "Can't you come and help me find it?"

"There's no point," she explains. "You can't recover anything, anyway."

"I did say I'm a dinosaur when it comes to technology. So I call my carrier, US Cellular, and they have no stores in the area. I can't get a phone for three days. The customer (no)service rep is getting a chuckle. I feel like a part of ME is lost, because, like a moron, I only have one of my kid's numbers memorized. Help, Maggie! (my wizard friend who remembers every number she's ever heard) I can't even recount whose numbers are stored in my phone, let alone what those numbers are. There was the day when I knew a hundred numbers by heart. Now? Gone. The rep asked me if I wanted to suspend service, until I got another phone so I didn't have to pay for the down time? It sounded reasonable until my daughter informed me that I should keep it activated so I can get voice mail. I'm thinking, 'Where does it go?' Like, somewhere in my understanding I assume there's a tiny recorder at the bottom of the lake that picks up messages!"

Side note: In my defense, that evening at my friend, Bonnie's, (she's a couple years older than me) she listened in total understanding as I related my ignorance of where the messages went."

"Well, why don't our kids explain it to us?" she asked.

"Because they can't dumb it down enough!"

We are beyond lame.

"It's such a sense of insecurity, bordering on adrift, a sea of uncertainty as I was driving to your house, no directions, and like where do you stop, if you're lost? Do gas stations even have pay phones anymore? Are they still coin operated?"

Twenty-four hours later I try to figure out how to retrieve my messages. Again, daughter to the rescue. Without her expertise, I'd probably be sitting in a corner of the house, drooling, mumbling, 'phone, lake, boat, water.' My friend, Tommy, says our kids are so smart because of all the LSD we took! Hahaha. Anyway, she informs me that I have no new voicemails.

I was right. Back to Vera and my monologue in the back yard, who thought it was hilarious, holding her sides laughing uproariously as I related the fiasco.

"I don't know how I get myself into such absurd shit shows. My first clue, on the kitchen counter were four pages of typed notes, which I painstakingly pored over, not wanting any upset to the darling's lives. Four—count 'em—one, two, three, four dogs, no less! Two miniature dachshunds and two

King Charles cavaliers. A ton of work. The routine; pottying the dogs, playing with them in the back yard, in the lake, hosing 'em down, because the lake is mucky, etc., and of course, the furnishings are predominantly white. Here I am picking up shit several times a day for a measly forty frikkin' dollars a day?! Explain to me why rich people are so cheap! They're always looking at me (the pooches) with those eyes. Pet me, talk to me, touch me, pay attention to me—four sets of eyes, begging, imploring. I need, I need, I NEED. OH MY GAWD! Lay down already and stop looking at me! I had to stand up and just walk around so they wouldn't sit there and stare at me. When I'd stop, they'd bob their heads into my shin trying to get my attention. HEY, YOU, LADY! HEY, PET ME!"

I rambled on about poops on the carpet. No universal signal for wanting to go out, one would stare, one would sit by the door. The other two? I had to be psychic. So if I didn't pay attention…plop. Feeding, everyone had specialties and I had to police them diligently or the only male would scarf down everyone's portion. Night time, you guessed it. They were supposed to sleep with me. I'm the lightest sleeper on the planet so that was impossible. I let them have the master and I tiptoed off to another bed until 6:30 a.m., where they whined at my door raring to go out. Oh, and one was deaf so needed hand signals!

"God, THOSE GERMANS!! What is in their genetic code that makes them so horribly aggressive?! I'm speaking of dogs now, you understand, me having a thread of German descent, so, anyway I'm walking the miniature dachshunds (although aren't they German?) well, so this large, menacing Shepherd comes loping out from a garage with these steady paces, very deliberate, intense, in attack mode with a leash dragging along the ground. My teeny dogs go berserk, as if they'd engage the monster. So the Shepherd charges. Sheeeeeeit! The owner comes tearing across his yard yelling for his dog who pays no heed whatsoever. I squat down holding my two between my knees, thrust my free hand out, screaming NO! as boldly and emphatically as I can muster. Goddamn wild, uncontrollable pets! What business do people have keeping animals like that without a secure tether? What if a child was walking there? It took this diminutive man a long, scary minute to finally get a grip on the leash."

He goes, "Sorry."

"Yikes," is all I say, hurriedly trotting away. Asshole!

"Finally, a welcome hurricane threatened the vacationers so one couple cut it short by a day. Hallelujah! They have this face-licking gross-out reunion. They lick asses! and any other gross thing they can stick their tongues into! And here I am, watching this mother of the dogren getting her face slobbered on by said tongues. Anyway, I had the remaining two dogs for another day which was when my phone met its demise."

"What did happen with your phone?" Vera asked.

"After I got a new one the dog owner called to say they dredged it out of the lake. From the Radio Shack guy I learned that the data could be retrieved if the battery wasn't still in it. That's the element that has the corrosive factor and as luck would have it the phone had bounced on the dock ejecting the battery before it splashed into the water. The gods smiled on me. They were able to transfer all my numbers with their magic box of codes. BAM! My life restored in full. Oh, and get this. The dog people called a month later to see if I could dog-sit for two weeks. After busting out laughing, picking myself up off the floor, I managed a civil, "Ya, for two hundred bucks a day."

"I love to hear your stories," Vera said, after the long saga. "How do you remember all that?"

"I know. You'd think it just happened. I can't remember telephone numbers or any passwords but that shit clogs my brain forever. It took so long to even get a smart phone, limping along with a flip phone, that even if it is an android, I still think I'm quite evolved. My kids, who are Apple users, have phone-shamed me for not getting an iPhone. The cost is the determining factor and I don't remember what I paid for this one but it was cheap."

5

Vera introduced me to her friend, Blair, having us over for dinner on a late summer evening. Vera always wowed me with her exquisite taste, whether it was her fashion sense or cooking and now I added the category of excellent friends to her assets. Blair was raised in California and there is something so unique about that coast that my impression was immediately one of the avant garde avec undertows of worldliness. With a northern Italian heritage Blair had grown up on her family's vineyard near Gilroy. When you're a Midwesterner through and through, California is tantamount to another planet in terms of panache. Definitely the cool factor, way ahead of the Midwest. I remember hearing about Haight Ashbury when I was sixteen thinking how completely bizarre yet nonetheless enticing. Consequently, Blair was involved with the counter culture scene at a much younger age than me. Along with Vera, we connected powerfully aligning on politics, environment, and spirituality, among others.

Blair invited us for dinner a few nights later. They were both sensitive to my depression over Crystal's untimely death, trying to pull me up and out of the funk. Grief is exhausting, threatening to spiral me into a dark place. They both did their damndest to encourage me, listening to my miseries and underlying resentment.

"I'm tired, depressed, unhappy but still putting one foot in front of the other. And my lower back has acted up, bunions ache at night, God, what next? Oh, and I'm having these floater black spots across my field of vision. I'm falling apart," as we clinked our glasses. "Tits up!" I declared.

"Well, it's good to see you haven't lost your sense of humor," Blair quipped.

Vera and I'd switched to beer having ODed on wine during a recent outing. I think I was binging over my emotional turmoil and Vera was a sympathetic drinker. Both of us decried the next day's hangover.

"God, my head wasn't right for two days," she confessed. "I'm getting too old to sustain that kind of debauchery. How's that for a word?"

"Love it. I'm rubbing off. But I do need to pull myself out of it. Everything is pissing me off. My job is so annoying. Trying to convince people that they need diamonds, baubles, superfluous bullshit when I know they are probably hard pressed to make house payments. It goes so against my grain, the tightwad in me. Jesus, what I had to make do on when raising four children. I'm pushing this merchandise and in my gut I'm thinking how totally stupid, wacky and wasteful to spend all that money on jewelry. I'm a jewelry pimp. Oh hell, who am I to say?"

Blair said, "You need the job, right? You have to suck it up and do what you have to do. We all do. You know the saying, it doesn't matter how many times you fall, even seven times, and what matters is you get back up eight. Have to. You will. I wish we'd win the lottery."

At that juncture of her life, Blair was an interior designer. Her talent and creativity evident in her home, replete with gorgeous textured walls, stunning window treatments, imported fixtures, custom made counters all in a restored turn of the century bank building. She had such élan for the unique, paring modern with vintage, antiques with new age

64

that it felt like I'd entered the pages of House Beautiful. With a gorgeous oriental rug to tie it all together, is oriental rug PC?, anyway the living area was exquisitely decorated. The pleasing atmosphere extended to the luscious cooking she was noted for. Italian cuisine dominated most of the menus, never quite the same, fresh salad fixings from her garden, we enjoyed scampi with homemade pasta, linguini with clam sauce, pesto, risotto and ravioli served on heirloom green and cream colored dishes complemented perfectly by green Depression glassware. You'd think she would have been a butterball but she maintained one of those 'just right' figures. Shorter than both Vera and me, Blair's proportions were not quite petite but compact with what I'd call firmness overall. Legs, derriere, arms, all put together in a package of feminine appeal. She exuded Mediterranean warmth, a depth not quickly penetrated, layer after layer, fecund and confident.

"It's really a godsend to have you guys to talk to. I mean it, this is my salvation. You can never move away. I was up in the middle of the night last night. 3a.m. with my thoughts."

"What do you do?"

"Well, I came up with this brilliant drink, the perfect remedy for seniors— a PRUNE-TINI."

"Sounds disgusting," Blair said.

After the eye roll and guffaws, I continued, "I lie there and regurgitate all the things wrong with this world. Ecology, education, homelessness, pay inequity, women who won't stand up for themselves. The male gender. God, you know this type, right? He cleans something, anything and has to announce it. 'I cleaned the toilet, give me a medal! Or oh, oh, I changed the baby's diaper.' Today I was waiting on this woman who started telling me about her pathetic life, her lame-ass husband who won't lift a finger, her kids taking advantage of her and I want to scream, 'DO SOMETHING ABOUT IT, FOR CHRIST'S SAKE!' Don't let yourself be walked on, bullied, put upon."

"What did you say? I'll bet you gave her some sterling advice, eh?" Blair's mocking tone was dead on.

"I wanted to make a sale. I know this is awful but I told her a nice bracelet would make her feel better. I know, I know. I'm an asshole hypocrite. Seriously. I don't get it. Why do so many knuckle under to that dynamic? Defer, be subjugated? Even that phrase, balls to the wall is totally about men. I prefer the saying 'tits up'."

"It's learned over a lifetime, from childhood," Blair offered. "Dealing with over-bearing authority figures, dominant bosses and boyfriends. My mother did not do anything to bolster my self-esteem, on the contrary, she continually put me in my place, even resorting to physical violence. It's ingrained from our earliest memories until we're enmeshed so deeply we can't recognize it let alone get out of it. I know I have a fair amount of that going on, but I see it and am working on it. You both give me courage. And I hope you know, Anne, you are strong and bold and will bounce back from this funk, whatever it is. One day at a time, right?"

"What I need is a sinecure."

"And that is?"

"Oh, it's the perfect career. Doing very little work for lots of money."

"We all need that," Blair agreed.

"So you were not technically a hippie," I said. "But you alluded to some experiences that aligned you with the counter culture?"

"For sure, I identified with the ideals and even had some unique encounters, the best being my personal face to face conversation with Sir Paul McCartney."

Vera and I both screamed, "No way! We have to hear the play by play."

"Ah, let's see, that was a million years ago, you know. I was sixteen, a junior, in Gilroy, California, that is. I was spending a glorious summer studying history, and various subjects in European universities with a group of students. First in Rome, umm, then Paris and on to Switzerland with the final destination, London. While there, my good pal, Cindi, learned that the Beatles were recording an album at EMI Studios in St. John's Wood."

"Oh God, what perfect timing," I exclaimed.

"Right. We cut class that day, sneaking off on our own to track down this studio. By ourselves! In London, mind you."

"Ya, how did you even know where to go?"

"Thinking about it now, Cindi heard about it and researched it, I can't remember, it seems pretty incredible we found our way around in that unfamiliar and sprawling city having never navigated the public transport. The Tube, they called it."

Vera and I are shaking our heads in wonder.

"So we got off at St. John's Wood."

"What is that?" I interrupt.

"It's a neighborhood west of London in Westminster."

I'm nodding as if I have any clue what that means.

"Okay, sorry, go on."

"Cindi and I ambled along a quaint, residential street, it was the quintessential summer day, like nary a care, so naïve. We passed other walkers but didn't bother to ask directions and then, just like that, here was this enormous mansion surrounded by a manicured English garden within a six foot stone wall, a placard signifying the studio. And to our delight the gate was open. We just walked in, like we belonged there, and sat down on a bench joining several young British women, chatting with them, getting more excited with their revelations. They'd been there often and usually saw the Beatles exiting the mansion after finishing the day's recording."

"So how long were you there? Like, were you at all concerned you needed to get back or anything?"

"At that point, it hadn't occurred to us. We were *going* to see them. Maybe it was about an hour, and then the front door opened and out walked John, Yoko, Ringo, Paul and George. RIGHT THERE! John and Yoko got into the back seat of a Rolls Royce that'd been parked and waiting. John put his feet up onto the back of the front seat and waved at us as they drove through the gate.

Then Paul, descending the stairs, looked up and walked straight over to me, honest, and said, 'Hello Love.' I can still hear him. His tone. Accent."

Vera and I were drop jawed.

"He was so adorable, smooth, natural, friendly. I thought I would die."

"Oh, I can't even imagine. I think I would have been paralyzed, speechless, completely tongue-tied."

"I had my little Instamatic camera and tried to keep my hands from shaking while I snapped his photo, while he signed Cindi's subway ticket. Then, just so cool, he asked me where I was from, what I was doing in London and as he handed the pen back to me we touched hands."

She said this last bit raising her voice and opening her hands in sort of an imploring gesture, like these very hands.

"You know how things happen like that and you have no idea of time, like it could be an hour or two minutes. But it was fast and I think I was almost in shock. Then Paul and the others got into their cars and drove over to Abbey Road. That was it. I didn't wash that hand for days."

"Did you get into trouble or anything."

"Not really. Sort of like no one noticed. It was all so charmed, the entire day and experience."

"I love it. I had a lot of concert stories back in the day but I think that's the topper."

"Truly. I treasure it. I was only twelve when I had seen them at the Cow Palace in San Francisco when they first toured America but you could not hear anything above the screaming."

With a sigh, I said, "I'm forever a groupie or star-struck, something like that. It's always been, who knows why? I could listen to those anecdotes all day. It was such a spectacular time or era to experience. I think we're lucky. A singular life."

It'd been one of those evenings, memorable in ways I hadn't expected, exploring histories that formed our particular characters, solidifying our bond. This trio of friendship was a gift. I so appreciated their advice and support knowing how lucky I was to connect with two such stellar women. As much as I projected this dynamo persona, they'd become well aware of my insecurity, the dissimilar cautionary aspect of my psyche. A control even when I felt out of control. The brakes, the reins that I utilized for protection of myself, my heart as if I always had to be defensive about my standards, especially when sizing up a potential partner. That seemed unlikely when I delineated my criteria, but I'd recently become open to that very possibility purposely setting the bar unattainably high. I'm in no rush. I won't compromise. I have an actual list: no dependent offspring, financially independent, fully divorced. It's quite extensive. It's not the worst thing to be alone, a mistake to be with the wrong person. So I remain one. For now.

I'm not such a prize, I am aware of my oldishness. Sometimes comparing myself to a dead tree, the bark loosely hanging or falling off, crinkled, pock marked, spotted, maybe a bit of life in the roots. My gray hair resembles the stubborn way a trunk or limb leans in one direction for eons. I take pains to curl and style my coif, thinking, 'okay, that's pretty good,' and in less than an hour it's decided to revert to its usual rigid bent. I'm glad I don't have the money to alter my body cosmetically. It seems deplorable, pulling, tightening, sucking out fat cells to achieve eternal youth. As if. But it might be tempting if I had enormous amounts of disposable income. As I age it takes increasingly more effort to maintain my weight. Fewer calories, more exercise. Jeans tighter, not wanting lip singers, as in singe. Ouch. Sitting in my back yard the other morning, eating a muffin and as I set the plateful on my lap the thought occurred to me that that's exactly where it would end up. Right there on my lumpy thighs. But the face-lift adherents, envisioning some of those outcomes, instead of younger they just look freaky. I like to call it the G- force expression or permanently surprised.

It was only a few days and my mood shifted. Journaling last night I found myself fairly upbeat, writing:
I'm wise, resilient, knowing some things, truth, knowledge, experience, depth coming through, getting back up, getting back up, again and again and again, one more day. I can do

it, only one day, that's all I have to accomplish. It's enough. There's always another day, another chance or opportunity to do well, do better, succeed. Just don't give up, never give in. Rest, let it go. All of it, the fear, let it go, the pain, let it go. Open your hands, reach out your arms. Let it go. Come in, good, light, energy, warmth, healing, love. Peace.

That's what I have to keep uppermost, the same old philosophy of make love, not war. Stop the fighting, the contention, quit contributing to that mindset. Does that include Jane? Not yet. I still fantasize about her 'accidental'demise.

Jesus, sometimes I impress myself with profundity. Anyway, as I'm writing in longhand in my journal I bemoan the fact that cursive isn't taught anymore. I continue my lifelong practice scribbling away. There's such an artistry, ink meeting paper, fluid, flowing, penmanship signifying so much more than letters or words that are simply punched. One of my favorite authors, George Sand, pseudonym for Aurore Dudevant, is said to have written throughout the night, after first partying until midnight. Not willing to lose the thread of her story, she'd fill page after page laboriously dipping her pen, accomplishing what is reputed as the most prolific female career dedicated to social change. I doubt if I'll ever give up the practice, longhand, that is, especially because research notes a definite difference in brain function when both methods are tracked, even concluding that the connection is more profound when written as opposed to the punching of a key.

George Eliot said, "It's never too late to be who you might have been." And I am believing that more each year. The 1970's were my first taste of empowerment, diving into the hippie, women's lib rebelliousness of the era. But after thirty years I still consider myself a work in progress or process aligning with particular social issues. The rural agricultural practices of our area are of particular concern as the expanding CAFO industry steamrolls across the Midwest and other parts of the country. Confined Animal Feeding Operations have 1000 animals in small spaces for their entire existence, producing millions of tons of manure every year, posing risks to the environment, both in air and water quality. Twenty to thirty times a year, on average, CAFOs have serious problems resulting from mismanagement. Discussing the upcoming meeting at the city offices, Blair, Vera and I determined to lend support and our voices to the growing movement against the farmers in our county who were trying to push through building proposals to increase hog numbers.

"I'm so alarmed that this is legal," I said. "Who's protecting the river, the run-off? What about the tourist revenue from trout fishing? This part of the state is so reliant on that money."

"You two are in town, maybe a small buffer, but I'm seventeen miles out and directly downwind from one of these farms. It's horrible, the smell, with my asthma. Some days I have to close up the house and not even venture out to my garden," Blair said.

Vera added, "I've got a friend who's had to sell his farm due to that very thing. One day he was outside and literally choked, couldn't get his breath, like he was suffocating. The methane gas was so dense that it shut down his esophagus. He was able to make it into his house where he called 911. He survived and sued the farm directly adjacent to his and actually won. The agreement stipulated they buy his farm, which I don't know if that did any good because the culpable party just expanded their operation to include another CAFO!"

"Goddammit! How can our legislators let this happen? God we've seen what they're doing, right? Doesn't anybody give a shit? Our property is going to be worthless," I said. "When is this meeting?"

"Tomorrow night, at 7:00," Vera answered. "The agriculture lobby is the most powerful lobby in this state, so it'll be interesting. It's the money that's driving them. As usual. How do they not understand about the long term consequences? It's the same with the big oil companies. You've heard about the frac sand in our county, right?"

We both nodded our heads.

Vera continued, "Don't they think about their grandchildren? The CEOs? I mean, don't they want a planet for them to grow up in? It's mind boggling."

"No they don't. They don't give a shit. Maybe they are so insulated they believe they won't be affected, that their money will shield them," I said.

Attempting to lighten our heavy hearts we emptied the second bottle of wine.

The hall was packed the following night, standing room only and when the meeting was over we felt even more hopeless for our precious mother earth. Evident was the animosity between factions, splitting along party lines, conservative, liberal. Our community was fractured as both sides voiced strident opinions and convictions.

"Come on over for a night cap," inviting Vera and Blair to debrief in my back yard, "we need it."

Always a respite, I considered my yard a sanctuary, reserved for only my closest friends. Fireflies drifted lazily up from the lawn, crickets serenaded, and in a buoyant breeze, branches softly whispered their ballet dancing atop the seventy foot tall ash trees.

"I love it back here," Blair said. "How long have you lived here?"

"Ah, let me think. Going on five years."

Knowing she'd want to get into the saga of my moving and Nick dying and way too much for that evening I steered the conversation into the frac sand issue.

"Oh that's completely bizarre. You haven't read about it?" Blair asked."

"Not enough."

"The short version is that mining companies want to utilize the sand in our county for the practice of fracking. It is a specific type of sand, crystalline silica that is a known carcinogen. It acts as a proppant, technically small ceramic balls, to keep fissures open so that oil can be extracted. Let me read you this from the Gazette newspaper, I happen to carry this in my purse, 'silica sand mining produces the dangerous silica dust. Prolonged exposure to the tiny mineral particles can scar lung tissue resulting in irreversible and sometimes fatal respiratory damage.' The dust from the sand affects air and water quality and with minimal oversight of the industry, our way of life will undoubtedly be negatively impacted."

Vera added, "We've got a good board of supervisors working on this issue and with public support, I think we can either institute a moratorium or even get it banned."

"I love it that we can do something about it. Or at least it feels that way. I hate to think we're powerless against big oil." Raising my glass, I said, "Here's to empowerment. And to strong women, daughters, and granddaughters."

Observing my plethora of flower beds, Blair asked, Did you design and plant all of this gorgeous landscaping?"

"I'd like to take credit but honestly, most of it was here, cultivated by previous owners. I did have humongous gardens when the kids were growing up but now it seems like another life. I've filled in some things here and there, arranged the rock borders, giving the whole aspect a funkier feel with my clay pots and various figurines, even that wrought iron cross," pointing out the three foot ornament. "I like to joke that Nick is buried there."

"That's awful, but I can see some people believing you," Vera quipped.

"I suppose. Gullible, eh? Sheesh."

"We're going to have to do a high tea some afternoon, sipping as we walk among the blooms, you regaling us with florid descriptions, you know, arm in arm as we stroll along," Blair suggested.

"Of course, sounds enchanting," I agreed. "We'll have to wear long dresses, right?"

6

Seriously people! Ranting and raving, obsessing about the breakdown in our society I retreated daily to the oasis in my yard, so grateful for the respite. The double lot was filled to overflowing with varieties that staggered from spring to fall with mostly perennials and wherever I could, I'd fill in with annuals spending more than I should have but it was so worth it. The delicate bright orange poppies were my favorite, but a close second were the enormous soft pink peonies lining the entire south side of my house. There must have been at least thirty cascading bushes. I'd cut off the spent blooms to allow the smaller secondary crop to have their day. Maybe two to three weeks I would garnish the house with vases of the arrangements, finally gathering the stems together to hang upside down in the basement to dry. They'd last in my dried creations until the following spring's crop emerged. Hostas, fabulously lush ferns, day and tiger lilies, daffodils, hyacinths, tulips, and bridal veil bushes flowed out from the front of the yard. I'd never seen naked ladies, technically amaryllis belladonna. The leaves would shoot up in the spring with all of this drama and then nothing. I couldn't figure it out that first season, why there were no flowers. But then in the late summer here would come this plain stalk with a delightful pink orchid atop, and not one leaf, hence, the naked lady. Mother nature's gifts.

How fun was that?! I was really coming into my own. We attended a concert at the local college. Blair, Vera and a couple of other friends met for happy hour and then headed over to the music. Bill Miller, a native American singer, song writer, and native flute player, was the performer. A Mohican Indian with roots in northern Wisconsin, Bill had been the recipient of three Grammy awards including one for best Native American album. His Indian name, Fush-Ya Heay Ka meant bird song. So apropos. Enraptured by his ethereal, awe inspiring performance, I was almost in a trance. For the wrap-up he asked the audience if anyone wanted to come up and do harmony on *Knock, knock, knockin' on heaven's door.* It's one of my Bob Dylan faves and after hesitating, no one responding, I marched up there. I've always done the alto part and knew I could nail it. Leaning into the same mic, it was one of those experiences where you wonder, 'is this really me?' And it was. Blair and Vera said I sang like an angel. I could tell Bill was duly impressed, we meshed so well. In the zone. Powerful energy went into my soul, watering the seed, fanning the ember, my will to succeed, positive ions spiraling through the universe like meteor showers. That's what went through my psyche. So star struck, it's always been this fascination, with virtually no effort, remembering who was in films, what celebrities were hot, cramming my brain with extraneous, inane details for no apparent reason. Maybe it was genetic, the interest. My mom pored over *Modern Screen* magazine back in the 50's and still never misses her favorite soap. I floated on the concert high for days finally gliding into a week's vacation to New Hampshire to visit my son, Aaron.

Flying from Minneapolis to the east coast afforded me probably too much time to reflect on society's ills especially having to endure the airlines. A bygone era, one that included manners, faded into obscurity. What happened? Decorum? A decade ago still recognizable, parents taught and expected comportment, although Nick would always point out, that manners and civility were better 'caught not taught.'

Remarkable that after losing my luggage, with marked consideration after traversing back roads, the airline delivered it amid apologies for the lateness of the hour, 2a.m. to be exact, me, nonetheless relieved to have my own toothbrush. My bonus for suffering inconvenience was a first class upgrade and, AND! a voucher for future travel. What was this present masquerade we'd become inured to? Remember when it was exciting, even luxurious to fly? You dressed up! A decent meal was routine, legs stretched out completely. Now we had been relegated to something akin to a hog confinement facility. Customer service used to be standard. How did we slide into this farce we tolerated today? One culprit, well, my theory, may be the scourge of social media, no more tête-à-tête. Shifting sands, we are removed, oblivious to social cues, body language, subtle eye allusion to imply propriety. Remember this edict: 'if you can't say anything nice, don't say anything at all?' I'm the bane of wait staff, who condescend to serve me. Now it's shocking, indeed, to get a simple nod of appreciation! I'm almost done with the rant. But it's interesting, to say the least. We're virtually unaccountable in our own walled world, while we slide further from civility.

When Nick and I bought our first computer our youngest, David, was still at home, hence the built in tech support. Laboriously he repeated the basics only to be met with blank stares. Exasperated, he'd finally answer our pleas for assistance by efficiently punching whatever key was needed and saunter off ignoring our recurrent 'slow down, tell me once more, and can't you write it down again?' When he went off to college we said 'take the damn thing with you because we will be lost and will totally screw it up left to our own devices.' For years I resisted the information highway stymied by that first ineptitude. I still prefer 'old-fashioned' letters and hand written note cards, but I have ultimately succumbed. I allow there are numerous benefits to this modern age but can't rid myself of the urge to dig in my heels. I don't much care for change. Am I alone in this? I like the familiar security of what I know. My kids whittled away my fear, first insisting I email. I like to talk, preferably face to face but also on the phone. My brain reaches critical mass too quickly, on overload with the PC. But I wanted to stay connected so I plugged away proud of my meager achievements. Next the little twits informed me I had to do Instagram if I ever wanted another picture and of course, Facebook. I drew a line. I couldn't be spending all day on social media, which I refer to as anti-social media. Their voice is what I crave, my ears hungering for kind words that show caring, enough to actually call and converse. Is it too much to ask, a heart to heart, after squeezing them out of my lady parts?!

When they were all home for Christmas in '06 I witnessed what to me was a heartbreaking phenomenon. With laptops open they sat in the living room heads tilted, eyes locked on the screen 'talking.' No speaking just an occasional chuckle. I sat watching, observing sans computer. Not that I'm still so averse, not entirely.

After a couple of lame attempts to engage them in conversation, frustrated, I asked, "Can't we look at each other and have a little communication?"

"We are," they said.

"What do you mean? On your computers?"

"We're IMing."

"Can't we just talk to each other? Here we all sit together in one room and everyone's in their own world. There's nothing wrong with this picture? A room full of people, no one looking at each other, silence. Isn't something missing?"

"We *are* talking to each other. We can communicate better this way."

"How?!"

Appearing slightly impatient with my tedious interruptions, they proffered, "This *is* how we talk. It's better with access to so much information. We're not missing anything."

Worlds away in the same room I tried to hide my agitation at their resistance.

My oldest daughter told me, "You're the only one I literally talk to on the phone."

Admittedly, there *are* aspects that make life easier, like when you send the text, it's read and efficiently responded to. Unlike voicemail that someone may or may not answer. Social network, in my opinion, is a contradiction. Our connections, our relationships are being redefined, often times about as deep and interesting as a mud puddle. The implications tear at my understanding of social mores. For instance, if you believe the eyes are the 'windows of the soul,' aren't we missing that depth by neglecting to engage face to face? Bolstering that sentiment, I love this from Emily Dickinson, 'True friendship multiplies the good in life and divides its evils. Strive to have friends, for life without friends is like life on a desert island. To find *one* real friend in a lifetime is good fortune; to keep him/her is a blessing.' Moral of the story: if you want a friend, be a friend.

Of course, these experiences brought about the yearning for my soul mate, the alignment that Nick and I treasured, on the same wavelength, one. I knew I'd never find that love again, so unique, so rare. How could I get to the place of memory where I appreciated what we had for all of those decades? I had no clue.

I've been called snobbish, a dinosaur not only by my kids but friends too, for resisting Facebook. It might hearken back to that 60s hippie mentality. Don't give any more information than you have to because *they* will use it against you. I marvel that deeply private, innermost thoughts are posted randomly to whomever is out there. In Jane Hamilton's *The Short History of a Prince*, Walter laments Lucy's boys "glued to the glow of their computer screens, communing in sentence fragments with people they would never meet."

Parallel to this canker, if I Google typing vs. printing the question turns toward another aspect of society that echoes this theme of disconnect. Pondering the fact that the brain functions differently when pen is applied to paper, I wonder how many parents are aware of this. When a child is taught to spell you can chart in the brain a more profound connection when she forms a letter as opposed to the punch of a key. One high school teacher related how she has to write on the board in block letters because her students can't read cursive. I've mentioned George Sand's technique how she'd socialize until midnight, then spend the next six hours writing in bed. I relate through my longhand journaling, watching the words flow along the page relishing the creativity of sentences taking shape. And yet here is this missive in typeface! That's the Gemini in me.

Even decades ago this was penned by Anais Nin in her journal entry, July 1951: "The art of writing. Will it become obsolete? Speech, already inadequate in America, will soon disappear together with the ability to derive significance from the printed word. This is as radical a change as from monkey to man …"

The lack of accountability and responsibility for our words is so alarming, cyber-bullying being one of the most destructive examples. How will this affect us, say ten years hence? Will the capability to verbally communicate all but disappear? A seventy-five year-long Harvard study concluded that the success and happiness of a good life is achieved not through money or fame but with serious and lasting relationships. Deep relationships along with the facility to express ideas and feelings through the spoken word are vital components that set our species apart. Isn't our ability to converse and relate intelligently, utilizing words, sounds, eyes and body language one of our significant advances? There are now detox retreats for those who want or need to be disentangled from their devices. Rehab for a bonafide addiction. At a lecture I attended given by a ranger from the Chiricahua National Monument in southern Arizona, she voiced concerns over millennials' disinterest in visiting our scenic parks opting instead to learn of these treasures by burying their heads in their personal devices. She pointed out that because of the parks failure to provide cell coverage or remote access it could very well contribute to their inability to be sustainable in the near future.

I may be a conversation addict. One may call it the art of speech. When I see a gaggle of pre-pubescent girls shuffling along, narrowed eyes downcast oblivious to brilliant fall colors I want to scream. Missing golds, blazing coral, crisp indigo sky their opposable thumbs speak from magnetic screens that plunder nature. Conversation? Relationship? Mono y mono slips away along with expression, subtle eye fluctuation, body language, intonation and nuance. It's the unraveling of society that deigns to connect on a level deeper than a single post. Soundlessly they move along the sidewalk masquerading as friends. I'm struck by their apparent isolation.

Can we promote and preserve a deeper connection through an authentic voice? My family has evolved into compliance these past years albeit not without the requisite eye rolling. Unwilling to ignore my conviction, I've pulled rank instituting a policy of MOM- minimum of media. Discipline, limits and moderation need to be employed to control a habit having the potential to seriously harm society in terms of life experience, enjoyment, creativity and imagination. Will we participate in life or only observe it?

On my uneventful flight home from the relaxing New Hampshire visit, minding my own business, having no conversation with my seat mates as is standard, approximately a half hour from the Twin Cities the captain announced, "We have received word from the control tower that thunderstorms prohibit our landing at this time. We don't have enough fuel for the thirty minute circling pattern so will divert to Sioux Falls, South Dakota."

The instant reaction took all eyes in unison to the atmosphere at ten thousand feet. Clear, no storm clouds, and questioning looks at each other. The cabin became a bee hive, all barriers and social norms ignored as we queried those in our respective row.

"Have you ever been in this type of situation? This seems weird," I said, engaging a woman to my left.

She was a striking African American about my age, and I thought this was providential, a professor of sociology at a St. Paul, Minnesota college.

"No, it does seem curious. I don't see any evidence of thunderclouds," she answered.

"I find it incredible how all these strangers are instantly concerned with each other, like one huge sociological experiment."

She agreed, asking me about my life, family, work and then we were landing in Sioux Falls, South Dakota. With 9/11 not far off in memory, scary thoughts swirled through my imagination. Bravado plus fear made for an eerie atmosphere of curiosity.

My oldest daughter, Zelda, and her new boyfriend, Kurt, whom I'd never met had arranged to pick me up at the airport and drive me home. As they watched the flight board, in a matter of seconds the ETA changed twice. Marching over to the ticketing counter, a bit miffed by the delay she asked the agent, "What's the deal with flight 7175 from New Hampshire? The board's all over the place."

"It's the captain's call," she replied.

Zelda asked, "And that meeeeans?"

Giving her that put-upon glare, the agent monotoned, "It could mean any number of things."

"Such as?" Zelda asked, never one to be put off.

Somewhat defensively, tap, tap, tapping on her computer, "It could be weather related, fuel issues, even an unruly passenger. It's their call. That is all the information I have." (Go away, now)

Kurt looked at Zelda with a sly wink, "Could that be your mom?"

Smirking, Zelda quipped to the agent, "Define unruly."

Not ready to acquiesce, Zelda pressed on learning that the jet was refueling in Sioux Falls and was expected within the half hour.

As the aircraft approached Minneapolis, I scanned the horizon for any storm clouds, anything at all that would have given credence to the detour. Nothing. Beautiful sunny, blue sky.

Deplaning, promising to email and call each other, I bid my new friend adieu. After retrieving my luggage I noticed quite a hullabaloo coming toward me down the corridor. It was some high profile entourage replete with bodyguards and five people protectively encircling a man with black square framed glasses and a classy black Fedora. From twenty feet away I recognized Elvis Costello. Wowza, as my heart did a noticeable pitty-pat! No way. Right there. As they neared, it was as if every member in his party, one by one, had to quickly attend to some other duty until there he was—five feet away from me standing completely alone and adorable. We looked at each other. He returned my smile. I perceived a gentle aura, not necessarily inviting, but neither was he off-putting.

I've got to go over to him, I thought, I can't let this pass. Oh shit, what can I say? Think, think, c'mon you've got to say something. What?

Slowly extending my hand, taking the few steps, I said, "Elvis?"

His eyes assented, arm reaching out as he gave my hand a light squeeze.

"I love your music."

"Thank you."

God, think of something else, quick, idiot, brain don't fail me now, I'm reasoning, and don't ask him for his autograph like a dolt!

Meantime, Zelda and Kurt were heading toward my baggage carousel. Anticipating the meeting, every few feet Kurt would point to someone, asking, "Is that your mom or oh, there, is that her?"

Each time Zelda shook her head in the negative until totally flabbergasted she declared, "That's my mom, **there**, talking to ELVIS COSTELLO!"

How cool was I?!

Nonplussed, drop-jawed, Kurt exclaimed, "NO WAY!"

After hugging them, Zelda introduced me to her boyfriend, and I introduced them to my 'friend,' Elvis!

And then just as suddenly as it disappeared, the entourage swept back around enveloping him into the cocoon, ushering him toward a waiting limo driver.

"So were there any storm warnings here?" I asked.

"Nothing. It isn't really even cloudy," they explained. "What was going on up there?"

"No clue," I said. "One of those enigmatic coincidences that put me face to face with one of my favorite artists who had one of the softest hands I've ever felt."

You gotta love the woowoo!

Another mind blowing night out in Dendrobia with my girls, Vera and Blair. Again with the assault, harassment, flirting, however you want to categorize it. We're all friends with this particular individual, and know he wants to date me but it's so not happening. Kelsey's not my type. He's alright to hang out with, dance with but I'm still on my guard wanting to hold that line because I know if I encouraged the least little bit, he'd be splaying his innermost soul across my life. How do I know this? He's too eager. You know my list, criteria for prospective suitors/partners: financially independent, fully single, divorced, no dependent children, blah, blah, blah. Kelsey did not have even one of these qualities. The last time we were together on the dance floor, he sidled up to me even thrusting into me, pissing me off. I'm like, "Back up!" So he pulled me into him as he pushed his leg into my groin. I returned the favor with a forceful knee. Maybe more energy than necessary but what fucking moron doesn't know that that's out of line? Apparently, a lot of them! Well, he crumbled to the floor as I pivoted, retrieved my coat, exiting post haste. It's called respect, Kelsey, and if I have to use that overt of an object lesson, you're a moron. I'm not taking this shit anymore. Dickbrain-thinking with his little head. If I have to demand respect, I will. Be mindful, I tell myself. Don't let anyone take advantage. Be wise, smart, bold, unequivocal, determinate. My husband was always such a gentleman, always faithful, honest, a man of integrity. I'm not settling for anything less. DON'T SETTLE!

Of course, I rehashed the situation with Vera after work. With a delightful bottle of Sauv Blanc we basked in the twilight lounging in my yard among the nightingale serenade. Late fall blessed us with a balmy seventy degree day. We took advantage of the gift while watching the coral sky tinge hazy gray.

"Get this," Vera said. "Blair told me she heard Kelsey, the immature weasel, is accusing you to whoever will listen, saying you led him on, encouraged and pressed into him!"

"Oh, that's just great! Whatever. You know that's not true, right? What is his problem?"

"Of course, I know it's not. That's his ego, his mindset, trying to save face, I guess. Rejection is hard to take and he's so insecure in the first place that it's not surprising."

"I wonder how long it took him to get off the floor?"

We both had to catch our breath, laughing so hard, taking care not to choke on our wine.

"Goddammit, I pretty much have to join a convent or something to keep myself safe from lecherous males," I grumbled, saddened but also somewhat disappointed in myself. "Are we to blame? I really don't understand the rules. Or I do but no one else does. I think I project a fairly wholesome persona, not overly revealing clothes, make-up minimal, some mascara, light eye liner, nothing heavy duty. But it's ridiculous to think we're still in this cave man era having to be on the defensive or someone will take advantage of you."

Vera commiserated, "I don't think so, to blame, we're just out having a good time, being loose, yes, but why does that say, 'come and get me?' We shouldn't have to be all straight laced and sober to merit respect. I'm exasperated with the whole situation. Let's just stay here, you and me. You want a refill?"

"Do you think we drink too much? Should we maybe consider that?"

Laughing, Vera eyed me intently, "Oh, you're serious?"

"Hah! Have you heard this one? The only twelve steps I'm interested in are the ones from the bar to the ladies room. But this is even better, if I give up drinking, I'm worried I'll have to replace it with murdering."

"Oh my god, did you make that up?"

"No, my daughter, Zelda, my type A daughter, so take charge, in your face, doesn't take any shit from anyone. She told me that line. By the time she was ten she was babysitting for her three younger siblings. As to murdering, I continue to entertain scenarios that make my old work nemesis disappear. I've told you about that catty cunt, Jane."

I'm pretty sure I was kidding but then …

After a couple more glasses, a cigar and airing of grievances we'd sorted it all out, getting quite absurd with the inebriated exchange, all over the map debating whether it was Native American or American Indian or even First Nations or if human interest news reports were all about exploiting the victim, invading their most private horror and trauma, laughing at the Keith Morrison/Bill Hader lampoon, inanely asking in that sing-song mode, 'how did thaaaat make you feel?'

"Friends, or should I say, a few fabulous friends, are the best tonic. And I read this, apparently attributed to Caesar, 'A friend, as it were, is a second self.' Here's to that, my dear."

"I'm curious about your cult background. You mentioned that in passing one night but we didn't get into it. When was that?" Vera queried.

"Really, you want to hear about that? Christ, it seems like a million years ago, another lifetime."

"How did you go from hippie to religion? I can't imagine you involved in that way of life."

"And I'm so glad you can't see it in me anymore. Purged. It wasn't that much of a stretch when you consider our idealism. Sometime I'll tell you about the Mesa. Mesa Poleo. That's another saga. When the cracks appeared in our life style, the 'hips' on the Mesa were faced with glaring humanity, all its foibles and hypocrisy, so the Jesus People message of forgiveness, grace and love of God looked like a reasonable alternative. Plus we were very judgmental,

89

espousing peace with our anti-war rhetoric but in actuality believing we were so superior to capitalist middle class society. Christians were the epitome of self-aggrandizers having all the answers."

"I can follow that," Vera said, eyebrows scrunched. "But why twenty years?"

"God, I marvel at that myself, and will probably forever. They told us it was the way, the only way. The way, the truth, life. We bought it. Were ripe for the picking. Why not morph into Jesus freak? We'd traveled the distance of our life, the gamut, all of our years to find that elusive, undeniable utopia. If it had stayed on that mountaintop, it probably would have been alright but we followed down, down into the abyss of blind faith. Brainwashed, I'd have to call it, in hindsight. Twenty years until the scales fell away. The last straw was Nick's and my involvement with the gay rights movement. All the love and grace didn't apply to that community. We thought it was exactly what Jesus was talking about and joined a group that supported AIDS victims. Didn't Jesus hang with the lepers and prostitutes? What a travesty some religions have devolved into. Our fundamental church warned us against that direction, you know 'pray the gay away' but we dug in, knowing in our hearts what was right. You know, there's that aspect of religion, the practice of judging anyone who isn't exactly aligned with you doctrinally, it is so insidious and flawed. I love this one: If you don't like gay marriage, don't get gay married."

"Good one. You know, I can't even imagine you a Jesus Freak."

"Right? It took many years to shed the cloak of fear. They rule by fear. Have you ever noticed how guys our age react to gay rights? Not that Nick was at all prejudiced, like I said, we were nothing but supportive and sympathetic, but he'd have this sort of shudder and expression when he'd actually think about it, as if someone was trying to shove something up his ass. I called him on it, asking if he had a problem and he, of course, said not at all but it makes me clench my butt cheeks. I've talked to other friends my age whose husbands have a similar response so I do believe Nick's explanation but I think it's their generation with the sort of indoctrination they may have been exposed to early on, that needs to be addressed, educated out of them."

"Hmmm, interesting. I'll have to remember that. It's not something you'd notice. Like I wouldn't be looking for it. Kind of amusing though. You come up with some bizarre anecdotes, I must say. Always enlightening. But how did your kids all turn out so liberal and normal?"

"Good question. I've thought about that a lot and am so grateful they weren't damaged beyond repair. Maybe they could see the hypocrisy more clearly, they did know we were doing the best we could, trying to be honest with them, be decent human beings. I believe, in our heart of hearts, Nick and I had a core mindset that although often may have been cloudy or over-shadowed, our love and integrity remained clear and evident. But truly, I just shake my head, like what a relief. We lucked out. Or it's a miracle. Nick used to say, 'you can't take the credit if they turn out good, and you can't blame yourself if they turn out bad, you just do the best you can'."

I never neglect to brush and floss, no matter how hammered I am. Gum surgery is an indelible imprint ensuring unflagging oral hygiene. As the Sonicare hums away I reflect on Nick, the conversation bringing him to the forefront,

91

conjuring images of my beloved. Sliding between the covers, I have that pang of loneliness, the empty bed and I silently wish for what was. Will that ever go away? He's not here. Where is he? Good question. My philosophy encompasses any and all persuasions, mine toward the theory I read about in *The Alchemist*. To paraphrase; when we die, we spread out to everything, knowing everything, being in and amongst all. Who knows? It's not hard to envision Nick in such an altruistic way. It's comforting to me.

[I'll write a few lines in my journal, express this gnawing thought so that it won't keep me awake. I have a headache so much, like eye strain except I wake up in the morning with it, in my right temple. Is it a brain tumor? I try to listen to my inner voice—you will live longer, realize your dreams. Don't expect to die. But then I never know. It's not guaranteed, not a sure thing. If I go, I go. C'est la vie. I do feel like I have to write all the things I want to write so my life can't be done yet. My justification. Goodnight.]

Now what? Huge upheaval. I'm laid off. My job is done. The jewelry store didn't make it. Big surprise. I didn't figure our small town needed another such business in the first place and with a faltering economic forecast, people are lucky to afford groceries. I'll apply for unemployment tomorrow and am determined to make it on whatever comes my way. Scary but I'm relieved to not have to go into that store again. I don't wish her, the boss, any ill-will but given her inexperience and naiveté, she really didn't stand a chance.

"I've got a new significant other," Vera confessed.

That evening we met at a local bar to debrief after our announcements. Vera was deeply concerned about my predicament, lending helpful suggestions for employment.

We split a Greek salad, a pitcher of beer and peanuts. Cracking, throwing the shells on the floor we downed the first glass too quickly. That standard salty marketing tool.

"I'm blown away. When did this happen? How long has this been going on? Who is it and tell me all about it," I gushed, excitedly.

"He used to live here but now is in Pennsylvania. We were good friends when he was here and we've kept in contact, talking fairly often, and then it just evolved into this deeper connection as we shared more of our lives. He has two kids that live here, teenagers, so he visits. It's been going on for a few months and now I want to take a road trip out there and see what happens. Are you up for a road trip?"

"Hell ya. It's perfect timing, out of work, enough money to split the gas. Can we stay with him or something else free? When are you thinking? What's his name?"

"His name's Gabe. Gabriel, but he goes by Gabe. I'm excited. I'm thinking in a couple of weeks," Vera said. "I think he has room or someone he knows could put you up."

"Oh man, I so need this. My thinking has gone through a metamorphosis of sorts. I feel like I'm ready to move on, as in dating. I'm thinking someone will materialize, pretty much out of thin air! Or a mutual friend introduction, and I'll consider going out. There. I said it."

"That's huge. Where did this come from? It seems abrupt, right?"

"Who knows? Some out of body experience. I know it is out of my comfort zone, but I don't have to get serious, don't have to have sex, or even see them more than once. My

93

choice. I mean, I haven't even seen anyone interesting in Dendrobia so I know it'll be elsewhere. Seems like a widower would be an option. I don't have to have all my ducks in a row before I make a move."

"I'm pretty flummoxed. But it's a good thing, going forward, taking a risk, frightening but I know you know your heart and mind. I'm right there with you."

"I'm so full of questions. Not the least of which is, how's the sex with Gabe?"

"My lips are sealed."

"No? Not even the least little hint?'

"Well, it's great and he's totally aware of my needs. I feel so lucky. And that's all I'm going to say about it."

"Hmm, not even a little dirt? No, I'm kidding. I respect you for that. Obviously, I know we're better than that. Plus, I'm sure it's too early to notice any faults. With the religious thing I do remember a few valuable lessons. One was this teaching about respect for your spouse that so impacted Nick and me. If you disparaged him or her, gossiped about their shortcomings it was like bringing him up in front of a crowd, standing him on a table and undressing him one item at a time until he was naked. That visual has always stuck with me."

"Thought provoking. What other tidbits?"

"Just this one. Nick and I would hold hands in the morning, facing each other and speak a blessing to one another, wishing for a peaceful and productive day ending with 'I love you.' Giving that intention was always so positive, so affirming for our relationship."

"I like that. It's like it sets the tone with encouraging energy."

"Anyway, you can see how hard it's going to be to replace that. I need to make some adjustments, eh? I always want to be in control, to know all of the particulars. How, when, who? I still have connections in Minneapolis, friends from Santa Fe, contacts. We'll just see how it all unfolds. If. "

"Well, the wheels are turning, I can see. I'll keep you on track. Maybe someone in Pennsylvania but we won't get ahead of ourselves. I've got to get home," Vera offered, rising to hug me.

Our hugs, so warm, so constant. Mmmmm.

So, that happened. Someone in Pennsylvania. Shit show. Mistake. Learning experience in that now I had one under my belt. A starter boyfriend. But Christ on a cracker, totally weird. We connected at the local diner in Gabe's town. Just struck up a conversation and let it take us on the ride. I guess I wanted to see where it would end up but should have turned right around the first time I entered his house. He was one of those pack-rat types where you couldn't see the floor. You couldn't even see the chairs it was piled so high. Simultaneously, I had been attracted and then instantly repelled. Could it have been something so simple as a spectacular back rub, kneading me into compliance, submission, malleability… my feet, my back, my shoulders, up my neck to my scalp. Liberatingly delicious. But he lived in squalor, imprisoned by a bizarre lifestyle of defense mechanisms insulating himself with piles, mounds of detritus hiding his cordoned soul.

The only thing that even gave it another day was that his sister had a condo in the Poconos that we lit out for the following morning. And I'd had my own bedroom that initial night and no, it wasn't jammed full to the ceiling. It was the one walled off space with some semblance of civilized habitation. My judgment was clouded by emotional components that were in need of an encounter. At least, that's how I see it in hindsight. And he did have deep pockets, showering me with gifts along with love and attention. If I would have pressed him on politics I'd have seen his right wing bent and worse was his disenfranchisement of his gay son. I did have sex with him, which was well, not good. He blew into my vagina? Never had that one. At least he's in the vicinity, I thought. It lasted six months but only because we weren't in the same state. Some back and forth, tons of phone calls and emails and I had to call it.

This unemployment thing is my salvation. I'm surprised at how I can go with the flow and not be freaking out. Dear, dear friends from the old days, hippie days in New Mexico where Nick and I lived for three years, keep in close contact extending invitations to come and visit, stay as long as you want. It hasn't been possible until now. I secured a house/cat-sitting gig in Nambe, north of Santa Fe for three months traveling the 1400 miles in my trusty old Camry, 'Cammie.'

Vera, Blair and I'd had a martini night the day before I was to take off at E.T, our moniker for Etoile Cuisine. Not the brightest idea but we needed a bon voyage.

"What am I going to do without you down the block for three months?" Vera queried. "I'll still have to go to your yard and just sit. I will keep an eye on your house, look in on it for you, but I can't imagine you not right there."

"Me too," Blair intoned. "I love that you're going, you need it, but we'll miss you so."

"Let's not get too sappy and sentimental. I'll be back. Soon enough and it'll be like we never skipped a beat. We'll talk, email. C'mon, let's have one more."

We knew it was that last one that did us in. Walking the six blocks to my house from the bar I'm surprised we didn't get arrested for public consumption or disorderly conduct. Something. We were loud, laughing at ridiculous bullshit trying to stay upright and not take a tumble. It was a good wind-up but now I was driving down Interstate 35W with blurry eyes and a muddy brain.

97

Plenty of thinking time alone across the states into Missouri, Kansas, Oklahoma ruminating over the previous night's conversation. I'd asked Blair about her rotten luck with men. She had two children with her college professor, splitting with him when the kids were very young.

"I had this connection to Wisconsin, visited, met my next husband and hung in an abusive situation for too many years," Blair explained. "The next man was truly a gem when he was sober but his addiction practically destroyed me. He was a good dad to my kids but I couldn't trust him to be honest with me, never knowing if he'd be driving drunk, lying about it."

This turned out to be the same dude who drove his Harley up the courthouse steps that particular 'lawn chair' night during the concert. What a train wreck and she was with him for a dozen or so years!

"I'm so sorry to know this, you deserve so much better. It makes me feel so lucky to have had my husband for three decades."

"You better believe it," Blair added. "I don't know many people who get that. Our parents typically stayed together that long but how many of them were happy and in love?"

Recalling the feeling that swept over me, the once in a lifetime love, my eyes teared up. That'll never happen again. I'll never have that, I thought. Alone the rest of my life. It was a vulnerable sense, especially driving through Kansas City and Oklahoma City, the undertow of fear. Scenarios skittered through my brain imagining a flat tire, some engine malfunction, and what would be my line of defense? You'd hear of horror stories like that every day. Wrong place, wrong time. As soon as I'd get back into my car after gassing up I'd hit the lock button, aware of my surroundings while projecting strength and inner confidence. I didn't drive at night and was careful to keep to the well-lit areas of motel parking lots but I hoped, even sensed Nick was watching over me, guiding me along the lonesome highway.

I was eager to reconnect with my hippie crowd, catch up on, God, how many years had it been? My kids and I'd brought Nick's ashes out to our mountain site the summer after he died. He and I said the previous year after a reunion with the old friends that someday we wanted to come back for good, live here again. We honored his wish and scattered him at 9,000 feet among the towering ponderosa pines of the Santa Fe national forest, up the winding dirt road from Mesa Poleo to Rio Puerco. Sydney and Blake, Maggie and Mickey, Lillie and Dylan, our dearest and closest friends arranged everything making an extremely difficult journey less so. Their love and support were my anchor and even though we hadn't been together regularly over the decades the bond was indestructible. Driving from Texas across the border into New Mexico I could hear my spirit voice, 'I'm home.' Yes, my physical address is elsewhere but it's apparent my spirit dwells in the mountains of the Southwest across this desertscape. Sage brush, pinon, scrub oaks, foothills ascending to rocky climes. The softly hued clay gradually blending to deep green, grayish blue crest, my route along Highway 285 captured the essence of northern New Mexico. In the distance I could now make out celestial frosted peaks defining the separation with shaded mounds, earthly to ethereal but truly, it's all one, my centering force. A tumbleweed rambles along the fence line finding others in the arroyo with which to congregate and commiserate. My breath exudes, and then as I inhale my soul is imbued with enchantment.

The cat sitting job was for one of the Los Alamos lab scientists. Talk about strange folks. Scientists are so out of my league and purview that I was intimidated in his presence. Not that he even said anything. His wife did all the talking, instructing, not the four pages of my dog sitting gig but detailed, nonetheless. A nineteen year old cat named Mosca, Spanish for mosquito, required several medications every day, special diet and of course, extreme deference to each and every need. She lived up to her name and I've always been more of a dog person so the challenge was formidable. Mosca wanted to sleep on my pillow next to me but that was out of the question. I mean, those feet are in the cat box, for god's sake, and now I'm having them right there where my mouth is? Yeah right.

That first morning Maggie called. Me, all excited to hear her voice, ready to make plans. She stopped me cold.

"You better sit down."

"Oh shit, what happened?"

"Blake had a heart attack and he's not going to survive. Sydney did CPR immediately and paramedics did all they could but he hasn't regained consciousness and brain function is, for all intents and purposes, gone."

Sliding down the wall, rubber-legs, I asked, "When did this happen?"

"Three days ago. When they said they couldn't do anything more for him at this hospital Sydney found the best brain center in Houston and moved him there. Private medical jet, the whole nine yards with hopes for a different outcome. You know our nurse, Sydney, knows more than the specialists, kinda nuts."

"Oh God, Maggie, when I think I may have had Nick hooked up to life support and waited for the kids to come to

Mexico, all the second thoughts wondering if anything could have been different, I am grateful I'd had that conversation with him. He told me in no uncertain terms not to keep him alive, not to do anything extraordinary. And too, I didn't have the funds to engineer something like Sydney."

"Maybe Sydney has to ease out of it this way, her sons, everyone. You know she has more money than God so maybe that's what you do. He's already gone though, it's obvious to everyone else."

"Maggie, this sends me right back to the trauma of Nick dying so suddenly. The shock is actually a blanket or insulation against the trauma. God, poor Sydney. She can be so out there anyway. I cannot imagine what this is doing to her. Blake was her balance, her normalizing influence. All I can think of is how much pain, agony and heartache she's in for. How the broken heart almost kills you, almost as if *you* had the heart attack. There's something to be said for quick, even instantaneous. Merciful for them, excruciating for us left behind. No adjustment, no processing, no saying goodbye."

"Sorry to have to be the bearer of such awful news. I'm in shock myself, we all are," Maggie said, choking up. "I'll see you as soon as I can. When will you be coming in?"

"Soon, for sure. I'll see what I can do to secure this place, the cat and I'll call you."

I called Sydney and was amazed when she picked up.

"I won't keep you, Sydney, but just want to tell you how much I love you and I'm here for you."

"I love you too."

And we hung up. I sat on the kitchen floor in stunned silence, petting Mosca curled up on my lap as if I was comforting her, me visualizing Nick's lifeless body, the light gone from his eyes, never to hear him laugh, too many nevers. You should always ask if they're sitting down, when you're delivering horrible news. I instinctively knew this when I called my kids from Mexico. Don't ask me how. It is really true that your legs give out, buckle. Haunting images of friends lost, too soon, too young, all of it beyond my reason. You simply can't make sense of the death. Unanswerable questions compound my despondency as I ponder why, always *why* such beautiful people are taken out too early and so many goddamn evil assholes sail along. I think Clarence Darrow was onto something when he said this: "One reason why we don't kill is because we are not used to it. I never killed anybody, but… I have had a great deal of satisfaction over many obituary notices that I have read. I never got into the habit of killing. I could mention the names of many that it would please me if I could read their obituaries in the paper in the morning."

It's all so unfair. It brought it all back in vivid frames as if I was right there hovering over Nick. PTSD has that ability, to crush you, at any given circumstance. I wasn't ever formally diagnosed but in therapy and through reading I'd deduced my reactions and symptoms enough to know when I was going down the abyss. And my doctor was wise enough to prescribe anti-anxiety medication. I still found it helpful to talk to Nick, at times like this, when he'd have known how to calm me, how to be firm but gentle, completely one with me. So I poured my heart out to him and you know what? It always felt like he somehow comprehended and even if I didn't hear anything, which most times didn't, his spirit reached into mine, into my heart and it was better. How can I explain it? There's no figuring out what happens when one dies. No one can say exactly where one goes. I do sincerely believe you're still somewhere, energy, essence. It continues.

102

What form? Who knows? Here's a bit of a science lesson from my research into the cycle of life and death:

In life, the human body comprises matter and energy. That energy is both electrical (impulses and signals) and chemical (reactions). The same can be said about plants, powered by photosynthesis, a process that allows them to generate energy from sunlight.

The process of energy generation is much more complex in humans. At any given moment, roughly twenty watts of energy course through your body, enough to power a light bulb, and this energy is acquired in a myriad of ways. Mostly, we get it through food, which gives us chemical energy. That chemical energy is then transformed into kinetic energy that is ultimately used to power muscles.

We learn through thermodynamics, energy cannot be created nor destroyed. It simply changes states. This so aligns with my intuition, my sensory receptors, confirming that my beloved husband is still out there somewhere. That is extremely comforting to me. The total amount of energy in an isolated system does not, cannot change, and thanks to Einstein, we know that matter and energy are two rungs of the same ladder.

The universe as a whole is closed. However, human bodies and other ecosystems are not closed, they're open systems. We exchange energy with our surroundings. We can gain energy through chemical processes and we can lose it by expelling waste or emitting heat.

This is especially significant aligning with my philosophy. In death, the collection of atoms we are composed of are repurposed. Those atoms and that energy, originating during the Big Bang, will always be around. Our 'light,' the essence of our energy, not to be confused with our actual consciousness, will continue to echo throughout space forever. Till the end of time!

Through my study of the topic I've gleaned various truths that form my basis of faith on the subject.

A physicist could possibly comfort at your funeral with this explanation. They could tell us all energy, every vibration, every BTU of heat, every wave of every particle that is our departed one remains with them in this world. Amid energies of the cosmos, that suggests to me that karma, in some way, does enter in. Photons created within our constellations of electromagnetically charged neurons contain the energy that will go on forever. According to the laws of conservation of energy, not one whit of you is gone, you're just in a different state.

Anger hits after the sadness, at the universe, the powers that be. When I was a Jesus freak I had the typical attitude that now they were in heaven and what a fabulous reward and they were so much better off. No more! I have no idea where anyone goes or if there's an afterlife but if you believe in the continuum, energy endures through other forms or incarnations. I entertain multiple theories that make me arrive at these conclusions, that enable me to recover and reignite my mostly positive attitude. I sincerely want to put encouragement into and around all of those within my sphere of influence. A glass not only half full but *full* kind of person. Part of the solution.

Here's a thought. What about being pro peace, instead of antiwar? Positive versus negative. Not fighting for peace but allowing peace, joining in an embrace of harmony. I like that.

This I'm sure of, I do not want to go through that again, the loss, morphing into someone I can't stand. That Debby

Downer for an inordinate amount of time. I know I don't have that kind of control, to orchestrate the universe, but I have learned so many important tenets from the sum total of my experience, not the least being that life goes on, life is short and it's our choice how we're going to live it. More therapy would be helpful and one day when I can afford it… truly, counseling has been so very beneficial, meantime, I will press on, have to, learn as I go, stumble with probably another relationship, comparing it to the 'gold standard' and find it wanting. *He* has to understand this depth to my temperament, not necessarily agreeing with it but sympathetic to it, has to have enough of a feminine side to be willing, not threatened, finesse as well as manliness, more evolved and balanced, ideologically. I may be asking too much.

After a week in Houston Sydney brought Blake back to Santa Fe to die, in their home, setting up an ICU in their bedroom with feeding tube, trach, catheter, all the equipment monitored by the more than capable nurse, Sydney. Around the clock she gave every last ounce of her being to circumvent the diagnosis, to no avail. Even researching anything and everything about obscure instances where an individual ostensibly came back from the dead. We all spent time with him complying with Sydney's last ditch effort but were essentially humoring her. Truthfully, we were saying our goodbyes before they pulled the plug. Tethered to machines is no way to end one's days and even if his brain wasn't comprehending, somewhere I sensed a sadness in him. Maybe it was my imagination but sort of spirit to spirit I felt him yearning to be set free.

When MRSA invaded his body even Sydney had to admit defeat, unplugging him. The silence that ensues when the clamor of the machines ends is deafening in its emptiness. One by one the beeps, the inhaling/exhaling halts and the life force disappears, an invisible fog to the senses. I've been with enough dying people to recognize the phenomenon.

The memorial was at their home, a gathering of loved ones, catered with prodigious amounts of adult beverages. Emotions all over the place, at the same time hearing laughter, sobbing, a constant din of sympathetic conversation, the occasional tranquil pause. I had this moment with a guy, somewhat of a ghost from hippie days, you know where you think you knew this person at some point in your life but can't place where? Anyway, Mickey introduced us, his name is Frank Bunde and we had a, and the only thing that describes it is, we had a vibe. A bit of an electric current, unspoken attraction, seeing into someone's soul, something in the eyes, his cool, soft grin. One tiny brain wave that makes you say, 'hmmm?' And it was maybe all of thirty seconds. Or a minute.

Sydney's doing as well as can be expected, seeing a therapist, taking meds and talking tons, and I'm actually glad to be that sounding board for the first time since Nick died because I know what I know, know what to say about death and heartbreak. It gives me credibility. Not that I'd ever *choose* to go through it but there are things I've learned and am not afraid to verbalize because I've experienced it, such as not skipping over turmoil by trying to bury it. It takes the rest of your life. I dread the next loss but I don't live there. It will happen as sure as the blinding sun rises or like sand washing out to sea, just as waves roll in … out, pummeling the shoreline, the undertow overpowering. I know the anguish it brings but have to risk it or give up on life. It's not defeatist or morbid but realistic and pragmatic. As strong as their presence was, that's how strong the absence is felt. Powerful and profound as that life lived, the depth of grief will surpass, continuing forever.

It was about a month later Maggie drove out to spend a night with me, just the two of us. Girl time. We were best friends forty years ago on the Mesa. Mickey and Nick also. Such extraordinary years, treasured memories, the indissoluble bond.

"It kind of freaks me out being here alone. Even with an alarm system and a gate I can't get past the isolation," I explained, "God, the coyotes were screaming last night like we'd hear them on the Mesa. It penetrated my spine."

"Ya, I don't hear that in the city. Sometimes I miss the wilderness but I don't want to live there. There's supposed to be a meteor shower tonight with an almost full moon. We'll see if we can catch it. This sky is so spectacular, so clear, so vibrant. I miss that too with all the lights in town. I gave Rob your number, by the way."

"Hold up. WHAT? Why?"

"We were at his art show, you know, what was it, two weeks ago, and you talked to him so much and you said positive things about him and you can talk to him, just see what he wants. He called and asked for your number. What's the big deal?"

"Just see? See what? Oh, Maggie, I'm not ready for that. Especially after Blake's death, all the heartbreak it churns up. You should have asked me first. I would have told you, 'get his number and if I want to, I'll call him.' Damn, I am not in the right place."

"Well, can't you just tell him that? Why make such a big deal out of it? You don't have to marry him. Have a drink with him."

"You really don't get it, do you?"

That put a damper on our whole evening and I ended up wishing I hadn't reacted so severely. It's not like we couldn't move on, yakking well into the night, imbibing, but there was a shadow, a constraint and we both sensed it. I felt blindsided. Like a girlfriend should know these things, right?

"Do you remember when we found that teenage girl lying on the highway? We were taking our laundry into Cuba, tooling along in your red VW bug."

Maggie immediately chimed in, "How could I forget that? I've thought about it many times over the years, forty plus years, and what actually happened. You know that story about her sleep walking out of the camper, falling onto the pavement, dying? That's bullshit. None of it adds up."

"Right. Why didn't we question it at the time? How could she fall out of the camper going down the highway at whatever speed and be completely serene, lying on her back, not even mussed up or askew in any way. If you fell out of a vehicle, you'd roll and be twisted, smashed and bloody. She looked like someone simply set her down, smack in the center of the road."

"Exactly!"

Engrossed in our conversation on the highway to Cuba that morning, we both gasped at the body, Maggie hitting the brake, "What's that?"

She slowed, approaching close enough for us to recognize a young girl looking like she was asleep in the middle of the road. I grabbed two of the baby blankets in the back seat as we both jumped out. Sort of like a vision of sleeping beauty, she had no visible injuries, not even any blood. We were stunned, to say the least, deciding Maggie would drive for help and I'd remain to flag traffic. But just as Maggie climbed into her car a truck pulled up.

Waving my arms, I heard him downshift, halting near me, "This girl is unconscious. We found her lying right there. Can you get help?"

"Ya, I'll get to the closest phone and call the police," he assured as he drove away."

Maggie and I stayed there, by her side, not knowing what else to do, so we said a prayer asking for divine assistance, insight, knowledge, anything that might help.

"So the thing I can't reconcile now is how she 'fell' out of her parent's camper, they were supposedly in the cab, right? The camper on the truck with a back door and she is napping, sleep walks out and lands on the highway. And she's not one huge, crumpled mass of blood and guts. Remember what they told us in town? Maybe a week later we heard that explanation and that she was pronounced DOA in Cuba. And the parents finally realized she was gone and turned around."

"It's a thing we'll never understand or figure out. Was it '72?"

"Ya, that sounds about right. And why were we the ones that found her? One of those very strange woowoo things, that makes me wonder if we could look that up somewhere. You know, fatality on highway by Lindrith, now that we have internet? I mean, if we're that interested."

We left it at that knowing neither of us were that vested.

"Anne, HI! Oh, it's so good to hear your voice. How are you, how's it going? I miss you so much," Vera gushed into the phone.

I had to call her to get her take on my predicament. Rob kept calling me daily and I never picked up.

"Vera, I feel like such a shit having this weird, almost harassing thing going on."

"Tell me, what's happening?"

"Oh God, Maggie gave this artist guy my number and he keeps calling me and I ignore it but he doesn't get the hint."

"And what's his deal?"

"Turns out, we're both from Minneapolis, similar upbringing, connections around that locale but he's the typical starving artist and bottom line, I don't want any attachments or involvements right now."

"Well, get this, Gabe is talking about moving here. Dendrobia."

"That is huge. When? Are you bouncing off the walls?"

"Of course. Within the next year. There's a lot to work out, figure out, details. But I'm hopeful it is going to happen. And I'm trying not to get ahead of myself."

"I'm so happy for you. Truly. You so deserve that, someone you love and trust and laugh with and dance with. It is the best news."

"God, I wish you were here. How are things going otherwise? Any work prospects or other house-sitting possibilities? And how 'bout your friend, Sydney? How's she doing?"

"It's so rough, day by day, but she's hanging in there and I'm hoping she'll make it. Sometimes she's so on the edge, drinking so heavily and completely losing it. Like I fear for her mental state but at the same time know that I was very much like that in the early days and I came out of it so I mostly encourage her to let it vent, don't hold back because then you'll get it out. I hope that's right. But it does scare me when I see her in the morning looking as if she'd been run over by a steam roller. I'm giving her all the grace I can muster. As far as work, nothing is panning out and this job is over in two more weeks. I'm scrambling for the next option. Maybe I'll go over to Arizona to my folks. That's getting desperate though. If nothing else opens up I'll be heading back up North, just in time for winter! First though, I'm going up to the Mesa for a few days, stay at Sydney's cabin, be totally alone and unplugged."

"You won't be afraid with all the crazies and wild animals? Isn't it dangerous?"

"I'm not going to think about it. I need to go. It's calling me. You know Nick's ashes are up there, well, were up there. Who knows where they are now? I need to hear something, understand or learn. I need direction so I tell myself I'll be alright, sort of on a quest. Don't worry. And I did have this encounter at Blake's memorial. Someone I'd heard about through the friends out here but never formally met. Tall, nice looking. Maggie's husband, Mickey, was talking with him and there was this magnetism, gravitational pull that made me sidle over to them. You know how that unction gets you? Pheromones."

"So what happened?

"Not a lot. We said 'hi,' had a few exchanges about hearing of each other through the years from our mutual friends. But the interesting thing was, there was a vibe, when we looked into each other's eyes. Some deeper spirit thing."

"Interesting. Why don't you get *his* number?" Vera laughed, zinging me.

"Well, this is the really weird part. He's the artist's brother! Anyway, his name is Frank Bunde and it's the first time I've felt the remotest connection since Nick died."

"I'll be glad when you're back at the end of the block and we can hash it all out. Gotta run now. Be safe my friend, be watchful. I love you so much."

"I will. You too, Vera. I love you. Bye."

Before I headed north Sydney invited me to spend a spa weekend in T or C. Truth or Consequences. It's the bona fide name that they changed upon winning a contest on the old game show, Truth or Consequences. Don't ask me how it was judged. I'm sure you can Google it. Ralph Edwards, I recall, was the host.

"You know who lives in Silver City, eh?" Sydney asked.

"No, but what's that look?"

"Frank," she revealed, with this sly, sideways glance.

I knew what she was up to, having had that conversation, her wanting me to find someone. She could envision it for me but of course, not for her.

"Tall drink of water, Frank? And what do you propose to do? Go there? How far is that?"

"Ya, that Frank. It's not far. I thought I'd call him and say we're in the area and would he like a visit."

"You could just do that? You're that comfortable asking? He probably won't remember me. Are you sure about this?"

"I'll call and see. I'm thinking he *will* remember you."

So she called. I couldn't believe her chutzpah. Like 'who are you right now?' I'm listening and she's telling him we'd be able to drive over and she'd love to see his place out there in the Burro Mountains and my friend Anne is with me, you remember her from Blake's memorial. Ya, that's the one. Right. Aw, damn. When will you be back?

Her smile fades as he explains to her he's actually on the road right then and he won't be back for several days. I'm wondering if it's subterfuge. She insists it is not and he did remember me because she could hear a lilt in his voice. I'm doubtful. And relieved he wasn't home. It felt like going down a precarious rabbit hole, so quick and spontaneous. Way too fast. I asked Sydney why, if they were all in Tucson together in '70, he didn't come to Mesa Poleo when the rest of them did. She revealed he'd been busted with four hundred pounds of pot and was serving time. Jesus! We'd all been dealing at some time or another in those days, maybe not in those amounts but nonetheless, I thought it some very bad luck and was curious to hear the whole saga. Sydney didn't know many of the specifics but he had to leave a wife and baby daughter behind to fend for themselves. It cast somewhat of a pall on my expectations but I didn't want to be too quick to judge deciding I'd have to hear his side of things before coming to any conclusions.

The spa was wonderfully relaxing, rejuvenating, our evenings peaceful as we processed the upheaval in her life. Shattered beyond recognition, I affirmed she'd never be the same.

"I read Joan Didion's book, *The Year of Magical Thinking,* when it came out in '03 gleaning so many helpful insights, particularly that your grief is totally personal to your own experience, your relationship, and the way she wrote, with her honest perception, enabled me to believe I didn't need to second guess myself or apologize for my emotions. I could be at peace with my situation in all its complexity and confusion. When Didion lost her only daughter two years later I was so impacted that I wrote her a letter. It actually got to her and, AND she wrote me back a short but poignant card which I treasure. Nick died in Mexico, in the state of Quintana Roo on the Yucatan peninsula which I wrote to Ms. Didion. Her daughter's name was Quintana Roo. Sometimes it's such a small world."

Sydney listened mopping the tears, finding release, a respite in the collective spirit of bereavement, commenting, "It could always be worse."

8

Grief. Where did the phrase 'good grief' come from? Well, it's not that complicated but I take issue with the incongruity. What it actually does to you, how disastrous and destructive it is really begs the question. You won't hear me ever using that term. With deleterious consequences to one's psyche, as well as body, one may attempt to mask the emotional upheaval, like Jackie Kennedy after the assassination. What we didn't know at the time was how medicated she was. And rightly so. It will work for some things for a while but grief will not be assuaged, ignored or minimized. One cannot skip ahead or waylay the fates. It will happen to all of us. The question is when? All the way back to my best friend, Sallie, who died at nine, losses have shaped me. Inevitably, we will all follow. The question that plagued me was how do I get from here to there? Seasons passed, flew by me. I resisted not wanting to grow separately away from my union, my best friend. No, it wasn't as strong as it was and I even found myself hating the relief this new direction took me, forcing me further away from what I held so dear. Would it be so awful to be stuck in the past, threatening mental illness, emotional dysfunction? The pain always a thought away? Grief is so damned hard, tiring and yet harder if I gave up, neglected to pull myself out of bed another day, instead wrapping my cocoon around and around with the safety of isolation. No. I couldn't hide. You know how people tell you your loved one would want you to move on, be happy, find someone else. God, I hate that notion.

Sydney and I were trying. Wanting to share my experience with her, praying she'd survive, we were taking those initial steps. Included in our spa experience, of course, were massages. Sydney informed me she wasn't at all partial to the practice, not wanting anyone soothing her, touching her in an intimate manner. I got her to acquiesce but only after she adjured the masseuse that she didn't want any of this namby-pamby, touchy-feely shit.

His stellar reply, "I'll whip you around my head and throw you on the floor, if that's what you want."

"Sounds perfect," she quipped.

Back on the road to Mesa Poleo, north of Abiquiu, O'Keefe country, heading on Highway 96 between Coyote and Gallina. The forest road takes you to our old stomping grounds, isolated, totally impossible to navigate, unless you know where you're going. As I drove up the highway, serenity settled over me like blessing, grace, tranquility. Belonging, as in 'this is where I long to be.' I could trade in Cammie, for a four wheel drive vehicle and be set for the winter. Something was summoning my heart. Blessed peace. No pressure, no arguments, no false fronts, utterly quiet, stone still. Fantasy is so enticing. That first night all of those notions were challenged. Wind howling, creaking, strange house, I did not sleep soundly, interrupted by each foreign noise. The second night was better but by the third day all of my resolve gave way to practicalities. With a significant snow storm threatening the next day I played it safe and headed back to civilization. Slightly ashamed of my quick flip-flop I rationalized Sydney needed me to help her with all the red tape and complications surrounding death. Such a mysterious journey. And then it is the fullness of time. New

Mexico, my second home, but I will turn northward soon, the soto voce intuition that reinforces decisions one at a time. The four months flew by, the hour is determined and I'll drive across country arriving in the Midwest December 21st, barring weather interruptions.

Sitting at my friend, Dylan's, kitchen table in Santa Fe, he helped chart my journey home, tracing the route with his yellow highlighter in my atlas. The trip included a stopover in Sidney, Nebraska enroute to my home in Wisconsin.

"You're kidding," Dylan remarked. "You've never been to Cabela's in Sidney?"

"Ah, no," I said, scrunching my eyes like, why would I go there. "I'm not exactly the hunter type."

"It's only their headquarters and most impressive store in the entire chain."

"Aaand??" I teased.

Dylan, one of the most avid outdoorsmen I know, no THEE most avid, was incredulous at my ignorance, commanding, "Well, you've gotta go. If you're passing through Sidney, you have to stop. It's like nothing you've ever experienced. You'll see," he encouraged, and launched into a most persuasive litany of the wonders and attractions therein delineating the vast selection of hunting, fishing and camping equipment.

That was what our family did for vacations. Camp. Every damn year, because that is all we could afford. So with four youngsters we braved northern Minnesota to be eaten alive by mosquitoes, me having to produce meals without the convenience of a modern kitchen. Been there, done that. No thanks. Here's another practical quip from my arsenal: if by camping I can see the forest from my motel room, then yes, I'm in.

With my curiosity piqued following Dylan's profusely florid description, I agreed, mostly to humor him. Heading out at dawn I wove, is it wove, how 'bout snaked my Camry up the route through northern New Mexico, Taos, over to Ordway, then cruising along highway 71 in eastern Colorado. I was increasingly struck by the remote landscape, no cell coverage, no other vehicles for miles on end, not even any noticeable dwellings, just long dirt driveways leading to, one would suppose, a ranch. God, Dylan what did you get me into? Maybe fine for a guy but a woman traveling alone? I already decided this would be my last trip on Highway 71. What if I had a flat tire or engine trouble? I'd be hiking for many miles in search of rescue.

Well, none of that happened and I was relieved to cross the border from Colorado into Sidney, Nebraska. As Cabela's came into view, built atop the hill on the outskirts of town, I was astonished by the sheer magnitude of the sprawling complex.

Entering the front door, eyes agog, I was drawn to the 8,000 gallon walk-through aquarium. The staff must have been familiar with this dazed stare, several of which offered assistance within seconds of my arrival. I just shook my head no, floating along in my reverie. The enormity of the showroom was surprising enough, but then viewing the contents, every imaginable animal trophy displayed in flawless taxidermy, including an elephant!, was utterly mind boggling. After the fifth guy asked me if he could help, I noticed something peculiar. Here was a veritable wealth of handsome, rugged, virile males. Being single, I wondered if there was a Cabela's match.com included in their official web site. Maybe it was the pheromones or the testosterone levels, but I was definitely feeling a primal energy.

When the next man asked me if I was finding everything alright, I replied, "I could use some help. I'm a Cabela virgin."

His look was priceless, accompanied by a wide grin. Granted, he may have been an avowed womanizer, but maybe I needed 'izering!' At any rate, the entire experience was a boost, not only to my ego, but also my mood. Kudos to the fabulous atmosphere, remarkable store, exemplar staff, and if they ever *do* get the Cabela's dating service up and running, I've got my profile ready.

Sadly, not long after my enlightenment, Cabela's went the way of the conglomerate takeover. Their new owner, Bass Pro Shops, offered buyout packages to employees at the once preeminent headquarters in Sidney, where the company once employed more than 2,000 people in its heyday. A fraction of the employees remained in the store that now functions under the dual name. I guess I'm fortunate to have experienced the burgeoning megastore in its prime and bemoan such a loss for yet another American small town. And even prior to Cabela's I'm sure there were several mom and pop establishments ravaged by the huge box store's invasion. Would that we could have a thriving economy in all regions of the country but the bottom line unfortunately being the driving force, relegates a growing segment of this nation to the scrap bin. I wondered how long my small town would survive suffering the same invasion by Walmart and Menard's.

One takeaway after being home a week, my independence is so much stronger, feeling empowered and free. Out there, all alone, it showed me, revealed my inner core in a way I haven't seen up to now. I like her. 1,400 miles alone is ample time to contemplate my beliefs, issues, and either reconnoiter or solidify many of them. With a plethora of NPR programs, I am challenged, educated and fascinated by this world we inhabit from controversy surrounding free speech, the economy, women's rights to our dysfunctional prison system and the political jungle, to name a few.

It'll be six years next month. SIX since Nick died. How did that happen? Life is good so to commemorate getting back up, I'm contemplating a tattoo. It will be my second. I have Nick's initials inked on my left breast, not exactly on top of my heart but close enough. That was three years after he died.

"Hey, when did you get back? When are you coming over?" I queried Vera when she called, just back from a week with Gabe. "I can't tell you how much we have to catch up on. And Nick's death anniversary is in two days and I need a hug."

"Tomorrow after work, I'll stop by. How's that?"

"I'd prefer right now," I said, even though it was practically my bedtime. "I understand and will see you tomorrow. Can't wait."

"See you then."

At 5:30 we were getting comfy in my living room with a chilled white Bordeaux, rosemary crackers and sharp cheddar. I could almost live on cheese and crackers. Easy, delicious, no prep or clean-up along with sterling company. It was perfect. Even when we stayed in I could always depend on Vera to look haute couture. We both had the same penchant for shoes, clothes, and accessories, but she had a singular panache that continually wowed me. Our closets bursting with choices, my trademark was a scarf draped around or threaded through my blond hair in some unique manner. I must have possessed thirty or more. And shoes, we both verged on obsession with wedges, loafers, and slides, clogs, cowboy boots, sandals. Her legs looked stunning in heels which I'd had to eliminate from my wardrobe sighting neuromas, bunions and ingrown toenails. I still saved one pair of stilettos for a future walk from the bedroom door to the bed in the event *he* responded to that. Who didn't?! We justified the superfluity by shopping almost exclusively at second hand and vintage boutiques. And there was Goodwill, Savers and garage sailing. Our keen eyes honed in on Wolky, Dansko, Merrells and the like, smelling, perusing and ascertaining if the item was worth our precious dollars. Maggie, from Santa Fe, had introduced me to Wolkys with one step. I had admired her sandals while we were standing in line to buy tickets for a movie. She bent down, undid the strap and said, here, put your foot in. That's all it took. It felt like instant relief and comfort unlike any shoe I'd ever owned. Saving for months I purchased a pair new, an extremely rare occurrence. Over $170.00, YIKES! but so worth it.

Tonight Vera donned jeans with a stylish black leather belt, tucked in crisp white long-sleeved shirt, several strands of silver necklaces with matching hoop earrings and a chic tan toque. She wore her auburn hair rather short, spiked, just the smallest bit poking out around her ears beneath the hat. I had this imagination, a short story, where our clothes came alive at night, taking on personas as they assembled themselves together with reckless abandon to dance and lilt their way out the back door venturing through the neighborhoods. Ephemera Escape, I'd entitle it.

Settling in I began, "It is always the same, reliving the day Nick died," tearing up. "Like he let go, he left me, and I wonder if he knows what's going on. That is the only way he would have ever left me. Through death. I'm not going to dwell on it but just need you to know how it is, every single year. I used to think it would go away and I wouldn't hurt but now I believe I will forever have this same reaction on the date, albeit less painful."

"And is that okay, can you handle it?"

"I am. So far. I mean, if I made it through the first two years, I know I'll keep on. I'm always learning and am so grateful for you, to be able to unload like this. It's like living in an emotional fog, less so now but initially I could barely function, the shock was so severe but the second year the depression all but smothered me. I would have this recurring dream where Nick was struggling in water, drowning, I'm trying to get to him and can't make any headway. I waken completely exhausted and overwhelmed. My parents visited just four months after he died, trying to shame or guilt me into being better. I actually kicked them out, screaming 'I never want to see you again.' I couldn't believe they could be so insensitive. But they were of that generation where you suck it up, don't express your feelings, don't ever appear weak. They told me I was nuts. My dad said that! I can't disagree. Nice, eh? If it wasn't for my kids, my friends, I don't think I'd have stuck around. Anyway, enough of that shit, tell me about Gabe. When's he moving here?"

"He says soon but I am taking a patient stance, wait and see attitude. He will do it but I don't know if he realizes how many things have to happen. It's complicated, selling his property, consolidating or liquidating possessions. We talked through many of the details so we've got some idea but to see that accomplished, that's another layer or half a dozen layers."

"It will happen. I know it," lifting my glass to her, clinking. "I believe it's meant to be. Here's to true love."

"Wow, that bottle went fast," Vera remarked, as I emptied the last into our glasses. "Do you have more? I'm not ready to quit and we've barely scratched the surface."

"Is the Pope Catholic?" I quipped.

"I love the idea of your tattoo. Where are you doing it? And when?"

"Not in this little burg. Want to go to LaCrosse Saturday? Mind Altering Tattoos. I've heard good things and looked them up online. Here's the picture of my idea, modified slightly."

"Mmm, nice," Vera confirmed.

I'd combined a tribal eagle with butterfly wings and omitted the head because it had a menacing aspect, determining to have it branded between my shoulder blades. I'd had just two dates with a guy who was a birding expert that disparaged my design because it wasn't anatomically correct. Asshole. As if that was the purpose. I told him it was spiritual, not his purview and further he didn't have any right to critique any aspect of my life.

Relating the exchange to Vera, we had a few brutally skaggy remarks relegating him to oblivion, "What nerve to think he had a right to question my decision. Some people are on such ego trips. Can you believe it? Mr. Specialist! He goes, 'you don't have to look at it, though.'

And I shot back, "Oh yeah? Neither do you! BAHAHA!"

"Ya, I know you know your own mind. So much for him. That was quick. Two dates? Good to know before you wasted any more time."

"There's this part of me that yearns for strong arms to envelope me, pull me into him, feel that nuzzle against the back of my neck. In reality I know my desire for the ideal is way out of whack. Like I don't want to be a part of his life, I want to BE his life. Real sane!"

"Well, to be honest, that's a sick, narcissistic thought," Vera offered, laughingly.

"I know, I realize, he'd be possessed, I'd be smothered, devoured, fleeing for the nearest exit. You know, Disney ruined me with all that Prince Charming crap!"

"Oh, OH!" Vera interjected. "Jane died!"

"Wait! What? That Jane?" I shrieked, astounded. "What happened?"

"Really bizarre. I heard it from my sister. She had an infected tooth, abscessed, and the infection, sepsis, went to her heart and that was it."

"Oh my GOD, I said, holding my arms up in a mock praise the lord motion. "There is a god! I'm incredulous, trying not to rejoice and jump up and down. I won't. But is that ever payback or what? Not that I really believe it works like that. There are too many situations and circumstances where the bad guys get off scott free."

"Right, we'll try not to revel in it too heartily," Vera concurred. "But what were you saying about Nick?"

"Oh, ya, I was telling you about how Nick was truly close to the dream or ideal in so many ways and now that he's dead, he's sainted. Saint Nicholas. My English literature bent is tangled up in that romantic element always loving the Austin, Bronte, Wharton novels. I know I had another life in Great Britain. My descendants date back to the 1600s, eleven generations to an Eliphalet Bristol. In, you guessed it, Bristol, England."

Vera asked, "Do you know what that name means?"

"I researched it and love this, 'leading light or beacon of hope.'

"Nice, I like that."

"He was one of five brothers sired by William. Less than remarkable, mildly interesting but I believe it explains why it was the only subject I ever excelled at. Not a single teacher was ever successful in engaging my attention long enough to drum anything into this complicated brain. In my thirties I embarked upon a study of history through the love stories of Napoleon and Josephine, Victoria and Albert, as well as Wallace Warfield Simpson and King Edward the VIII. Dates and battles, facts and minutia miraculously sunk in. History finally made sense capturing my interest and veneration. Anyway, Sydney called today, too, just to encourage me, knowing the date. I was so proud of her ability to look past herself, her own situation, to reach out to me. Definitely kindred spirits now more so in loss. In this particular conversation she was on the giving end and told me I was her hero. I believe she's going to make it. I'm heading back out there in a month and a half so we better jam in as much girl time as we can. There's a couple of house-sitting gigs, some organizing stints they've lined up for me and I can stay with Sydney on the off time."

That Saturday Vera did some shopping, wandering along the river walk in LaCrosse while I got my tattoo. I asked the artist to soften it with a watercolor effect, dark blue but diffused. He'd ask periodically how I was doing, with the pain, whether I needed a break. I told him I had four babies without anesthesia. Bring it on. I'd like to think he was impressed.

125

Sydney's offer was timely. She'd invited me to come and stay in her lower level, be her companion, as it were, on the road to perdition. Well, to try to bring her back from it. She offered a stipend, of sorts, to help her organize, eliminate and simplify not just her closets but her life. Tall order. The hardest part would be sorting through Blake's belongings but she was resolute nothing was being discarded. We'd haul everything up to the Mesa where storage space in her barn was ample.

The uneventful drive to the Southwest was perfect for reflection and meditation allaying the anxiety I consistently felt about a single woman on the road. Defensive driving, mindful living, aware of my vulnerability I always took precautions, traveling strictly during daytime hours, sizing up situations, keeping doors locked, not even going to the motel pool or hot tub, even though it would feel so relaxing. I've seen those exposés where someone jumps a lone woman in the hallway. Maybe a little paranoid but hey, I'd rather be cautious than dead. I know men don't or usually cannot understand this, they're just wired differently. Plus that typical upper body strength doesn't hurt either. I never take for granted that something could not happen to me.

It is tough with Sydney, her recent widowhood, stumbling, flailing in the throes of despair. Not all the time but most evenings involve heavy drinking coupled with various medications. Not wise and I see the danger but am loathe to say anything. Yet. Her appearance in the morning is so telling. On a good day she resembles Sally Field, on a not so good, Elton John. Sorry Elton. We'll see how it goes after a month or so. I encourage her to let it out, cry, wail, whatever she needs. It won't be too much. Honestly, on my worst days I would carry on howling in agony until my nose bled. I could never imagine it would hurt that much. And *I* came out of it. Ultimately, I got through it so why not Sydney? But I missed my fun with Vera, our life. More and more I felt torn between two realities: the Southwest enchanted existence and the Midwest mother, nana, practicality person. Both necessary. Both woven like a tapestry throughout my very soul. Questions surface: where do I want to be, what do I want to do, with whom do I want to be? To thine own self be true, right? Most of the time I am fortified against involvement, barricaded against vulnerability, seeming to dread the need or any semblance of closeness that might leave me open to loss, or brokenness. How can I do it again?

I do love my freedom. Somewhere inside me there's courage to try again and I will know when it is time. Not yet. I know I'm still comparing every guy to Nick and they fall short. Every single one. When I recall our long spiritual discussions that ran the gamut from euthanasia to nonsensical, half-sense hippie day acid trips, I'm confronted with a huge void and yearning for that singular union. Words unspoken but understood, thought-melding looks, his soft eyes, tender embrace, standing in the kitchen leaning into each other. On so many levels there was this tacit connection sharing knowledge, intellectually challenging each other for over three decades. I'm convinced it's an eternal bond.

Fun, fun, fun. What a crazy scene movie making is. I loved it and hated it. Truly grueling work. Rising at 3:30a.m., to be south of Albuquerque, in Belen, New Mexico at 6:00, I drove the one and a half hours from Santa Fe. By a fluke, I'd discovered the nmfilms.com website, where I learned that Kevin Costner was shooting his new movie *Swing Vote* and

127

needed extras. I sent in my stats, (height, weight, and age) along with a head shot and received a call, telling me to report with black tie fancy outfits. I was to be a high end party-goer at a gala benefit for the Democratic presidential candidate, played by Dennis Hopper. I just happened to possess a gorgeous, black beaded, floor length gown (drag queenesque), and borrowed fabulous rhinestone jewelry from Sydney, that made my skin break out with a ghastly rash from my metal sensitivity. I'd gladly risk another alloy reaction, hazardous as it may be, for the experience.

After make-up, and a two hour wait, we hiked over to the set, a three block distance, in spike heels. Stupid. The following day, we ladies wised up and kept our flats on, stashing them under the tables before the 'take,' saving our tortured feet.

The scene: a banquet for the purpose of garnering the single vote that would decide the election. Both parties were, essentially, trying to buy Kevin's endorsement. By some quirky electoral fluke, the choice to decide the presidency was left to one individual. The extras were arranged, hob-knobbing in clutches, and in walks Nathan Lane, escorting Kevin and his stage daughter, eight year old, Molly.

Kevin, gawking, definitely out of his element, as a back-woodsy, hillbilly sort of character, observes the decorations, and jokes, "Looks like prom."

They stop and chat with a few folks, one being Judge Reinhold, and then Nathan ushers Kevin to the front of the room to meet the Democratic Presidential candidate, Dennis Hopper. I've loved him since *Easy Rider*. Dennis had a ranch in the tiny burg of Lindrith not too far from Mesa Poleo but he never interacted with us hippies.

All of the action takes place two feet from me. I'm right there, practically face to face with the stars!

Between one of the innumerable takes, hour after hour repeating the same sequence, Kevin stops by my group and asks, "Are you guys doing okay? Is everyone alright? You're not too hot, are you?"

"No, we're fine, thanks," we lied.

I thought, how considerate to even care enough to stop and ask. And he *was* completely genuine, concerned for our well-being. He was so normal, so not full of himself, a decent human being. The air conditioning in the pole barn didn't have a chance to keep up with the couple hundred, over-heated bodies. As soon as the scene was reset, it was turned off to quell all noise interference. It must have been a hundred plus degrees in there.

At one break in the filming, Kevin carried in his two month old baby (for real), wife, Christine, by his side, and walked through the extras, receiving all the oohs and aahs.

Kevin announced, "Cayden's first red carpet walk."

It was a tender moment for the proud Papa.

The second scene I took part in, Kevin joined his band onstage for a mini concert. Yes, he actually has a bona fide rockabilly band, in which he plays guitar and sings. They performed two benefit concerts around the area, during the filming, one in Albuquerque and one in Santa Fe. So Kevin gets a rockin' with the other two guitarists, a kick-ass fiddle player, a bass, and drummer. I was duly impressed. The three songs that they taped for the film got progressively wilder as the audience swilled virgin libations throughout the evening. The third number took on a Chippendale effect with tidy whities being thrown onstage, by Judge Reinhold and his buddy, whose name we could never figure out … sort of like the three tenors, you can remember Pavarotti and Domingo, but not the other guy. I'll be surprised if those antics make the cut. I got to be one of those picked to rush the stage, due to my superb dancing skills (tongue in cheek) and bumped and ground to the country beat. My poor hi-heeled feet were near blistering. Like most white, Anglo Saxons, I need a drink or two to bust my moves. Hence, the concept of acting. I poured it on trying to be included in a nanosecond of the edit. If I'm lucky, I'll be able to pause the DVD and point out a single lobe by my flashy, obtrusive earrings.

At long last, we were dismissed for the evening only to be trapped in the holding area by a forty minute thunderstorm. Pummeling the tin roof, dripping through cracks, the rain continued until our parking lot was one enormous sea of mud. The crew did their best shuttling us in ATVs, but I still had to slog the ten feet to my car, sinking half way up my shoes.

On to my next adventure, I had to find my way to the Hub Motel (aka Bate's Hotel), a once cute, pink adobe Motor Court. With a wall around it displaying a for sale or lease sign, I had the distinct feeling that a serious bail out was requisite. The courtyard past the wrought iron gate was replete with decrepit fountains, pathways and crusty ponds that were probably quite charming twenty years ago, maybe thirty. With thirteen units along the walkway I found a door midway, stating PRIVATE NO TRESPASSING. I pounded on the door. No response. At this point, I'd been up for nineteen hours! My senses were keenly aware of a seedy looking character walking towards me, a cigarette dangling from his skinny lips as he smiled a toothless grin.

"I'm looking for the office," projecting a steady, sure tone. (NO FEAR)

He didn't say anything, but walked closer, extending his hand toward a grated window. There was a doorbell type button next to a sign: Push for Service. He pushed it.

"Thanks," I said, to which he replied,

"Yah, ya gotta push the button."

Like I hadn't grasped the concept from his demonstration.

"Thanks," I restated.

Then he walked back down the sidewalk to his room. The four by ten inch slot opened behind the metal bars and a tiny woman's head appeared.

I thought, "Geez, where the hell am I?"

"Are you Priscilla?"

"Yes," the tiny head replied.

"I reserved a room. Sorry I'm so late."

"One night or two?" she asked.

"One."

Priscilla handed me a card to fill out, along with the key and said, "Ordinarily I'd ask you for your I.D, but it's late."

The opening slid shut and I found my way to number twelve. The 'dude' was leaning casually outside his unit. I avoided eye contact, quickly locking my door behind me. As I stepped inside, I was transported into another dimension. My mouth dropped open as I took in the décor. That *Twilight Zone* theme began in my head: doot, doot, doot, doot—doot, doot, doot, doot. Rod Serling walked out from the bathroom. No. Seriously, along the inside wall, stood what once was an over-stuffed couch. But it had been reduced to a frame with a thick, printed, flannel blanket to camouflage its skeleton. The bed, two feet into the room, was built with 6x6 inch beams, including four posters with a canopy frame sans canopy. Barely a foot from that, along the next wall, stood a huge dresser that allowed just enough space to edge through, sideways. Following to the next wall was a five foot round, glass table. They may have been trying to disguise the grossly stained carpet which I vowed my feet would not touch unshod. But the most garish feature was the dozen or so artificial floral arrangements placed every six inches, around the room. On the table, hanging on the walls, free standing, the dusty blooms dated from the inception of the motel, the faded colors impossible to discern. My artistic senses winced, dried up, and went comatose.

After standing ten hours in heels, I didn't give a rat's ass! Carefully pulling back the bed spread, exposing sheets that seemed to have been laundered, I sunk down and put a pillow under my feet. Taking the remote, I pressed the power button. Nothing. Damn! Well, of course it wouldn't work. I rotated the probably ten year old batteries, still nothing. The TV was hung at the ceiling in the corner. I had to position myself so that the canopy frame didn't cut the screen in half.

Damn! Getting up, I slid my flip-flops on, and pushed the POWER button manually. Lo and behold, it came on. But surfing the channels up and down until I found something to watch proved more taxing than I could endure so I shut it off and resigned myself to sleep. And straight into the depths I went until the train whistle demanded consciousness. Belen is the fueling point for every train traveling the Southwest rails, so all night long the horn shook me awake. I was so exhausted, however, that I readily returned to dreamland. Adding to my consternation, the following day someone informed me the whistle was standard operating procedure through small towns. There were no intersections to cross. Everything through town was an overpass. What a monumental annoyance. Every night?

Day two of filming began, mercifully, at 9a.m. It was all so interesting to me, so unique, everything a learning opportunity that I soaked it in, carefully listening to the cues, observing directions, trying not to screw up. You weren't yelled at or humiliated, but if anything wasn't perfect, if anyone didn't follow directions to the letter, you were immediately informed, with precise corrections for remedying the mistake. It astounded me how utterly particular the takes were. Continuity was paramount. For example: the first day, I wore the stunning, rhinestone necklace, earrings and bracelet ensemble. Being vintage, the earrings had the old screw back closure. Late into the evening I lost one of them. I had to borrow another set from wardrobe, trying to duplicate my prior look.

"That hangs lower than your other set," the wardrobe staff critically stated.

Hardly noticeable to me, the trained eye kept track of over a hundred necklines, trying to keep the takes seamless. As the director yelled, "Cut!" crew members, make-up, and wardrobe workers appeared, to dust off, pat dry, and straighten all of us up for the twentieth time.

We took up action where we'd left off the night before, dancing wildly, as if we'd been drinking all evening, but this time, Judge Reinhold and his buddy were up on stage, with Kevin's band, singing like drunken sailors. We positioned ourselves in front as we'd been directed to on all the previous takes.

"What's this nudging me? It feels like someone's fat ass," I thought to myself.

One of the extras had put herself forward. You know the type, a stereotypical wannabee, hogging the spotlight. An obvious vapid vixen, we'd noticed her on numerous occasions, sidling up to the crew, making sure they were aware of her presence. With garish make-up and jet black hair, we dubbed her Elvira. So as she nudged, I exerted equal pressure, letting her know I would not be bullied.

I'd kicked off my shoes to dance so when I felt her heel come down on my toe, I yelled, "Yowww, you're on my foot!"

"Can't you move over?" she whined.

Incredulously, I looked at her, answering, "No, this is where I've been, where they told me to be, and I'm keeping the continuity of the shot."

"They haven't ever done it like this, so it doesn't make any difference," she argued.

"This is where I'm stayin," I reiterated, planting my feet.

When the director yelled, "Action," it was push and shove the entire song. I fantasized jumping her, slamming her to the ground with hair-pulling, WWF style. God, I never resort to violence. Honest. But maybe it was sleep deprivation.

Turning to the guy on my left, I asked, "Are you seeing this? Elvira's trying to butt her way into my space."

He was aware, as was everyone else around us, "I can't believe some people. They'll do anything it takes," he bantered.

"I'm right here. I can hear you!" Elvira responded.

Comic relief was worth it. But when the next shot resumed, I'd had it. I decided to let her and her ample backside fill up the space. I slid alongside a soft-spoken Hispanic woman who whispered, "I saw that whole thing. She shoved me too, right out of the way to get down there, in front."

I thought, "Ah well, life's too short…"

Back in the holding area, when lunch was brought in, I observed Elvira jump up to be at the head of the line.

On this particular occasion, the crew stepped in, instructing, "We're going to line up by tables, so everyone stay seated until you're called."

My table was summoned first, so I sashayed past her, trying not to gloat too obviously, but it was deliciously rewarding. Karma's a bitch! The next time we passed each other I gave her my best sparkly toothed smile, trying to kill her with kindness.

Filming lasted until one minute before midnight. Child actors have to be finished at the witching hour so thankfully, Kevin's onstage daughter became our godsend. The last scene had been shot at least thirty times, taxing us to such a degree that many extras simply walked off. I never worked so hard for eight dollars an hour!

The entire experience was such an exhilarating education that I concluded it was well worth the hardship. The stars: Nathan Lane, Dennis Hopper, Judge Reinhold, and mostly, Kevin Costner dispelled every preconceived notion I'd held about egotistical Hollywood types. They were all so decent, cordial, and down to earth, sweating right alongside us. Oh, and I forgot to mention Stanley Tucci, who was not in my scenes but nonetheless, noteworthy.

Before being dismissed, Kevin, extemporaneously, addressed the weary performers, "I want you all to know how much this film depends on you, how much I am indebted to you for your efforts. Your hard work is what makes this industry successful. This is how I started. This is what first gave me a love for acting. I want to thank you all for making this possible."

I was so impressed with his sincerity, with his character. He didn't have to take the time. He didn't have to say one word to us. To be reinforced, reminded of humanity's innate decency is always welcome and admired. In this world that is one of the things that separates the mediocre from the truly superior individuals—genuine human kindness ... or really good acting!

9

Talk about non sequiturs. Duty calls and I'm back on the road with a northern trajectory. Since Nick died, an only child, I'm saddled with his mother who lives 150 miles from me in St. Paul, Minnesota. To say she's a handful is a gross understatement. (Note to self. Don't be like that when you're in your eighties) Suffice it to say, the burden is one that I hope affords me some excellent karma. More than once I've shaken my fist at the heavens declaring, "How could you die and leave her to me?!" So not fair. She's survived several bouts of cancer beginning with breast and now uterine and how can I not be sympathetic?

We're on the discovery regimen, myriad doctor appointments, deducing treatment options, pain management and she's one of the most stubborn individuals you would ever encounter. Doesn't like medication so won't ever take enough to manage her pain. And this cancer is painful. God, if I could figure out how to dose her covertly, I would. Violetta is a proper, impeccably dressed and coiffed clean freak that appears utterly congenial and wonderful to everyone except her immediate family members, most notably me having resented me all of our thirty one years of relationship for steering her only child into the counter culture. Me? You're welcome! I felt duty bound to step up and care for her, to take one for the team as if I was doing it for Nick. She had lost her husband a few years before Nick died and that in itself gave me extra patience but oh my god, there was a virulent need for drinks at the end of the day or depending on the particular day, at any given hour. Which she didn't do either, much to my chagrin. So I was furtive about it. Vera's words would pop in at various moments, "Do you think we have a problem?" Jesus! Taking care of aged and infirm parents? Hell, that's what drinking is for! Now my right pinky is acting up, probably arthritis, not my favorite guy, Arthur Itis. It may be alcohol. Culprit or savior? It gets to be five and I am ready for happy hour. I'll endure the ache.

Every few months I allow myself to reflect on life without Nick, when I let myself sink into my forever broken heart without fear of losing my equilibrium. Enough time has elapsed, six and a half years, and I've experienced the pattern sufficiently enough to trust the process. Reminiscing about his very singular penchant of holding my hand too tightly, those strong fingers pressing the metal of his wedding band into my knuckles. I'd yell, yeow, easy honey, not so hard. But you wanted to hold me that strong, hanging onto my hand, like you could not let me go. I loved your desire, how you touched me, couldn't take your hands off me, never sated. It was always exciting. God, how spectacular your love made me feel.

After two weeks of nursing, Violetta rallied enough for me to take my leave. Promising to return when necessary I meandered the long way home following the Mississippi river down Highway 61 spotting eagles soaring overhead, lighting in aeries along the bluffs. Taking stock of the most recent situation, meditating on Nick I came to the conclusion that I needed to take my health more seriously, at this maturity. You could call it a cleanse. Of sorts. Nothing too drastic. More fruits and vegetables, one cup of coffee, juices, tea, very little alcohol. It will be experimental to determine any noticeable difference in my body.

Vera was not too thrilled with my direction but with Gabe possessing more and more of her life, we weren't able to engage in our 'decadence' as frequently.

Blair was the instigator of the fall from grace, inevitable after a month of reserved behavior, "Let's meet for drinks, first at your house, Anne, and then we'll wing it. There's music at Wally's, I heard it's a decent band. I'm overdue for some dancing. How 'bout it?"

"Fine by me, and I'll see what Vera's doing."

"It's a date. Saturday at 6:00."

The three of us were hungover for at least two days. It was Tuesday now meeting for lunch, comparing notes, Vera remarking, between bites of her cheeseburger, "We were so young Saturday night."

She and I split a juicy burger, piled with tomato and lettuce, a dill pickle on the side. Onion rings, crispy and thin. Just right. Blair, a vegetarian, but not one of those judgy ones that made you feel guilty eating meat in front of them, nibbled her cranberry, pecan salad. In a small town you were aware of eyes and ears hovering too closely, honing in on private conversations, especially given our topic.

"That's a great way to put it," Blair stated. "My feet were so sore, I don't think we sat out more than two songs. What a fabulous band. Blues, rock and roll, everything was danceable. I think I lost five pounds."

I confessed, "Someone told me we were dangerous. Loose, a bit slutty, just enough, eh? God, you two are so fun. And why don't more men dance? There's always a dearth of male partners. I don't get it. In junior high they'd have these sock hops and all the boys would be lined up against the wall watching the girls dance with each other."

"Gabe likes to dance," Vera countered. "He's really good. When he moves here I'll share him when we go out. If he can keep up. But knowing him he'll never admit he can't handle it. Three ravishing partners."

"A fourway," I said, laughing. "We were so young last night," repeating the phrase, storing it in my arsenal.

"You'll like this adage I swear by, 'you get a lot more cleaning done, a lot faster, if you don't wear your glasses.' It goes along with my questionable cleaning practices trying to keep up with four kids, six years old and under. Christ, it was a miracle if I could squeeze in a shower every few days."

"Did you make that up, about the glasses?" Blair asked, cracking up.

"Of course. Doesn't it sound like me? But then there's this downer. I've agreed to help my mom out for two weeks when she has her hip replacement. My dad is there, marginally alive, but too crippled to do any good, in fact, he'll be a hindrance but there's nothing I can do about that."

Both their faces dropped, honestly empathetic, Vera even taking my hand across the table. "You have thought this through?" she asked.

The three of us had delved into all of our family dynamics enough to be aware of certain pitfalls and challenges. I seemed to be in the thick of it with Nick's mother and now, my own.

"I'm duty bound. Something is triggered in my psyche or heart or soul that compels me to do my due diligence. I was no picnic growing up and she didn't kill me."

Of course, that got a big laugh.

But true enough, I explain, "Someone who gave you life, well, you owe them, I figure. Also, I think karma's a fairly real philosophy and this will increase my account, eh?"

Blair, a bona fide tarot card reader, Reiki master for real, offered, "I'm not sure it works exactly like that, but I admire your dedication. I really had to step up when my mother was sick and have to say there was significant healing between us before she died. I believe you know what you are doing but it will certainly test your limits. When is this happening?"

"I'll be heading out to Arizona, the land of 10,000 Town Cars or golf carts, in two weeks. I'll arm myself against the histrionics, the passive aggressiveness and all around intimidation. If nothing else, they're an endless supply of material. Both Mom and Dad had other 'intendeds' but something derailed them. They settled for each other and it only took sixty years for them to get over that loss. Mom used to bronze all summer long, hours on end slathering herself with cocoa butter. You know those sticks deceptively wrapped like candy bars. The smell was inviting but the taste acutely bitter. She smelled like a chocolate treat, a double fudge brownie baking in the blazing sun. Along with her girlfriends they competed for the darkest shade. Now, in her eighty-sixth year living in Sun City West, she maintains a permanent darkness but upon close inspection it's this bizarre pigment of age spots and scars rather than an actual tan joined together in a translucent layer of epidermis that rips and bruises with the slightest bump."

Regaling Blair and Vera with amusing anecdotes, they were incredulous about the weekly disasters between Town Cars vs. golf carts. I've never seen the statistics but octogenarians habitually and fatally drive into houses or plate glass store fronts mistaking reverse for drive or the gas pedal for the brake.

It'll be fine," I quipped, sarcastically. "I intend to take the high road. My feet won't even touch the ground."

"I can always count on you to have the perfect line," Vera said. "I hope you write this shit down."

"Oh, I do. I've got notebooks and post-its and stacks of intention covering my desk, in my bedside table drawer," I opined, as I dug out a tablet from my purse to prove my point, turning to a particularly good line, "You'll love this: my metabolism's so slow I'd come out of Auschwitz looking svelte. And this, 'he tells me I'm a prick tease, ya well, you're a clit tease."

Attracting too much attention with our raucous cackling, I reined it in. Rising to go, Blair offered some more advice for the moribund parent, "You know you can call me any time of the day or night. Right? And take some time every day for yourself, even if it's a twenty minute walk. Promise me. I know your desire to be a force for good but don't be a martyr."

"Well, and it reinforces my belief in euthanasia, to choose our exit when life isn't fun anymore, eh? We baby boomers aren't going to go out like that, wasting away with a dreadful quality of life, losing freedom, mobility, wearing diapers, possibly spending years in a nursing home."

The discussion ensued with a declared agreement to not end our days being 'cared' for by some meth head who didn't give a shit, spending every last penny of our savings to vegetate till death. No, we were going to die with dignity, me stating I'd research more about the movement and report back. Another thing we were aligned on.

Out on the sidewalk we hugged and I promised, "I'll remember this lunch, this loving support. I can't tell you both how I treasure this," our eyes welling as we hung on longer than social norms allowed garnering the usual double takes from staid observers. Jesus H Christ, it's a hug.

My ace in the hole was the escape from winter. Sunny, desert Arizona held that reprieve. I'd keep reminding myself on the road. Each day, about a hundred times.

It felt like my new job, this latest mission of mercy tending the declining parent. Another twilight zone, again, Sun City West, a bubble filled with tremendous wealth where charitable giving was common at church but homeless dare not venture (the Posse will get you). Not my chosen habitat but a requirement, maternal need deteriorating. No more fooling me. Decaying visage, twisted body decrepit 80's, confused Swiss cheese memory clinging to independence, facility to appear eternally vibrant, ever in control, now waning but still able to admonish with age-old sanctions this crumby, messy daughter who will never measure up to impossible standards. I'm obliged to manage the crises, the magic of Lifeline propping one vertical. I won't shirk making the hundred phone calls, please hold, maybe a call-back days later, home health-care interviews, ER, urology, GP, dozens of errands, My God! the errands. Standing in line at CVS with Depends, "They're not for me!" I want to scream to noting eyes. Likely not the rain shower depositing a puddle on the recliner, "Why do you do all this for me," gratefully Mom asks, "how do you?" I hope someone will do it for me, I explain (but I've made my daughter, Zelda, promise to Kevorkian my ass in lieu of diapers!)

Anyway, more details of the parental fiasco aren't worth telling because I don't want to relive it. Suffice it to say it was horrendous and bearable all at once. I hope I never have to go there again. The toxicity level is all but lethal, with no happiness, no peace. They don't know me, understand me and never will. I worked getting Mom back to health, drove back home and now I'm on my way to Violetta's for another one two punch. Or maybe the K O. It would seem I'm due for some payback. Where's that karma train?

Blair's got a new guy friend, seems alright, but she has consistently bad luck with men. I know a few things about him so I'll reserve my opinions and see how it shakes out. Will. That's his name. Not William. An attorney which suits Blair. She likes the intellectual type having done para-legal work at one point in her career. They're in the throes of new, fresh infatuation. Vera and I are happy for her, them. But I won't make any prognostications or lay any money on it. Not that it can't be IT. Nope, that's all I'm going to say about it. I don't want to send any negative energy their way. I did confess to Vera, though, that I wished they'd slow it down a mite. They had an impromptu Easter dinner for ten friends, his kitchen so woefully under outfitted that Blair had to basically cook at her house and then schlep everything into town. We all brought things to fill in, even glasses and silverware along with side dishes. Rather short sighted. And here I am saying more about it so shut the hell up already.

Driving out of town to meditate alone I pulled alongside the river under a line of huge cottonwoods. Silence enveloped me as I reclined my seat, windows down, a gentle breeze rustling leaves slightly, when a screech grabbed my attention. Jumping out, searching the heavens, there was the eagle, then another circling in tandem, upward across the treetops. I laid my head back against the roof observing their flight, their grace radiating this message: effortless, soaring, two together, watching over … let it come, let it happen, keep on keepin' on. It was as if I could hear the words, they were so distinct. I grabbed my pen and paper jotting it down. Uplifting, affirming, comforting. It was exactly the tonic for my loneliness. I truly believe in a spiritual force, some sort of other worldliness, if you will, that has influence and direction, if we're tuned into it. The wing span reminded me of the tattoo I'd drawn. Love the energy along with an inner voice, speaking to my soul. Things like that happen and I feel so strongly that Nick is out there somewhere still connected, even protective. I know I can't prove it, that Nick is somehow still vested in our lives, but neither do I attempt refute it. We can access those particular methods or systems that center and balance us. It works for me.

That night Sydney called, feeling rather desperate.

"I've got a proposal," she said, rather too seriously.

"Okay, shoot."

"I want you to go to Alaska with me."

"Ah, okay, you're ready for something like that? I mean, this is pretty huge so soon after Blake died."

"I know and I've been in such a state. It feels like I need this or I won't make it."

"Do you have a time frame?"

"Ya, next month. I've researched it, spent hours looking online and I've got it pretty well narrowed down to two weeks. But I know I can't do it alone. I need you to help me get back up. I'll cover all the expenses so that doesn't have to concern you."

"Wow," I gushed. "I do want to go but will you let me think about it, at least overnight, and look at my calendar and maybe talk to the kids and Violetta?"

"Oh, that old bag is going to outlive *us*. You watch."

I laughed, thinking, I will do this. I will figure out how to make it work. How often did an invitation like this come along?

"I'll call you tomorrow, okay, and I will think positively."

I was not going to let this elude me, dammit. It *was* happening. Sydney and I dated back to 1971, she having helped birth my daughter, Zelda, in our log cabin. We'd suffered the deaths of our husbands and dealt with devastating shock so pervasive it was a miracle either of us survived. Sydney was so integral to my recovery that I knew this trip was predestined. Time to give back. Calling both Blair and Vera they echoed my thoughts telling me I'd be crazy to pass up the opportunity, Vera declaring hopes she could meet Sydney someday. My fantasy is to have all of my loved ones in the same vicinity, kids, grandkids, best friends, but I know, realistically, that'll never happen. Too much of a stretch.

"Alright, I'm in," I announced the following night. "How will we work this?"

"I've got all the particulars. We'll fly to Anchorage where we'll meet up and then travel all around the state ending with a cruise down the Bering Strait to Vancouver. The web site will give you all of the stops and what we can do at each town."

I could see right off that we'd be pushing our bodies and minds to the limit signing up for the most outrageous side trips offered on our excursion. Transported to another state, one that hardly felt like part of the U.S., on each leg of our journey by land, air and sea, we moved further from our comfort zone and a little closer to the edge.

A single engine, five seater plane was our first mode of transport. It took us above the Talkeetna glacier. Talkeetna was the strange little village quite accurately depicted in the early 90s TV series, *Northern Exposure*. We were supposed to be able to set down and walk about, but the weather was snowy with low visibility. Our veteran pilot wisely opted to forego the hazardous landing.

Exchanging air for rails in the pursuant train ride to Denali, glimpsing the singular beauty throughout the isolated countryside, we were very fortunate to see Mt. McKinley 'come out' on a couple of occasions. At twenty thousand feet it possesses its own weather system. Many visitors wait for days to observe it, only to be disappointed. It felt like our trip was charmed as we traveled from town to town, having evenings to ourselves to hang out, dining, listening to Sydney's admirable attempts at normal conversation, knowing her veiled grief was just beneath the surface. At any given moment her eyes would glaze over and I knew she was envisioning Blake's dead body and the pursuant nightmare trauma.

"You know, you can say anything to me, right? I won't be shocked. I know exactly how you are feeling, you do not have to try to mask it."

"What if I want to die?"

"Even that. I told you I felt like that for a year after Nick died. It hurt too much and I couldn't see how that was going to change and I could barely stand it. But I'm here now, telling you to wait and see, to hang in there, that it does let up. Meantime I will be here for you, whatever you need."

Sydney just shook her head. It was incomprehensible at that juncture, the fact that she could come back. I had to trust the process and my own experience of perseverance. I told her about my rage room in my basement, having one of those ancient stone dungeons. Collecting glass from garage sales for ten cents each I'd keep a supply on hand for smashing. When the anger reached explosion level I'd don my safety glasses, head downstairs and throw the pieces against the stone wall as hard as I could while I screamed, swore and oftentimes wailed. It was enormously therapeutic. All of my feelings were furiously hurled along with the glass. Before I abandoned the practice I had a pile of shards a foot high. I had many requests from friends who wanted to give it a try. Which I never allowed. It was my singular, solitary escape. And it worked.

The last time I'd talked to Maggie we both agreed Sydney was in tough shape possibly in need of intervention, especially in terms of her drinking, but how and when we could facilitate that eluded us. I convinced Maggie that Sydney's grief was not over the top, that I acted much like her in that first year. Yes, it was scary, even crazy but I contended we just needed to give it space. I determined to keep a closer watch for signs of distress. Was she spinning out of control? I was convinced she just needed time. For me, that was the miraculous healer. Pouring into her all of the courage I could muster I related instances when Nick visited me, either in dreams or paranormal occurrences. The first spring after he died I'm convinced he changed the clocks ahead. I swear I didn't do it. When I came downstairs the morning of, the microwave and stovetop clocks were switched ahead to the correct hour. Honest. I wracked my brain for another explanation but decided it was his handy work.

The next leg of our journey was an exhilarating white water raft trip down the Nenana River that included one category four rapid and several threes. I hoped this would release some of the angst. The 32.5 degree water left me breathless as icy waves blasted my face. Definitely an adrenaline rush! The guide explained that the water was a mere four hours from the glacier.

"Are we going to be able to do this?" I questioned Sydney, after an attempt to thaw out my bones in a steaming shower.

"Either that or we'll die trying," she joked.

Looking askance at her, somewhere in my psyche I did sense Sydney was entertaining a latent death wish. It was something akin to an angel of death, a shadow of morbidity, and nagging foreboding.

Almost every morning we traveled to a new destination. Fairbanks was low-key with a steamboat ride to an Athabaskan Village where we learned the native lore from two young women back from college for the summer. The Athabaskans, late prehistoric and historic period peoples of the American southwest, are considered ancestral to the Navajo and Apache. Athabaskan tribes originated in Canada and the Northern Territories, migrating into the American southwest sometime after 1400 AD. Sydney, having lived and worked for decades in the healthcare system of the Southwest, was able to converse in Navajo, rather lingua franca, with a ninety-six year old Athabaskan man that we encountered. Home to Iditarod mushers, one of the local sayings is: "Fairbanks—where men are strong and women win the Iditarod." Another is: "If you're looking for a man, the odds are good, but the goods are odd." No argument there. About five men to one woman. This was pre-Sarah Palin notoriety or we may have sported overtly offensive liberal paraphernalia.

Being two single women, we kept a wary eye out for ten men chasing us on the ride to Juneau. As if. We did get the vibe from folks wondering if we were a couple.

The fact that you can't reach Juneau via highway—you can only get there by plane or boat—was certainly telling. The residents liked it that way sporting bumper stickers, "If you want more roads, move south." Trekking around on the glacier was something similar to traveling backward through time a couple million years. Mendenhall Glacier field, North America's fifth largest ice field, located in the Coast Mountain Range blanketed fifteen hundred square miles of land. The vastness was incomprehensible. Trying to put the size of the Mendenhall Glacier field into perspective from the front seat of the helicopter was dizzying. After landing, we donned the provided gear, much of which, although likely to help us, could also injure us if used improperly. Crampons, the spiked add-ons that you strapped to the bottom of your boots, enabled us to keep a steady foothold on ice, but if you tripped you could easily slice a leg with the metal points. Gloves, we were told, had to be worn at all times. The guide warned us about the hazards posed to our palms sliding across the ice surface that resembled shards of broken glass. The icepick walking stick helped us stay upright on the slippery hike but could easily impale one. A helmet topped off the protective outfit.

Each and every guide had an impressive knowledge, ability, and genuine love of Alaska. Not many of them resided there year-round but returned for the season to infuse tourists with wanderlust. I positioned myself directly behind the lead guide, placing my foot in his imprint. To my untrained eye it was all solid, but you could easily break through softer spots with one misstep and end up in a

150

limitless crevasse. The astounding blue/white peaks glistened streaming sun rays, virtually blinding us if we took our sunglasses off. Two miles went by much too quickly.

Despite my enjoyment of our glacial trek, the exceptional beauty, I must admit my favorite adventure was the sheer rock climb in Skagway, coupled with rappelling back down. Each challenge was carefully prefaced with copious instructions and proper gear. I always felt secure with the tools afforded us. The intense physical exertion along with the technical difficulty taxed me to my limit. Being harnessed was fairly reassuring but as the forty degree weather turned my fingertips numb, I determined that faith and fortitude would have to guide my assent. More than once I thought, this is so nuts, am I crazy? Reaching the top, one, two, and finally, the third and highest climb, it gave me such a sense of accomplishment, well worth the trepidation. I would absolutely do it again. Hear me roar!

Sydney and I loved the looks we got from those younger and more experienced than us, but evident also, were the encouraging words, that spurred us on. ("You've got this. Go for it.") Some assumed we were an old, married couple, one individual even brash enough to ask us how long we'd been together. We smiled and answered since the 70s, but I whispered to Sydney I wanted to tell them, 'Oh, we've been vagitarians forever.'

In between the extreme challenges was the ship experience. We had an outside cabin with a sizeable balcony, top notch. I decided one cruise would be it for me. On the one hand, it was the most glorious part of the world with its invigorating temperature, energy, keeping us up all hours well into the midnight sun, cloaking exhaustion. Stunning snowcapped mountains shrouded in gauze amid lofty pines, a solid evergreen mass threading through, poking holes in the stark white blanket then fading into Denali's mist. There were the engaging locals, friendly after months holed up in the dark, below zero topography, and salmon, OH MY GOD, the salmon. Sockeye, SO fresh right out of icy water onto the plate in an instant, at most a couple of hours, nevertheless tasty doesn't even come close to describing it. King, dog chum, silver, pink, Chinook. What a goddamn surfeit!

Conversely, the dark cloud that imprisoned Sydney, undeniably ever present, even though she powered onward each day, was a constant and concerning challenge.

"I couldn't find you last night. It was so choppy, I woke up and your bed was empty," I queried Sydney that morning upon her return to the room.

She looked completely bedraggled, hair stringy, jacket damp, face blown up. Elton. Who knows where she could have been? I had gone looking at 3a.m., worried, checking the casino, the dining areas, bars. She'd been throwing down drinks the entire trip keeping bizarre hours but I'd mostly ignored it.

"I was out on the balcony, lying on the floor and I must have passed out," she explained, nonchalantly.

It was so wild out there, waves crashing, I never even checked to see if that's where she was.

I was incredulous, "You could have been swept right off," trying not to scold but Jesus, "weren't you freezing?"

My voice was intense, maybe too much.

"Well, I'm fine, as you can see."

Sort of a fuck off. With that she walked out the door and I didn't see her until lunch time. Spying her across the dining room I approached cautiously, telling myself to be gracious. Smiling, I asked if I could join her.

"Of course. I'm fine. Don't worry about me. I mean it. Get some lunch."

Taking my place in line for the buffet I was struck by the incongruity of the whole scene. Raucous clods, ill-mannered Yanks garnering foreign disdain piling their plates to further inflate their swelling waistlines, I could have easily lost my appetite. Disengage, I told myself, keep your walled space, fortressed psyche. You don't need to be bothered.

Sydney kept it together for the remainder of the voyage, to my relief. I couldn't help thinking she'd wanted the waves to pull her off the ship that night. Shit! Most likely we'd never have found her, forever entombed in Glacier Bay.

Completing our journey high above the treetops in Ketchikan, a zip line shot us across the longest and fastest of its caliber in North America. Eight hundred fifty feet long, with a height of one hundred thirty five feet, we clipped along at thirty five miles per hour! The platform swayed as each member landed, which meant the tree that it was built upon was alive and healthy. Good to know. Three suspension bridges mixed it up a bit, giving us ample opportunity to observe the black bears cavorting on the ground right below us, dining on blueberries. Upon finishing, we were all given medals, which I wore on the ship that night, delighted to exhibit my prowess. We had done it, and we hadn't died trying. Winding down in Vancouver for the last three days I grew increasingly aware of Sydney's fragile state and now I had to separate from her back to my home, she to Santa Fe trusting her to the universe. Even though I wished I could stay with her there was this sense that I had to let go. I had to trust her, reminding myself of this tenet, people will rise to the level of expectation.

Upon my return, first order of business was to clean up the rage room. It had served its purpose and I really was beyond it. God, it felt so healthy. The strength I had gained from the excursion empowered me to a new place, definitely mentally and spiritually but possibly even geographically.

I barely had a week home before being summoned to St. Paul. Violetta took a turn for the worse so back I went to don my nursing hat. After only three days with Violetta I was ready to cut her loose. Put the pillow over her face. The metaphor was disturbingly plausible. Sink or swim. God, she was so mean, belligerent, and yet pathetic. Her pain level increasing which she masked with everyone but me, making me appear overly concerned, even alarmist.

She's in denial but has her funeral plans in order. How does that compute? Her hope is to not wake up one day. Don't we all? More likely, she'll waste away, bed ridden, in pain. So I'm lining up an outfit for the Greek funeral. Talk about judgy! That's why Nick dropped out of the church as soon as he could exert his will. Big bucks and a ton of ritual. She's dreadfully thin, frail maybe ninety pounds, all sinew and bone but still insists she can drive! I pray this infinitely stubborn woman won't have the strength much longer. The uterine tumor keeps growing, nothing more to do except try to manage the pain which hospice is assisting with. Zelda discusses the genetic testing with her because it began with breast cancer, and to my surprise, she agrees to have it done. I've nicknamed her Charmane for her charming persona when hospice visits. She is a delight. They think she's so cute, so together for her age. Instead of a dried up old prune, she's buoyant, engaging and apologizing because she skipped her makeup. Charmane's blood pressure was excellent, heart rate good, with only a slight reduction in air flow to the lower left lung. She talks herself out of nausea and brags to the nurse that she reads a book a day. The volunteer they hooked her up with is a disappointing eighty years old. Charmane wanted somebody younger. To keep up with her!

"I don't want anyone to clean," she told the nurse. "I do that myself."

She's still doing physical therapy for her previous torn rotator cuff! Wouldn't you think you'd say, 'what the hell?'

No, she powers on as if cancer is defeatable, declaring, "If I didn't have to eat or sleep, everything would be fine."

Because she can't get comfortable to sleep and food makes her sick. I want to ask her how long she thinks she'd survive without food but I forbear. Now I'm being educated as to her finances and anything else she won't be able to control when she's dead.

Her pledge to the Greek Orthodox church has four months to go for the year. "If you don't pay it off, they'll send a bill," she explains matter of factly.

I quip, "Do they charge interest?"

She's not amused, continuing, "A nice piece of fish, dessert, wine for the funeral lunch. Call Jimmy Chronis and get his recommendation for a caterer."

"I will," I say for the hundredth time. Her notes, all of her wishes, even what she wants her obituary to say are slid under the runner on the dining room table.

"Don't tell them my age and whatever you do, DON'T put my picture in. And don't put all that flowery stuff about beloved and sadly missed."

"Okay," I agree." Not a problem!

"Here's my list of female pall bearers, and their phone numbers. I don't know if Father Rick will allow it, but it's not his funeral," she says with a twinkle in her eye. "You'll have to go head to head with him. He doesn't go in for anything but tradition."

"I will. Not to mention your grandkids. If we're anything, it's non-traditional."

"I called the funeral director and he said I could do anything I wanted to. I wish the ladies would all wear pink."

She had a good laugh over that and I thought, 'if she wasn't dying, I think this would be the most fun she's had in a long time.

"Too bad you won't be able to see the look on Father Rick's face."

I don't tell her we've nicknamed him Father Prick.

"Nothing fits me anymore. I'm stick thin," she complained to the hospice nurse. "I don't have anything to wear."

I noted the unusual look on the nurse's face, Violetta so not the typical deathbed patient.

She offered, "The funeral director fits the clothes around the person," in way of reassurance. "Your outfit will look fine."

Violetta turns to me, "If they put that awful bright red lipstick on me, you better wipe it off!"

"I will."

"I'm not having a viewing anyway," she interjects to the nurse. "Only my immediate family. I went to my friend, Mary's funeral last week and they had a coral jacket on her and matching lipstick! Why do they do that? God awful!"

She pronounces it Gawwwd. That was one of her favorite expressions, God Awful.

"Coral lipstick next to that white, white skin."

The nurse was at an understandable loss for words until Violetta abruptly changed course, "I'm worried about when I can't bathe myself anymore."

"That's a valid concern. It's a difficult thing to allow. Some people prefer a stranger to a family member."

"Oh, I don't want a family member."

Phew! I breathed a silent, Thank you.

With yet another one-eighty Violetta brought out a photo album acquainting the nurse with her late husband and son, and then on to the grandchildren. I side-stepped to the front door, clearing my throat, ahemm, a cue, knowing the caregiver had used up her allotted time frame and had others on her schedule.

How do hospice workers do it? They have to be saints, angels. But I guess that makes them angels of death? My friend, Martha, back in LaCrosse had been one for decades. Helping people die. I could never do it. For family, yes, but strangers? Not so much. Every so often I catch a glimpse of the tender soul buried beneath the staid exterior, like when someone referred to me as Violetta's daughter and she failed to correct them by labeling me her daughter-*in-law*.

"I look like John McCain," she tells the social worker, who cracks up.

These inimitable asides disguise the circumstances in such a way that it keeps me going day after demanding day. Father Prick has called two days in a row to visit.

On the third day, with no call, Violetta asks, "Did God call?"

When he finally schedules his visit it isn't too awful until he asks, "Have you thought about designating memorials?" As in, 'leave us your money.'

She confides later to me, "I've given that church enough money." Completely unabashed, talking to her distended stomach, poking it she chides, "Well, c'mon, hurry up and get it over with. What are you waiting for?"

Next morning I look across the street to see a teepeed house. Toilet paper. I can't believe how things stay the same. Forty years ago we terrorized the neighborhoods of South Minneapolis with the same prank.

Zelda spelled me for a night allowing me to drive home and restock my suitcase, check my house and spend an evening with Vera and Gabe. He was visiting for a week and they had the run of my house for privacy evading her critical teenagers' censure. I loved the intimate energy they left behind. At least someone was getting off. Me? All I had during those long night hours was a pillow between *my* legs to alleviate back ache.

"It's so sad," I told Vera, absorbing her presence for one scant hour. "The way she's wasting away, bit by bit, barely able to ingest food, even water. And yet she hangs on."

"I'm so proud of you doing this for her. How much longer do you think it will be?"

"I'm baffled it's gone on this long. Never count someone out till their last breath. But I can't imagine how it can be much more. Before I left we had a tender moment. I told Violetta try not to be sad it's over, be glad it happened. I heard that on NPR. She really liked it and said to have it on her church leaflet. Oh, ya, she calls her lady pall bearers her bridesmaids and I told you she wants them to wear pink, right?"

"When you talk about her like that I get such a positive impression of this grand lady, powerful and admirable. A true gentlewoman."

"I know, it tears me up, the suffering but then she'll zing me with something that mystifies or hurts me and balances or negates that sort of tender impression. Mystery. And who knows how we'd be if we were dying? Get this, the day before yesterday she managed to get downstairs, lower level where the TV is and plopped herself in the rocker. I'm incredulous asking her why she's risking a tumble. She gets up, comes over to me and asks if I want to feel her tailbone? I'm thinking, 'do I have to' as she turns around indicating where to put my hand. It sticks out about a half inch from her body. No flesh around it. Ghastly."

"This is the most comfortable chair," she states.

With genuine sympathy I offer to bring the chair up to the living room. BAM.

Just like that she fires back, 'NOBODY'S HAULING ANYTHING ANYWHERE!'

"I see what you mean," Vera stated, shaking her head, pulling me into a hug. I melt into her shoulder.

"You are a tonic. I can't imagine what she'll do when they install the medic alert this week. Heaven forbid something should be different, displace one of her nick-nacks. Watching cancer eat her from within, the body, mind, but still the iron will. Unbendable. Thank you for this, Vera, I love you."

I walked her to the door having this secret desire or unction to pull her back in, to grab on and not let go. It was more like my heart was groaning for something permanent, continual, where we'd be together, even in a living situation. Of course, I didn't say anything, letting her glide away into the night, watching her turn left onto the sidewalk, listening as her footsteps faded down the block. I tamped it down, getting a grip, almost ashamed of my desperation.

10

On the return drive seventy miles an hour down Highway 61, I feel like I'm skimming across the tops of the tall, golden cornfields. If I look out over the stalks, it's like flying. The wind, slightly bending the tops that shimmer in golden sunlight. They'd wave if they weren't so tightly packed together. As the field turns at a ninety degree angle from the road, it's as if shuffling a deck of cards. I can see right down each row in nature's balance. The oak trees are past their prime with a brownish hue that colors the wooded area. And I love to see the stark limbs reaching skyward, naked as if stripped bare, ready to face the frost. Not me! I want fall to last. I want sunshine. I want Indian summer. Umber, rust, faded glory. If it stayed, it wouldn't be that spectacular but there's a week maybe two of the brilliance and then as if on autumn's dimmer switch, it fades, leaving glimpses of its former star power. Now why can't fall exchange time frames with winter? Winter be about three weeks, one month at the most. And we'd be sad to see the snow leave and the cold turn to mild days. Hah! That'd be prit near perfect. There's no perfect place to live.

Protuberant cell phone towers interrupt, displacing natural tree lines. They don't make a very good windbreak and I concentrate, holding the wheel to keep from being tossed by the errant twenty-five mile per hour gusts on the open road. The blue highway sign says, Concentrate On Driving. Hmmm, yeah. I don't know. I don't want to miss anything. I love where the tops of trees erupt from the hillside behind the thousands of planted rows, and I ruminate on the struggling farmers trying to hang onto their livelihood. I know when my husband was in the timber business he was eager to help farmers remain on their land by paying them as much money as he could for their precious timber. And they were glad for it. Maybe that enabled them to maintain, to keep on with their chosen vocation.

Thanks Ladybird for your Beautification of America. Removing all of those ugly billboards so that I can see the countryside. I'm reminded of the skit on the old SNL when they'd pan LBJ and his family, referring to his children, Linda and Lucy, as his semi-beautiful daughters. Still makes me chuckle.

I slow my speed, letting off the gas, mistaking an errant leaf for a bird sailing toward me, a stalk, sheaf ... the particular sheen on the leaves reflecting sunrays. Shimmering burgundy, plum, magenta, wine, a rainbow of painted landscape.

And every few miles in the midst of a patch of drab landscape a burst of brilliant yellow commands my gaze, wearing the crown in the pageant of leaves. Birch, maple, oak, walnut, poplar shooting out horizontally from the craggy bluff. Or are they aspens? I don't think aspens grow in southern Minnesota.

Not that there's anything wrong with brown. I like brown, but it has that washed-up, has-been persona, like a faded starlet. Nothing left for you but to fall to the earth and be ground to powder.

It looks as if the air force is trying to divide the sky with a long white tape measure. Why do fighter jets create such a beautiful drapery? Incongruous dichotomy. Is that redundant? One looks as if it made a right turn at a direct angle, zero degrees. I wonder if he had his blinker on?

Violetta died the following week. Early November. Over. Fini. She hated having her picture taken, even before she was ill, declaring, "I look so God-awful."

Nobody ever guessed she was ninety. Flawless complexion slathered with gallons of moisturizer, age spots zapped, sheesh, looking younger than me! Weathering life's struggles. Alone. Strength, courage and grace personified, refusing to own the enemy raging inside, never admitting defeat in those wiry ninety pounds. Truly an admirable example.

I'm exhausted a week and a half later, planning a Santa Fe trip as soon as things are settled here. I'm debating living in St. Paul but her domicile will need an overhaul. It's not comfy here and her ghost will encroach and dominate. Sunshine and the change of scenery will enable me to get my bearings and sort it out. I ponder the weeks with that fiery woman who claimed she'd read the riot act to her late husband and son when she got to heaven. What a picture, the tiny, proper, polite beauty with a tempestuous, wrangling, stubborn wench bent. Indurate, obdurate steel, her heart steeped in pain—the result, resilience and courage. What did she possess in her tenacious will that never allowed self-pity or depression? How *did* she talk herself out of it? Living alone, these last ten years from eighty to ninety permitting no divergence from daily routine, not missing a beat through three bouts of cancer. Except for this one, even you, little AliGma, couldn't back it down, your weight and age, now tied. Maybe that's all there is to your secret. Mind over matter. Getting out of bed, (making that bed perfectly), clomping down eight stairs, slippers flopping, unlocking the front door, both doors, to pick up the St. Paul Pioneer Press from the stoop for the fifty-thousandth time. Making your coffee to look like tea, doctored with mounds of sugar and Coffee Rich, cutting one slice of cantaloupe into bite-sized pieces onto a stark white dessert plate. Setting your place with napkin and fork, on the left, and one appropriately sized glass of orange juice. Sitting at the end of the kitchen table blocking the doorway, controlling traffic, spreading out the front page. Every single morning, without fail ... until. It waited, in its yellow bag on the welcome mat, for the gnarly knuckles to grasp it. But by eight o'clock with no clank of the lock those hands would remain milky white. No ink stains this day. No. The tiny, curled fist would be held up shaking, bold as you please, at two chins that had the nerve to ignore her iron will having their just reward— to now endure a tongue lashing, followed by warm hugs and tender smiles. Give 'em hell and give 'em one for me, beautiful, incomparable AliGma.

Sydney picked me up in Albuquerque, treating me to a scrumptious lunch of my favorite green chili enchiladas and two margaritas. A touch too, too for driving but I didn't argue. It was ample food to soak up some of the alcohol and it was a straight shot up Highway 25 to Santa. Installed in the lower level of her home I saw myself sliding from the frying pan into the fire. Nothing I could immediately put my finger on but Sydney was too chatty, amped up on something. Her standard arsenal included asthma meds, antidepressants, pain killers, you name it. How she procured it all gnawed at me. After unpacking it was nearing happy hour, which extended far into the evening. Drinking in the sunset as well as a piquant glass of white wine I let my emotions take over, tension draining like my glass. Sydney left me alone with my magical thoughts. This sky, tres spectaculaire, lying here on the slate stone courtyard, astral planing amongst lucent clouds revealing a canvas, contrails accentuating gossamer wisps, vapor haze fusing white with azure gray, innuendo of coral. Ahhh... what just happened? Exhaling, my breath makes the sound of longing, stay forever, cradle me within the tranquility of your spell, entrancing me till I blush crimson. Fuse me... with the vision I can witness only this once, this singular twilight. My eyes reflect the waning sunlight, still with soul penetrating rays, warming from inside out these somnolent bones, a surreal gift this clement evening, autumn in my enchanted land. Magic.

Sydney was driving up to the Mesa the following day allowing me to hang back doing absolutely nothing, except writing about sunsets and luxuriating in bubble baths. Pondering her complicated mental state I recalled our profound closeness, the time we took Nick's ashes to the Mesa, what was it now, how many years ago? Anyway Sydney handling every detail giving me time to unwind. The day had been so wrought with emotion, pouring him out, giving him back, I was utterly drained, retreating to my bedroom where I cocooned myself sobbing into the pillow.

"Can I come in?" Sydney whispered from the doorway.

"Please, yes."

Curling my legs up into a fetal position, I groaned in agony, suddenly not ashamed of the release. Sydney crawled under the covers, wrapping her arms around me in such a tender embrace. No words. She stayed until I fell asleep.

It was those last days with Violetta, crossing over into the unknown, that I attempted to unpack. She'd resisted morphine almost to the final hours not wanting to be out of control even though she was in the throes of agony. The on-call hospice nurse told me to give her thirty milligrams of liquid morphine under the tongue every three to four hours. The first dose was the only difficult one. After that I was the dutiful caregiver with pain alleviation my only concern. Society's sanction against death with dignity is beyond my comprehension. We are more merciful with our pets as far as a humane approach goes, allowed to put them out of their misery. What is the logic or sense of watching loved ones writhe in anguish, laboring to breathe, yes, with relief medication affords but those final six hours were murder to experience. I tried to rest on the couch listening for the intermittent respirations, a loud death rattle and I must have dozed off awakening to silence. Creeping up the stairs I knew what I'd find, Violetta, a strained expression, mouth agape, stone still. When I felt the icy cheek I was saddened and sorry she was all alone with no hand to hold in those last moments. At the same instant came the relief that her suffering was over. Anger rose up instantly, six months of days, hours and weeks spent to this end. I let out a deep groan as I sank to the floor. Time of death: 3a.m. Give or take. When I felt my legs could support me I rose and tucked the covers around her as if that would make her comfortable or warm. At 6:30 I called the funeral director as I'd been advised, not the coroner or police. They would have sent all the emergency equipment including fire trucks and ambulance, even if you told them the person was dead. Violetta detested any spectacle. She was loaded and hauled out as discreetly as possible, what with a hearse parked outside, no mystery to the neighbors.

And the funeral. Gaawd awful! Even though Father Prick agreed to her face that she could have a closed casket he proceeded to inform me, as they were about to wheel her into the church, that he would have to have it open.

"Why?" I inquired, completely nonplussed. "You told her it would be closed."

"We have to be able to anoint the body. The special dispensation of oils and herbs. We have to honor the traditions."

"You will honor *her* traditions," I stated emphatically. "You promised her wishes would be adhered to. I will have them load her right back up. She made me promise and if it's the last thing I do for her," I had to take a breath and not allow myself to cry, bolstering my resolve. "I am immovable so if you want this service to proceed, you will keep your word."

I stood, defiant, her grandkids, all in lock step with my avowal, ready to step in if necessary. If there was a scene then so be it. Fortunately, he relented.

"Can I open the casket to anoint her and close it immediately after?"

"Alright, but make it quick. Because if you don't, I swear she will reach up and pull the lid down."

Either that or she'd haunt the bejesus out of him for the rest of his days. He tried to come and sit at our family table at the luncheon but no one would make room for him. Very unchristian but I wasn't playing any games. After the argument on the sidewalk earlier I had nothing civilized to say to him, however I seemed to recall a single lesson from Socrates: "When debate is lost, slander becomes the tool of the loser." (As I slander the hell out of Father Prick)

167

Aaron informed me he was ready to march over to us and tell the funeral director to 'load her back up!' He's six feet five weighing in at 220. Everyone should have an Aaron on their team. I kind of wish it would have come to that. Furthermore, I was aware Father Prick wanted to talk to me about setting up the customary forty day service that of course, I'd have to furnish another lunch for, making donations in her name, blah, blah, blah. They really knew how to milk the bereaved and thankfully Violetta had warned me about the practice declaring I was to have no part of it. Done and done.

Liberation. Now here I am soaking up vitamin D in the gorgeous Southwest and I suppose the requisite wrinkles but who cares? I can't be bothered today. It penetrates my very soul melting that protective barrier constructed during the past six months. God, was it really that long? It's going to take a while so in the process my focus is intent on Sydney, her well-being or not so well. Like Goldilocks I decided to give her king sized bed a whirl since she wouldn't be home until tomorrow, staying overnight on the Mesa. To my shock as I pulled back the bedspread under her pillow I uncovered a loaded .38 special. Pulling the covers right back up, gingerly tucking in the bedspread I declared her room off limits. Jesus H Christ. This was going to require some tact. Ya think? What was I getting myself into now? Not much of a break but it was better to know the truth, to face the fact that Sydney was not coming out of it any time soon despite therapy. She's working herself to a frazzle, to keep busy, keeping the demons at bay but her health is suffering. I'm just her friend, not a professional and I hope that counts for something. It has to.

"I'm sorry to admit, but I didn't think you'd mind, I went to sleep in your bed last night and found your gun under the pillow. It's loaded, right?"

Full disclosure was my tack, needing to inquire when she got home. Fearful of the uncertainty, I wanted reassurance from her. I knew it wasn't foolhardy.

"I've got nothing to hide," her defensiveness evident. "I'm here all alone. I hear things and you don't know all the crazies wandering around."

"Ya, but you've got a fence and a locked gate. Do you feel that threatened?"

"You don't have to worry about it. I promise I'm careful, safe. I need it. Just don't surprise me in the middle of the night."

She said this with a grin and I was so not amused. Sydney's house. Sydney's rules.

I pressed on. I had to ask, "You aren't considering using it on yourself?" There wasn't an immediate response. I waited. "I beg you, Sydney, please promise me you won't do that."

"You can really be dramatic, Anne. You find my gun and make that leap. I'm doing fine, so let's just forget about it, okay?"

"I love you too much to not be honest with you, I care, that's all. You know that's where I'm coming from, right? It's the hardest thing you've ever been through, losing Blake, you don't have to tell me, but it will get better. I am living proof of that."

I thought it not prudent to acquaint her with my brilliant defensive plan of having my dad's ancient .22 rifle in my bedroom closet. If I heard a door or window break in, I

169

strategized to get in the closet and load the gun. If the closet door opened, I'd shoot.

She was on her third bottle of scotch in a little over ten days, and with her IBS and meds it was a long two weeks. I was so torn between duty and survival, so sapped, I was relieved to depart bouncing back to the Midwest. It was like she had to numb herself or punish herself for Blake's death. I get that. When a loved one dies it's natural to blame yourself on some level, as if there should have been something, anything you could have done to avoid it. It's the never ending question of WHY?

Shifting sands on the home front. Gabe is now inhabiting my best friend's home and life, seemingly consuming all of her, as so often occurs with a new relationship. Rightly so. One has to meld, become one with a partner almost to the exclusion of everyone else, at least initially, in order to solidify the union. It is a natural evolvement in the scope of things, coinciding with my focus and responsibility to settle Violetta's estate and my potential move to St. Paul where I have landed. In my darker moments I see the Tammy Wynette/Stand By Your Man element and it makes me gag but then I soften and only wish them the best. To determine the relationship balance takes the rest of your life together. Or that's the way it was with Nick and me. A constant juggling of wants and needs, give and take but women have to be careful not to subjugate themselves to the alpha male, which almost every man *is* to some degree. Is it worth it? All of my children hopefully got some wisdom from me when I told them to work on their relationship like it was the most important thing in their life, to commit one hundred percent, but as well, if it wasn't going to be fulfilling to have the courage to get out, to admit and concede the loss.

The season for so much togetherness between Vera and me and also Blair had run its course, at least in the recent incarnation. My indebtedness to Vera for walking into my life that summer day, my caged bird phase, even stultifying existence goes beyond my capacity to fathom. Incredible.

Sydney launched out on another wild adventure, alone this time, traveling to Greece to visit her son. I had not spoken with her to any great extent since our intense conversation after the gun episode. At least, not with any depth, sort of skipping around the topic skimming the surface. There hadn't been any opportunity with her being overseas so I was happy to hear her voice that evening upon her return.

Still at Violetta's, holed up that blustery January day, I had spent the majority of time sorting through bank statements, insurance documents and financial records. Weather included icy sleet with a three inch covering of snow, temperatures hovering around thirty-four degrees. I was trying to decide what to eat for dinner scanning the fridge for choices. Leftover shrimp tempted my palate and I did have parmesan to grate but no garlic and I wasn't hazarding a trip to the store.

Opening the cupboard door, "Pasta. Yes," I said aloud. "That should do me. And I ..."

Picking up my phone, I saw Sydney's name, "Hello! You're back? How was it?"

"Fabulous! You wouldn't believe how incredible. I was on the ocean in the most relaxing atmosphere. It was the best thing for me."

Sydney was definitely on a manic, jazzed up, yammering on and on about how we were going to go there.

171

"You want to go, right? You would love it, Anne. Spectacular. Everything about it. We're going. Yes?"

"Of course," I assented, blown away by her exuberance. So glad for the positive energy, there was something almost alarming in the way she was going on. "Have you slept since you got back?"

"No, I've been up all night and am so high, it'll be a few hours before I can even sit down, let alone lie down. You know, the time change. I've got tons of stuff to do anyway so it's fine. You will go with me, right? I want to go back soon. We'll go. You and me. It is just the most far out place."

Sydney barely took a breath, so intent on an answer. Like now, this minute. I'd put the pan on to boil the pasta water and it was steaming, bubbling over, "Hey, can I call you right back? I'm trying to get my dinner together and it'll take about a half hour. Are you going to be around?"

When she didn't answer later I chalked it up to her finally crashing, crawling into bed and hibernating. I waited till the next afternoon to call. She answered, somewhat groggy having just awakened but she launched right into a conversation again about my going to Greece. I told her I was so humbled by her generosity, how she was so caring and loving and how it made my heart happy. She was equally grateful to me for the support, emotionally, the hours and hours listening to her lament the loss of her beloved.

Abruptly Sidney said, "Oh, I've got to do some things. Can I call you back tonight?"

"Sure, love you."

"I love you. Kisses."

That was Sydney's trademark colloquialism. Kisses. Cutesy and endearing. Those were our last words. I kept leaving messages. Three that evening. Three the following day. Two the next day. I racked my brain trying to figure out if I could have offended her in some weird way. Had the jet lag caught up with her. Did she come down with Legionnaires disease, dysentery, something?

Maggie called me on day four, "I would have called you sooner but your new phone number wasn't in my phone and I couldn't find it and finally Lillie had it."

"What's going on? I've been trying to get a hold of Sydney. Is it Sydney?" I wanted to scream at Maggie, 'PLEASE, just get to the point' but I remained placid.

"Oh God, how do I say this, I'm so sorry, Anne, I don't know what happened and they aren't able to give us any information."

"WHAT! Is she okay? WHAT!"

"Sydney's dead."

Maggie was saying more but I couldn't hear. I crumbled to the floor yelling NO, NO, NO. SHIT! This can't happen. NO. How could this happen? What happened? Not again.

Maggie waited until I stopped, then only sobbing, both of us were equally overcome. We had talked about an intervention, Maggie and me, shortly after I had come upon Sydney's gun under her pillow. We knew something had to be done. Why, why hadn't we followed through? Goddammit! Would it have made any difference?

"Tell me what happened," making my way to a kitchen chair, laying my head on my arm on the table as I listened to Maggie's explanation.

"We don't know exactly the day Sydney died. The autopsy isn't done yet. I knew she was home and had one short conversation with her but she seemed confused, not even aware of the time or day. Someone else talked to her and she mistook 5p.m. for 5a.m. thinking she'd woken up too early and it was still dark. She told me she had the runs and if she'd been drinking heavily and taken any sleep meds she could have gotten dehydrated, had liver failure or possibly picked up something in Greece. I keep rerunning the tape, wondering how I could have, or should have gone right over there. But how could we know she'd actually go through with it? I went over Thursday night but the lights were out and both cars were there. She'd mentioned something about going to the Mesa but I figured maybe that was so people would leave her alone and let her rest. The next day I drove back there on my lunch hour determined to get into the house and find out what the hell was going on. I knocked, pounded, hollered, called on my phone. All silence. I looked for the key in the stashed spot but it was gone. So I called Dylan and he drove over. He was reluctant but I convinced him to call a locksmith but they couldn't or wouldn't help because we weren't residents. Finally, I insisted we call the police. They arrived and broke in and instantly the smell hit us. Awful. Sydney was dead, in bed."

"It hits me like a punch to the gut, Maggie," I sobbed. "I just can't believe it. What did the police say?"

"They were all business. They didn't even want us around, as if we didn't belong, were just some strangers or something in the way. But we were right behind them so we saw her in the bed. You knew right away. What a shock."

"Were there any marks on her, anything to suggest foul play or an accident?"

"No, we couldn't get close, we couldn't see except for the plastic bag over her head."

174

"Goddammit Maggie, I'm devastated. I cannot understand it. It's too sad. I can't believe it. I've got to call Zelda and see if she can come over here. Can I call you later?"

"Sure, sure, love you."

"You too."

It was a crushing blow, once again, to be torn from a loved one. 'Kisses' Sydney. 'Kisses.' Her closing word. I cried for hours, Zelda coming to my rescue, sitting with me, holding me. As the waves washed over me I felt a cave in, pulling me under, unable to make any sense of this latest tragedy. My heart broken again, the hurt so achingly familiar. She knew me in my heart of hearts, bruised, battered, crushed, and yet living, at times unwillingly. Don't be gone, Sydney. Don't you know how much I still need you, my dear, wounded friend? How much you helped me? How you said I saved your life? Well, you saved mine, many times over. Every single time I asked you to help. Instantly! Just like that. No questions asked. And you always said *you* owed me. I love you my crazy, beautiful friend. Your struggle is over. I can hope you and Blake are together in spirit. Your pain is gone both physically and emotionally and you are at peace. You are forever in my heart. You will always be a part of me. I will be stronger for yet another harsh, unfair lesson. You said what a good traveler I was in Alaska. I love it. Those were the times you relished. God, I'm going to miss you. I'm not ready to let you go and yet I know you are better now, so it's okay. There's a sentiment, even a belief in evangelical circles that one is selfish to commit suicide. That's such an idiotic inaccuracy, so sanctimonious and judgmental. If you are in that much pain, why not seek relief? I will carry on, regardless. That was one of Blake's catch phrases. 'Carry on, regardless.'

11

We'd spoken almost every day in those last few months prior to her trip. She was repeating herself more and more, especially in the evening. The conversation would ramble on until she was starting over again. I never called her on it, feeling like it would have been rude or some ridiculous prohibition, letting her vent hoping she'd come around eventually, like I did but then that gnawing in the back of my mind, the knowing if she didn't quit her virulent behavior, if she failed to make that choice, it was going to end badly. Soon.

Now the fresh pain of missing her, the questions, her loss unbearable, beyond what her shattered heart could endure. It was a taut thread to sanity and it snapped whirling irretrievably into that murky shadow, enticed into the web of delusion, the infinite sleep of amnesty. Me, being the control freak that I am, find it horrible to be confused, even vulnerable to weakness. Circumstances have overruled dictating the unacceptable outcome. The mission now to find peace and let go. Let it be. I tell myself it wasn't as much me you left but him you *went to*. I relinquish my dissension, [at least in this one circumstance] always striving for the underdog, chasing a happy ending to right the injustice.
 IT IS NOT FUCKING FAIR!

I'm throwing myself into renovating Violetta's house with thoughts of relocating to St. Paul. After fifty odd years of her habitation, I barely know where to begin. Deliverance.

Smudge. Of course, I have to unload the Dendrobia house first. Close the chapter and be released. The busy-ness can help with my mood. Sydney occupies my ongoing self-harangue as I ruminate over what ifs. She could not live without Blake. He was her rock, keeping her in check, the settling influence. But we never realized how much, how vital he was to her sanity. Those are my present cogitations.

After a month, the realtor wants to reduce my asking price. Nothing doing. It smacks of desperation, a bargain basement approach which I'm too proud to submit to. You drive by those signs, NEW PRICE or PRICE REDUCED and my thought is, 'what's wrong with it.' If it's meant to be, it will happen. That's always my philosophy. I listed the Dendrobia house with a mentality of if it sells, I'll reside in St. Paul. Vera and I have come to a very different phase of relationship. Both of us have priorities taking us away from each other and we've accepted it as a timing thing. However, I have had moments where I thought loneliness would consume me, wanting to pour my heart out to Nick, Vera, Sydney. Repeatedly asking where's my solace? Playing this waiting game, wondering where I'll live, the financial pressure.

I've said how I feel about technology. Not all of it but I'll repeat, God, how I hate having to deal with reps or service people, loosely described. Service! That's a good one. The latest Verizon phone plan I bought in St. Paul dropped, on average, at least two calls per day. The network that advertises the most coverage with the least dropped calls. Right? I've called, I've gone to the store—zip! No remedy. Finally, a customer service rep admitted that my area had a poor signal. It was due to the large trees. What? That was

177

their excuse. So I tried to convince them to buy back my phone since their plan didn't work for me. Impossible. Thirty days is the return window.

"But In January, when I bought it there were no leaves and I got service," I argued.

Tough shit.

"Try to sell it on eBay," he advised.

Ya, I'll do that. Assholes.

In my parting shot at the rep I said, "I am very disappointed in your company, your service and your treatment of me. I will be sure to tell everyone I know."

I got no response and clicked 'end' which is far less satisfying than slamming the receiver in their ear, like the 'good old days.'

Next up, my Comcast internet company that continually either disconnects or won't connect me at all. A trip to downtown St. Paul to exchange the modem wasn't too difficult but after the rep simply handed me the box with nary a word of explanation I should have known to press her further with my dumb questions.

"So I just hook it up and I'm ready to go?"

"Yep," she said, giving me that [what kind of an idiot are you?] look. You know—the one your kids give you.

Back home, I plug it in, connect the dots and no juice. That is, no lights in the proper sequence. I do all the things it says, unscrew this, unplug that, shut down the PC and wait twenty seconds. Dang. I call Comcast spending an hour with the first rep and a half hour with the second, who schedules a visit for Monday to check the wiring. She tries to sell me the service protection plan which I always refuse on moral grounds. Same with the extended warranty on appliances, TVs, etc.

What they're saying is, "we know this item is a piece of shit that will break in a few months so unless you want to pay for exorbitant repair costs, you better shell out x amount up front to cover what we know will occur."

So I tell the rep, "If your guy didn't wire my house properly, why is that my responsibility?"

"Well, I'm just offering the service, because if it's not the equipment, then you'll be charged for a service call and repairs."

God, I wanted to scream. Unbelievable. I want to go to the woods and dig holes ala the old Seinfeld episode where Jerry's friend runs into Central Park after the van misunderstanding. Instead, I get on my bicycle and ride down to Como Lake where I pump my frustrations out on the bike trail. The bikers at that particular time of day are few so in a show of abject rebellion [oh, you rabble rouser] I head the opposite direction of the arrows. Sailing along, the wind lashes resistance, which I ignore, determined to vent. Two riders, side by side, are taking up the entire pathway, obliviously yammering away, peddling toward me, so I slow, veering off onto the grass, courteously, I might add.

"Oh, oh," the woman says, passing by, a bit unnerved. Then mustering an admonition, she hollers, "You're going the wrong way."

Of course, I think of the rebuttal a few lengths down the path, you know, from the film *Planes, Trains, and Automobiles*, "How do you know where I'm going?"

Regardless, I push on, not recklessly, not a danger to anyone, thinking of my next encounter which is sure to come as we round the lake. Past the parking lot by the Pavilion, up behind the waterfall where the path follows the steep rise and then drops down bordering the golf course, I spy them at the

179

same instant they see me. Widening the gap between them purposely to edge me onto the grass, I welcome the confrontation. Hah, I think, boldly meeting their stare.

Again she pipes up, "You know it's a one way trail."

In the few seconds of hearing distance I shoot back, "Arrest me!"

Yes! Smarty pants. Yes! I couldn't see their faces, whether they laughed or grimaced or flicked me off but I know I nailed it. Fearing citizen's arrest, I *did* end my ride, peddling on home, not wanting to risk being thrown to the ground or possibly rammed on our next encounter. I'm really not imbalanced. For the most part.

As the sun set I realized I'd been fighting all day, or longer. Could be since I'd inhabited my mother-in-law's house. She did possess a formidable temper controlling every aspect of her sphere up until the final battle, Armageddon. With the smudge stick I'd brought from Santa Fe I performed a cleansing ritual to purify and bless my environs. From the farthest basement corner, I wound through each room with positive intention allowing the smoke to waft slowly detoxifying the kitchen, dining, living rooms, upstairs bedrooms finishing with the bathroom repeating peace, love, health, grace, forgiveness, and kindness. Spreading the pungent smoke with a circular motion there was a profound sense, a release of my spirit, allowing the aura to center me. It was uncanny. Settling into the couch, my favorite Bordeaux and notebook in hand I penned these lines:

Get Back Up (writing is therapy/therapy is writing) How much time do we have? Who knows? Keep on keepin' on. Go with the flow   ing   third glass of wine. Drink up. Hear me.

Keep me from falling. Powers that be, deafening crack of lightning. Universe, listen to my thoughts, heart. Console. Where is the reason, the meaning, the solemn promise that we adhere to, that echoes in a chamber so deep and primal solidifying our faith, our belief, our trust in life, humankind, that what?! That there is equity, karma, core goodness? I still possess a smattering of childlike innocence that believes in the fairy tale, if we live a certain way and do certain things and love and give and try, that someone, something, somehow, at some point a more civilized world will return to us. Even though life has treated me ill, even though removing myself from this planet was imagined, contemplated, even entertained. And though I could barely convince myself of the logic to keep on, there remained a shadow of this life, a fragile thread to cling to that ultimately justifies my existence here.

Just here. That's a New Mexico axiom. When someone asks you how you're doing, 'Just Here' is a typical response. Sort of like 'chillin.' My attitude has shifted today, this morning. Noticeably. Could be the excellent regularity I'm experiencing. Is it the water? The highlight of my day, taking a dump. I have the best shits I've ever had. No kidding. Big healthy pile, forming letters, shapes. It gives me confidence about my overall well-being. I don't know how many times I've quipped, 'if I ever sit around and talk about my bowel movements, shoot me.' Well, load up the .38. To change the subject. And you're welcome. I came across this quote and wondered how I'd missed it: "If Jesus would have been killed in modern times, would we be going around wearing little electric chairs on chains?" I'm a huge fan of Lenny Bruce,

181

one of the best stand-up comics of all time. Don't you wonder what he'd be spewing today? It's mind boggling all of the major talents taken out by ODs.

I can't deal with two properties, obviously. Without capital, energy, or time I have to decide on a course of action. My house in Dendrobia hasn't attracted the one, thee buyer, and after three months I'm not willing to extend the contract. My belief has been and still is if that house didn't sell, then it wasn't meant to be. Simple. I need to be done with it. I'll put Violetta's on the market and whichever one sells first, that will determine where I'll stay. At least, until I figure out some place else to be. A condo?

Vera, Blair and I had one short interlude when I was in town, trying to catch up and stay connected.

"I am sort of on the lookout in case a guy encounters my gravitational pull," I confessed. "Don't look so shocked," observing Blair's chin jut downward, eyes pop.

"Well, when did this change of heart occur?" she asked. "It seems sudden but you must have been contemplating it."

"No shit," Vera intoned. "We have spoken a bit in terms of entertaining the prospect but I didn't know you were READY."

This night called for more of a celebratory vibe so I'd gotten martini makings along with a scrumptious spinach/artichoke dip and chips. A nice block of Edam and rosemary crackers, rounding out our menu with luscious fresh peach slices. No fuss, it suited and sated our tastes, simple and delicious.

"I am not exactly pursuing anyone, not seeing any man that attracts me that much knowing it will be a minor miracle if anything develops. I am open, that's all. Being in the cities gives me more perspective with so many more possibilities."

"If you do get lucky, see if he has any friends," Blair said, with a delightful snicker.

We were getting jiggy with our second martini. This is when I'd hop onto my dependable upright and start belting out old rock and roll tunes. With typed pages of words, sing alongs were typical when the liquor loosened my fingers and vocal chords. Not with everyone. Only close friends. I did take the perfunctory five years of lessons learning mostly that I hated my piano teacher. She was the dreaded, fat old lady with a mothball smelling home, dust coated, grungy surfaces and at least two cats meowing to my efforts, brushing my calves under the bench. Blocking every smidgeon of inspiration, I never mastered basic music reading but fooled my instructress playing by ear. Which served me well enough for my friends. Abilities, not so much, but the shot of courage afforded me enough confidence to hammer away belting out some Carol King, Stones, Eagles, and Dylan, the usual suspects. Then, all too soon, Blair headed out, having to drive the seventeen miles home. We tried to convince her to spend the night but she insisted she was alright and would be careful and did eat enough over several hours. We're all adults. Make our own choices. Vera stayed another hour listening to my bellyaching, or should I say bitch fest? We both had some issues dealing with life, me grieving over Sydney, her adjusting to Gabe, he with her kids, both of us moving. After waiting many months the final word, autopsy confirming our suspicions of Sydney's decision to take herself out brought my heartache to the forefront. How did she decide to do that? My dear, loving Sydney. Such a tormented mind, a troubled soul with a crushed spirit. Her utter agony would not relent only getting worse as the reality of life without Blake became insurmountable.

"She was tricky and illusive conning us all, me, into believing she wasn't as desperate as she was, and I feel like I failed her because I couldn't comfort her or recognize that devastating need. I hope it didn't hurt or take too long. I hope at the end it was peace or relief."

"I'm sure you did all that you could. You can't blame yourself. It's no one's fault. Her brutal inner turmoil was the culprit."

"She did try. But she couldn't make it. I think we were all holding her here, on this planet against her will. *Her* will was to die. It was the only solution," now crying, reaching for the box of tissues, handing one to Vera, I continued. "I relate to Sydney's choice, I understand. I do. I hate to lose my dear, my deep, my true compatriots. Ah life. Forever missing beautiful people, gifts of my existence. It reminds me to cherish the people I still have. Not that they, you, are mine. You're on loan," as I reached over pulling her into my arms for a tender hug.

"Don't you wonder if they're watching what's going on down here? Or over here, wherever they are? It seems as if Nick's presence is still around."

"Oh, I don't doubt it for a minute," I whispered. "In my heart and soul I hold fast the purity of strong love and am grateful for what I had. And what I have now."

Such a tender moment to treasure, as if we knew they'd be few and far between going forward. How lucky, how blessed to enjoy the singular experiences unique to certain relationships. Friends are few, at least the real ones.

I'd marked a passage in *Leaves of Gold* and shared it with Vera. "Beautiful and rich is an old friendship, grateful to the touch as ancient ivory, smooth as aged wine, or sheen of tapestry where light has lingered, intimate and long. Full of

184

tears and warm is an old friendship that asks no longer deeds of gallantry, or any deed at all, save that the friend shall be alive and breathing somewhere, like a song." Eunice Tietjens.

On the drive back to St. Paul my head had time to detox, or just be quiet. Vera and I'd given in to one more martini, unwise but after two, well, there goes your resolve or temperance. No regrets. I am convinced I'm about to sell a house. A knowing. And I'm not sweating it.

Ace is the place with the helpful hardware man…la, la, la. And how. The Ace Hardware guy came over to service my lawn mower. It wouldn't start and I bought it at his store a while back. On that day, he dropped everything, grabbed his tools, made a few adjustments while engaging in a decidedly flirtatious exchange including a suggested meeting for a drink. The mower was now yard worthy. That was September.

Giving serendipity a tweak, I ambled into his parking lot Saturday last, the intent to find a space heater (ulterior motive) seeing if he remembered me from the aforementioned lawn mower repair, and yes, indeed, he did recall with noticeable alacrity jumping down off his monster front-end loader, to ostensibly break rank and personally assist me. Me?

So Ace Hardware guy rings up my space heater, totes it to my car, and I flirtatiously inquire, "Do you make house calls?"

He affirms offering to come over Monday to look at my mower that's again acting up.

On Monday I lead him to the garage where he effortlessly fires up the mower in one pull with his amply bulging biceps.

That's all it really needed, you know. A penis. (AKA upper body strength.)

His smile makes him look so young. I can't believe he's truly dallying with me. Because *I* am not young.

We go back into the house. I offer him a chair in the kitchen whereupon he proceeds to unfold the most heartfelt saga of his fractured marriage to a personality disordered woman with whom he propagated three offspring, the youngest being the same age as my oldest granddaughter, da dat, da dat, da dat. Jesus H Christ.

I have to reiterate what a genuinely nice guy he is. Big, attractive, fix-it man. Owns the Ace Hardware, did I mention? But during the course of the convo I calculate that he's maybe forty-two. No shit! When he gets up to leave, he asks for my number. He gives me this rub down hug, squeeze, mmmmm, ya, that's nice. And I think, seriously dude, do you know how old I am?! God, for ten cents I'd bite. But no, how would that work? Ahhhhgggg, can't do it. Not even for a booty call? He's so delicious.

This is all your fault Ron, (an old friend), for telling me if I dyed my hair I'd look forty!

Well, it turned out to be moot, that is, the wondering and calculating. After a month and no call, I gave up the fantasy. Could it be I'm not as attractive as I think I am?! Hah.

I added a word to my vocab: Pantasy. Musing, as I am wont, does anyone truly believe the skinny jeans lie? The size twelve body dexterously squashed into a nine? When will I ever accept the shape that I am? Maybe when looks aren't dictated by men. Pantasy. That's when the size eight fits these lumpy thighs which haven't actually attempted that since oh, junior high. It works, if you can suffer a camel toe squeeze

186

but watch out, hit the deck, if you hear me sneeze. Zozobra style, whatdaya say we burn Barbie in effigy? Come on Mattel, make a doll that looks like me. Function over fashion, that's the byword for life now. But the nagging thought still jeers, do I look like a cow? Does this make me look fat? Don't answer that! Liar, liar pants on fire. Did I try to rhyme that?

Drama back and forth with the St. Paul negotiations. First one, then two buyers, then back to one and now it feels like they won't close. Do I ever need to get laid! I'll take matters into my own hands. Literally. Clitorally. Someone wrote about chick lit calling it 'cliterature.' That's a good one. I crack myself up.

Done and Done. Final offer, accepted, closed, out of the cities and back to Dendrobia for December. Breathing easier, I'm hunkered down for the next chapter.

Meantime, a month ago a mutual friend, (the one and the same Ron who made the comment about dying my hair) had informed me that Frank was lonely out on his mountain by himself. You know, Frank, the man I met at Blake's memorial. Apparently available, my brain was percolating with scenarios about how to situate myself within his radius.

Garnering his number from Maggie I left him a rambling message about my intent to travel to Arizona to see my folks and continue on through New Mexico to end up in Santa Fe. I offered house-sitting services attempting to sound breezy, explaining I'd been attracted to Silver City and would take the opportunity to explore the area. Maggie called twice to query me about any response. Zip. Zilch. Nada!

"God, it's embarrassing. I can't call again. That's a huge matzo ball hanging out there."

Maggie offered, "Oh, well, then you couldn't have heard about his accident."

"Who would have told me that, if not you? Whaaat?"

"Oh God, he was visiting relatives in Pennsylvania, hit a patch of black ice and rolled his car. He broke some bones, his clavicle and some ribs, he's lucky to be alive. The whole top of his car was completely flattened."

"Jesus, how'd he get home? Or is he even home yet?"

"His brother, Rob, flew out there, they rented a vehicle and drove back. He is home in Silver City now, recuperating. So don't give up yet. I bet he'll call."

"Well shit, as if that's a priority. I'll be patient and if he doesn't call, that will be that. It's fine, really. I am honestly okay by myself. Like, I'm accustomed to it. It's been so many years since Nick died, you know and here I am, Maggie. I never would have thought it."

"Ya, I know but don't count him out yet. I've got a feeling about him. We go way back. You know Mickey worked on his construction crew for twenty years."

12

The world of shock I existed in the first year after Nick died, where I hovered between insanity and despair, was truly hellish. The only thing that kept me in this world was my refusal to saddle my children with the additional trauma of suicide. As the first anniversary of Nick's death approached I wondered if I would feel any differently, any better. Somewhere deep within my soul I wanted to recover but was powerless to achieve even the smallest semblance of wholeness. There is a plethora of material defining the one year mark as a watershed event. No such amelioration was noticeable.

It took me all of two grueling years to even decide if I wanted to live. Each subsequent year brought measurable recovery until this year, where I truly understand what valuable lessons I've been taught. I see how strength and resiliency undergird me in my daily choice to live intentionally positive. Using every means possible, I extracted some measure of benefit from a myriad of modalities: grief support group, counseling, yoga, meditation, reflexology, massage and Reiki, guided imagery, medication, and reading, reading, reading. Three publications in particular I highly recommend, Joan Didion's *The Year of Magical Thinking*, Donald Hall's *Without*, and C.S. Lewis' *A Grief Observed*. The faith and loyal support of a few friends, [an extremely narrow circle] held me in a place of secure love. The passage of time *is* ultimately the miraculous healer and my salvation.

I flipped back through my journal to find a note I'd written in April, reflecting on Nick's past birthday. It read:
April 6

"How would it be? We'd have a special dinner. I'd get you some small thing, a funny or poignant card. Right this moment, my dear, I can say I don't miss you. I say that with peace, with love and fond, fond memories. It has finally happened, Nick. It took so many years but it doesn't always hurt anymore to think of you, to see your picture. And it is not like I am over you. No, you will remain embedded in my heart forever but it is interesting, even profound the healing that's come to this psyche and soul."

Frank did call. A week later. We had an intriguing chat resulting in an invite to his mountain home. Any time. Don't mind if I do. His voice was warm, masculine, and calm. I said I'd call him when I got down there and set up a tête-à-tête. I've no designs, not exactly, just possibilities.

My sleep was interrupted several times that night. Anxiety over a new direction, rehashing scenarios ad infinitum, dozing, then dreaming about Nick but the face was a combo of him and Frank, then waking with a dozen questions. I always have a tablet and pen on my night stand, jotting ideas, to-do list, and anecdotes. At 3a.m. I can be quite voluble. It was as if Nick was not gone, touching me, brushing my lips, his tongue tasting stroke. The aesthete so knowing, so pleasureable. I basked sensing his fingers resting tenderly at home upon my neck, a slight squeeze inferring in his singularly quiet way all of the words he didn't voice.

I know I slept some but not waking until 9a.m. left me groggy swirling in second thoughts. Sipping my favorite dark roast quaff I'm reflecting on the direction, the course I've set, now feeling these familiar body aches, moving more slowly and deliberately as forces of gravity challenge. God, my body makes intermittent, uncontrollable noises. I remind myself not to groan or breathe loudly when I get up from a chair. The stomach gurgling is out of my control but my trick to cough so as to camouflage a fart is quite clever.

Good lord, the tension among so many former friends and lovers in this introverted town grows palpable, ugly and toxic. I'm determined to remain far removed from certain. What are we? Fourteen? Trusting, associating, I keep my circle very tight. Who needs it? Some individuals are clueless or insuperably naïve, others are plain and simply, assholes. Just stay the hell away from me. I need a break.

When I think of Frank I get a little giddy, our conversation, my intent to get acquainted. He's been on my short list for a couple of years and now it seems like a timing thing, the planets aligned. Favorable. Remember the Magic 8 Ball? 'All signs point to YES!' My Santa Fe klatch all say what a good guy he is. I can't count how many times I've heard, 'he's a lovely man.' I'm sure I'll decide pretty quickly. I'm really going to do this.

I call the side trip to Sun City West a 'trip to Hollywood' as if I landed on a different planet. If you've never been, don't. The entire neighborhood where the 'rents' live keeps green lawn year around. As if there's no water shortage. Unbelievable. Mom turns on the tap and walks away to assume another task. I, of course, immediately turn it off only to be admonished that she's waiting for it to get cool. Like that will ever happen. It's triple digits but they don't think they need to turn on the AC. Such a grand adventure. Didn't Winnie the Pooh have a grand adventure? I'll be Annie the Cuckoo. I don't need to rehash anything further.

"Hi, I'm about twenty miles out," I informed Frank.

We'd worked it out for me to meet him at the bottom of his road to guide me to the remote location, both of us not confident with his directions. When I turned onto his road there he was standing next to his well-worn Ford pickup, smiling, definitely a moment. Maybe even a heart flutter. I told myself to calm down. I got out, walked over and we had a somewhat awkward hug. You know, the one where neither of you knows whether it's appropriate or too anxious but a hand shake is lame and all of this is going through your mind. Jesus, just breathe.

"Did you have any trouble?" he asked.

"Nope, Highway 10 through Lordsburg and then up 90. God, it is beautiful through the mountains. Not much traffic."

"Ya, you have to be coming to Silver City. It isn't on the way to anything else. No major airport or freeway. But we like it like that."

He's handsome, used to be dark but now gray, in a grizzled yet unruffled exterior, faded denim jacket, jeans to match, a baseball cap. Attractive, reminding me of Sam Elliot. We had one of those interesting connections, like that little buzz in a look, a blip, definitely something. He's got lashes every woman covets, long, naturally curved, framing deep dark brown eyes. Lanky but still with impressive shoulders left over from his career as a stone mason.

192

As I followed him, turning onto the next road I noticed my odometer read 88,888. No shit! This means something. I called Blair, my on-call numerologist.

"You won't believe it," as I recited the numbers to her. "Is that significant?"

"I've got chills. That's an eternal number. Whoa. No beginning. No end."

"I don't want to read too much into it but wow!"

"So what's he like? What's your first impression?"

"Definitely favorable. I'll know more when we can have a conversation and when I can see where and how he lives. Which we're winding around a pretty narrow road so I'm going to let you go. Thanks for the insight. Love you."

"Glad you called. I've been worried. And please be careful. This is a bold thing to attempt and I need to know you're doing alright, okay? Love you too."

Yes, yes it was unusual to scope someone out and follow him up to his secluded mountain home. But my friends in Santa Fe had known him, socialized, and worked with him and vouched for him. Even though he was well over six feet and formidably built I sensed a gentleness under that gruff surface. No second thoughts. Not yet.

I did have an exit strategy. I'm not that shortsighted. He'd made it clear he had an extra bedroom for me (no pressure) and I was welcome to stay as long as I wanted. I'd lined up a rental outside of T or C for three days hence. Enough time to get to know Frank but not too much to overwhelm us. When he took off his hat I thought, why do you squash that shock of white. Sort of Billy Idolish and I immediately wanted to spike it up with some product. The first time my three year old granddaughters met him, they dubbed him Hedgehog. Their Calico Critters had a Pickleweeds Hedgehog character apparently sporting the same spikey hair style. He was instantly accepted and completely revered by them. Anyway, no makeovers yet. I told myself to cool it, he was not a fixer-upper. As we dug into our histories we discovered we attended the same high school in Minneapolis. He was five years older so our paths never crossed until we both followed the hippie route where we haunted the West Bank and the Triangle Bar. There were so many parallel experiences along with mutual drug dealing connections, same stomping grounds, we figured we had probably been in the same place at least once or twice. Uncanny. Nick and I would hear of Frank and Lenore, his ex, and he would hear of us throughout a forty year span of mutual relationships. The man is no stranger to drama as I discovered over the ensuing days. We discussed our god mentality, spirituality, death with dignity, no diapers or nursing homes for us. Neither of us had any tolerance or regard for organized religion. Me being a recovering fundamentalist, him avoiding the whole aspect while his ex was a life-long devoted church goer. It immediately struck me as a kindred spirit connection, an easy friendship developing without a lot of effort. On the same page with deeper beliefs including nature, Buddhism, Native American philosophy, mysticism peppered with varied interpretations, we both held that god was not one entity, one way, that it/she/he comprised a very personal experience specific to every being. He is a complete Luddite, way more than me, about anything more advanced than a flip phone which I do admire but still I admit, I need to live in the current century.

During the course of the evening I noticed a picture on his kitchen counter, turned upside down and from that angle I thought it was Nick. Seriously.

"Where'd you get this picture?" I queried. "And why do you have it?"

Rising from the couch to see what I was talking about, he gave me an odd shake of his head, "What do you mean?"

"This looks almost exactly like my late husband, Nick. I can show you a picture that would amaze you."

"That's me," Frank stated. "When I was about twenty-four. Ya, your old friends from the Mesa always told me I looked like their friend Nick Dovolis."

I definitely have a type, I thought. Almost spooky. When Frank revealed his sober date, when he got clean and joined the AA/NA program, I had this impression, or more of an electric shock that Nick's spirit somehow helped Frank have the strength to beat his addictions. Spirit is not finite. Why can't it go wherever? Even inhabiting another being? It sounds bizarre but the dates coincided almost to the day and year, nine years prior.

The three days went by like that. Blink. I was following him down off the mountain with a head full of what ifs and how tos, trying to stay centered, not take off on a whirlwind. But it had gone so smoothly, conversing so easily from one decade and topic to the next I already felt a closeness with him. Family dynamics, education, spiritual beliefs, health and well-being, this was genuinely promising.

My overall impression of his home I liken to a mirror of his individuality. Personifying solid, sturdy, steady, manly, definitely a bachelor pad with his imprint visible throughout, his personal touches fit seamlessly from the ten foot beamed ceilings to the red brick floors softened with woven Navajo rugs. The spiral staircase, an architectural feat, was enclosed in a turret-like structure capturing an English castle facet. When he explained the physics of the design I marveled at his

195

proficiency. But without a doubt, my favorite aspect was the kiva fireplace built with his own hands, his specialty, he pointed out, expounding on the countless establishments in and around Santa Fe he'd constructed kivas in, continuing with a detailed account of the mechanics and nuances. I didn't need convincing, his entire home the unmistakable example, showing artistry, mastery, and love. Chilly that first evening, Frank fired it up, I think most likely knowing the effect it would produce. Warm and sensual, the mellow glow invited the romantic with flames dancing, crackling, sizzling energy entrancing with its allure. Firelight is so flattering and forgiving, the shadows softening flaws. I was smitten.

As it turned out, the rental I had secured was a disaster. Not ready, light fixtures barely installed, windows open so a fan could blow out some weird exhaust in an effort to mask the distinctly strange odor. The sink in the kitchen and the shower dripped continually. There was no hot water. Frank and I decided to drive to Hillsboro, ten miles back, for lunch, savoring fabulous green chili cheeseburgers. My first. A surfeit to the senses after which Frank headed back to Silver City. We hugged affirming our intent to get together again but not exactly having specifics, maybe the rental, or possibly Santa Fe. I think we both knew something had germinated but at this maturity one realizes there are a lot of details to hammer out. For one thing I lived seventeen hundred miles away. You gotta love the bad boy though. I remembered asking Sydney why Frank and his wife hadn't come to the Mesa from Tucson like she and many others, all of them in the same circle. She gave me an abbreviated version of his prison stint. Intriguing, to say the least,. I'd wait to get that saga from the horse's mouth. Having ample time to ponder his early life digesting some of the fascinating details I'd garnered over the past days, an amusing anecdote had me smiling.

When he lived in Santa Fe, one day shopping at Trader Joe's, the cashier looked at him with a probing stare, questioning, "Are you Donald Sutherland?"

Frank grinned, shaking his head in the negative.

"Yes, you *are*," she argued, not to be dissuaded.

There was a resemblance and with the star power of Santa Fe she was convinced that he was, indeed, Donald.

Frank was born in Washington where his grandpa owned and operated a lumber mill at the base of Mt. Ranier. Grandpa had the auspicious accolade of cutting down the largest redwood, so they say, the mammoth accomplishment documented in the Guinness Book of World Records. There was a picture of said relative standing next to the treasure on Frank's mantle. Baby brother, Robbie, was a mere thirteen months younger and how the two managed to stay alive through one debacle after another is a real head scratcher. At a fourth of July parade that the family attended, Frank four, Robbie three, they escaped their parents' view marching off joining the parade. The foundlings were tracked down at the end of the procession whooping it up with revelers at a tailgate party.

His early public school experience mirrored much of my attitude, not ready, out of place, insecure. After his kindergarten teacher reprimanded him he retaliated by going into the bathroom and unrolling the entire roll onto the floor. At all of five years old, one might have predicted the direction his life was going to take.

197

With the city bus line route at the end of their block there was always someone waiting at the stop. Frank and Robbie cooked up this outrageous plan to shoot someone in the ass with their pellet gun. Upstairs in their bedroom, this was when they were eight and nine, they took the screen off, leaned out and nailed a man waiting for the bus. He looked around, side to side, rubbing his ass, trying to decipher where it came from. They hit the floor, carefully rising just enough to peer out. It was almost impossible to muffle their raucous laughter. But that one smote his conscience and he vowed to his brother he'd never do it again.

Pulling into the driveway of my rental I felt like turning around and following Frank. They were still working on issues insisting it would only be ten to fifteen more minutes. Cammie was my respite where I reclined the seat and opened my notebook to chronicle some of Frank's early years. How he was still on the planet I couldn't fathom. Incident after incident should have killed him long ago.

One of his friends, Dave, lived two blocks away on Aldrich Avenue. In seventh grade they went up to northern Minnesota to Dave's family cabin. Old enough to be left alone but not to have a driver's license they were dropped off at the cabin for three days of duck hunting, each with his trusty shotgun. For some reason they traded weapons, Frank explaining to Dave that his single shot twelve gauge had a hammer that you pulled back. There was no safety. When the hammer's back, it's ready to go. It must have fallen on deaf ears because after walking through the woods finally arriving back at the cabin, Dave reached out for the door hitting the trigger. It blew a nice sized twelve gauge hole right through it.

This same Dave was the partner in crime that dreamed up their bomb scheme. Back in their middle class neighborhood they hatched a plan to blow up a mailbox, starting off with a CO_2 cartridge that handily took care of the job. That initial rush of adrenaline quickly propelled them to produce more powerful pipe bombs. Threaded on both ends you'd cap one end, Frank explained to me, put the powder in, and have a hole drilled for the fuse on the other cap. With the sporting goods store closed on a lazy Sunday their final detonation required an extra measure of resourcefulness to fabricate the needed fuse. The boys improvised a substitution out of gun powder, estimating a three foot long trail to be ample. At the end of the alley, putting the pipe under a trash can next to a garage they lit the gun powder. Instantly, before they were even a few steps away the thing blew like dynamite with such force it flattened both of them as well as blowing an eight inch hole in the side of the garage. How lucky were they to not catch any shrapnel or smash their skulls on the concrete alley? Not even a concussion. The bomb squad, and yes, there was a bomb squad in Minneapolis in the fifties, showed up the next day investigating the scene, looking for evidence but the two boys were never apprehended. They were wise enough or scared enough to never utter one word about it. To anyone. Pretty good little criminals. A few months later they couldn't resist another blast. After all, they'd gotten off scot-free. In a galvanized bucket at the bottom of the bridge at Minnehaha creek Dave and Frank detonated one final bomb. The coup de grace obliterated every last shred of the bucket as they stealthily darted away on their bicycles.

God, when you consider the difference in the present day. Seriously. We didn't have car seats. Now playgrounds barely have equipment due to the myriad liabilities. Thanks lawyers.

Chronicling Frank's escapades, I continued jotting the treasure trove of material in my notebook. Beginning in seventh grade at the downtown Woolworth's Frank began his shoplifting career with LPs, easily slipping an album inside his winter coat. The Everly Brothers were carefully chosen for his maiden heist. To get downtown he and his fellow delinquents would hop a city bus, grabbing onto the rear rail careening behind. If it was icy they grabbed onto the bumper skiing along on their boots. Cars following behind would sometimes honk trying to alert the bus driver and if he did stop and head for the door, they'd just jump off and either run or wait until he resumed his route and jump back on.

Frank experienced his first drunk in seventh grade, coupled with a bona fide black out. At a sleepover in his parent's basement he split a pint of Vodka with another guy. The following morning on a bus ride to the public library downtown, sick and hungover, his buddy related the previous night's antics, none of which Frank recalled. Alcoholic amnesia. His brain forgot although the body was functioning, even appearing sober. By eighth grade his fast track to juvenile delinquency was at breakneck speed where punishment entailed remedial summer school to make up the subject he'd failed.

Reclining the seat in Cammie I nodded off grinning to myself, envisioning this intriguing character I'd become undeniably attracted to.

It couldn't have been more than ten minutes. Tap, tap, tap on my window, "Are you okay?" the goddamn landlord asked, stupidly.

"I'm resting, nothing wrong. Are you done?"

"Yes, you can come in and see what you think," he replied with such a ridiculous expression, like I should be so thrilled.

Christ, what a dipshit. Why hadn't I left already? Upon entering it was crystal clear this would really be a stretch. Proving its readiness, I was given a demonstration of burners and oven functions.

"It seems smelly, gassy. Do you notice that?" I asked.

He gave me this blank stare as if he wasn't in the same time zone or dimension. But by this time all I wanted was for him to have mercy, get the hell out and leave me alone so I could decompress. Rest was paramount and I figured I'd deal with any additional snafus in the morning. Exhaling, feeling marginally okay with a glass of wine and the crossword, I lounged on the portal, watching the brilliant, coral sunset paint the sky. As I reentered the kitchen the question could not be ignored. Do I still detect gas? Was it my imagination, my fatigue? Opening all of the windows I figured a proper airing should suffice but halfway through the glass I felt woozy. A half a glass couldn't be the culprit. It was too creepy. Testing my senses I walked back outside breathing deeply for about three minutes then I went back in. Damn! It hit me full force. If I fell asleep it begged the question if I'd ever wake up? That's it! I'm oughta here. In the pitch dark, suitcases, bags and boxes were hauled back out to my car. The owner was only a hundred yards away in another dwelling and I wanted no interaction, not one more word with the idiot. Leaving him a terse note, I fled into the night, destination T or C, approximately forty miles away.

Goddammit! Are we there yet? Pulling into the first motel I collapsed in my room sleeping amidst bizarro dreams of chase scenes and asphyxiation. Next day, first thing, I called the bank to stop payment on my check I'd been gullible enough to leave with him. The next order of business was finding a cottage or casita for two weeks until my Santa Fe house-sitting gigs. The population in T or C is, shall we say, quirky? That's generous. It may need some investigative journalism? Odd, in a word.

The new rental I found was a dive, even a little scary, in need of some elbow grease or possibly a fire hose, but beggars can't be choosers, right? It was Friday and Frank said he'd ride up, on his Harley, oh yes, he's a Harley guy, probably Monday for a couple of days so this is doable. The complex is named Kansas Court, built in the fifties. If these walls could talk, they'd most likely say, 'ABORT, GET OUT NOW!' There's a three to four inch hump heaving the entire length of the kitchen floor, a buckle, which I'll have to be careful not to stumble over on my nightly potty trek. I promised my feet they wouldn't touch this tile without protection. Exhausted, I look at the clock. Can that be right? It's all of 7 p.m. The hot tub out the back door provided the respite I needed to bolster my resolve, my initial goal, that of healing my ailing feet in the curative mineral waters. The entire town is built over natural hot springs that flow from a fifty million year old rift along the Rio Grande. The deep groundwater flows to the surface without losing heat or minerals typically ranging from ninety-eight to one hundred fifteen degrees with about thirty-eight different minerals and a neutral pH balance. Ahhhh, heaven!

When I get an internet connection it occurs to me to check the crime rate. On the other hand, probably not. One night down. No rodents, no extraordinary events, sleeping reasonably well on the futon bunk bed. Never seen that one before. There was clean bedding but I needed several more layers between my skin and whatever may have been left over from previous tenants. So I bought one of those waffle foam pads from WalMart, topped with a comforter I'd brought with me by another stroke of luck plus Mommie Dearest had unloaded two more outmoded bedspreads on me, both in an eye popping floral but spotlessly clean. Thank you Mother.

Speaking of mothers, I chuckle at Frank's childhood having had more time to ponder the differences in our parents' techniques. I did tear all over the county, biking, free to wander miles from home but if discipline was warranted you can damn well believe it wasn't lax. We've all seen the hovering, helicopter parents, right? The children with no sense of adventure, every detail regulated, watched, corrected, and explained ad infinitum. Children need to be allowed to discover. Figure it out, even fail. OMG. Fail? Lesson learned. Maybe. Or not.

I'll elaborate: Five year old birthday party, where all the parents come. And stay. And be at the beck and call of the child. Presents are given but birthday child can't open them. They're opened privately. This is to save other party attendees the heartbreak of being left out. Not being special. What?! Why deprive the giver of the lesson; seeing your friend joyful over your gift.

You give something to someone you care about, they express joy and excitement, and you derive pleasure from being that source. You have the ability to make that happen. Everyone gets a special day but not at the same time. It's about life's inequities. We celebrate with a person while realizing our own day will be another day. Deal with it. It's such a huge part of life, figuring out how the world works, and that it is oftentimes unfair.

When did this happen? When did all the rules change? When did parents become servants?

I get it. I've had four children, four babies and would have done anything in my power to protect them from pain, hardship, a hangnail—but now I'm a Nana with four grandchildren and the things they need are character, strength, stamina, resilience, and compassion, to name a few. You want to shield, be the fixer, the intermediary, whatever it takes but my same four children that played outside all day ramming around without helmets on bikes, climbing onto the garage roof, playing with fire in the trash burning barrel, and toughening each other's hide and psyche with kick fights and wet willies, are now mature, well-adjusted, successful adults. Honest. They weren't allowed much TV time, barely any video games. It was too much fun gluing ants to the sidewalk, using the riding lawn mower as a tow for a sled roped to the back. It didn't kill them. Neither did drinking Kool-Aid and eating Kraft macaroni and cheese practically every day throughout summer vacation.

Two of these rabble rousers are said parents of the grandchildren of which I speak. They are steeped with memories of a fun, free, exciting, adventurous childhood. Granted, we lived seven miles out of town. Far enough for neighbors to not be concerned but close enough for the fire department to arrive in time.

Last time I visited, I was delighted to see my daughter, Chloe, teaching her daughter how to blow a fart on the inside of her elbow. Hilarious! She's an only child so won't have siblings to rip one with. Never forget how funny those noises are. Farts never disappoint as granddaughter, Sophia, so succinctly put it. Bella had a stellar comment that I love sharing with friends. She was maybe four years old, having 'tooted' a couple of times, when her mom asked, "Do you have to poop?" Bella replied, "No, it's still loading."

About four years ago, two of my granddaughters, Bella and Sophia, now ten, displayed the normal curiosity concerning swear words and body parts. Bella had evidently heard the F-word and needed enlightenment.

"Mom, what is the F word?" she inquired one day.

Being the progressive individual she so personifies, Chloe replied matter of factly, "It means fuck."

"What does that mean?"

Tactfully, Chloe hedged, "It's when you're really mad at someone and you want to say something really bad. Like fuck you."

"Well, I want to say that."

"You'd make someone feel so bad if you said that to them, like *you'd* be so mean and it would hurt them."

"Can I say it in my room?"

"Ya, that would be okay."

Explaining the whole conversation to me, I agreed with her logic, "It's just a word. I don't think she should be prohibited as long as she understands the societal 'time and place' restrictions."

"That makes so much sense," I said, thinking how evolved it all sounded, especially when I thought back to Chloe's older sister coming home from kindergarten and dropping the F bomb after a few days. I figured it was probably the bus ride which included K-12 students. My reaction was definitely befuddled.

"What did you say!?"

Immediately Zelda deduced my chagrin, and speaking much more timidly said, "fuck, why, what's that?"

"It's a bad word and I do not want you to say it."

"What is it?"

"It's a swear word. You don't hear me and Daddy saying that, do you?"

"No."

"Then I don't want you to say it."

With no further discussion she seemed compliant, but I'm sure it gained a prominent position in her vocabulary by virtue of its reaction. It is an important milestone for a youngster to feel the power of such a word as well as learning the lessons of discretion and proper usage. I do wish I would have had a better sense of humor about the subject, like Chloe.

The following day, back to Bella, she asked her mom what this means, poking up her middle finger.

"That means, fuck you, like sign language," Chloe explained.

"Can I do *that*?"

"Not at anyone. It's a mean thing to do and it's as if you're super mad at them. And some people think it's the most terrible thing to do, like older people."

"But I waaaant to," Bella whined.

The forbidden attraction is so undeniable, so enticing. I remember getting my mouth washed out with soap for infractions of that sort. Mom would even grind it onto my teeth making it about impossible to get rid of. If that doesn't make you want to say it!

Chloe reasoned, "You can do that in private, in your room, or when no one else will see you."

A while later she walked past the bathroom and witnessed Bella with her face up to the mirror. With both hands her middle finger was extended pressing against her cheeks, a big smile on her face with obvious admiration as she practiced the newfound first amendment right. Sitting on the couch later that evening, Chloe and Bella watched TV, comfy under a warm afghan.

"Guess what I'm doing?" Bella inquired of her mom.

With one glance at her elfin expression Chloe knew the exact position of Stella's hands under the blanket. Like an illicit drug.

Bella's cousin, Sophia, is one month older. Their curiosity about the male body developed at exactly the same time. The big question being, how does the genital area differ from their own. Both sets of parents debated how to explain and educate, using correct verbiage and unflinching honesty. Anatomy books were helpful but it was obvious they both wanted to see for themselves, Bella even trying to bust in on her dad peeing or showering. Well, neither Daddy was comfortable with that option so the girls had to be satisfied with pictures. I heard considerable discussion about penises and vaginas during the next months, as the learning curve coagulated.

"Do you expect to get an irate phone call from parents of Bella's friends?" I queried Chloe. "I'm sure she's relishing informing her class mates."

"I'm not too worried. They are mostly of the same mindset. It's liberal Madison," Chloe said.

During my next visit with Sophia, she casually caught me up on her latest understanding, "I have a vagina," she declared, obviously proud of her anatomical vocabulary.

"That's right," keeping my tone interested but unremarkable. I'm so hip.

"My mom has a vagina. You have a vagina."

She stands up for this next part. Taking her hands upward in a victory salute, she brings them down forming a V shape at her groin area, stating, "But my dad has a penis," all with a slight grin, like having the most inside information she's ever been privy to.

"Yep," I answer with a totally straight face, knowing her dad and I will have a hilarious moment when I relate it later.

I gotta say, I do love being a grandparent!

And then this. Are children benefitting from all the hovering? It makes me kinda crazy. Get out of the way. Let them suffer consequences. Step in if and when the situation poses bodily harm, say, blood. Leave them alone. Seriously. Refrain from all the 'sit this way on your chair, hold your fork this way, jump here, walk there, wash hands, wash hands!' Dirt is not the enemy. Have you seen the study about Amish kids not getting asthma and allergies apparently because they're out in the farm fields with all the dust? It purports that kids are more protected if they live in a dirtier environment. It was actually published in the New England Journal of Medicine.

13

Back to my present environs. Across the alleyway sits a trailer park. It's one of a dozen such settings littering the vicinity spilling out into Caballo Lake and Elephant Butte State Park. This particular one appears to be teeming with men around my age, sitting for hours on end in folding lawn chairs shootin' the shit. This line comes to mind, 'one sandwich short of a picnic.' Full beards, straggly, long hair, some sporting pony tails, wheel chairs roll in and out and I decide, Vietnam vet enclave. Harmless, laid back, I'm mostly not sensing any danger but then again as I dozed off last night sirens and hollering broke my calm, enough to haul my ass over to the door double checking the lock.

"Be aware of your surroundings," Frank advised, after I related that information.

I will. Now this afternoon there's yelling outside my window so I sneak a peek to observe a young man, not in his right mind running back and forth. He's carrying a black and white print backpack, average build and looks desperately in need of psychotic meds. I'm taking note of details as if I'll have to describe him to the police. Keep on moving, I repeat, and don't start wailing on my car. Please. A line from one of my poems goes, 'still so much fragility in me, hidden by bravado' and at this poignant moment the truth is, I need to project confidence. Don't let them see your fear or insecurity. I can't, I will not be impeded by gender inequity. Right? Right!

Next morning the trailers have deserted, the battalion went AWOL. Hallelujah. Diana Krall croons on my laptop. Thank god for tunes. There's no other media. No TV. Media abstinence is good for me, especially a news 'fast.' How my outlook improves in a bubble. I wonder if the indigent purlieu is off attending church on this fine Sunday morning? It wouldn't surprise me, adding religious dogma to the misfits.

Frank's riding over on Tuesday, on his Harley, and I intend to take advantage of such an opportunity to scooch up to him astride the Road Glide. Hah! Nice line. Conjuring the twat squash on the back of him or even vibra-twat. Phew, did I need to get laid or what?

Relating my latest adventure to Vera on a marathon phone call, I told her, "It will be comforting to have a man in my corner/quarters. It's been unsettling and I only have myself to thank for that."

"I so do not like hearing that, the precarious circumstances, it makes me nervous."

"I know and I'm sorry to do that to you. It's my exercise in fortitude. Maybe it's foolhardy, stupid to do shit like this but I do revel in my imprudent, or maybe impudent spirit."

"I'll be glad when Frank gets there. And even better when you get out of there. I don't want you to become a statistic."

Always a barometer of wisdom, measured with love, I so valued her input and vowed to be more circumspect going forward. I decided not to take any pics of the strange neighborhood not wanting to draw any attention to myself or have my motives questioned or scrutinized. I was determined to stay under the radar. Frank and I discussed the sleeping situation, me having the one bedroom. The perfect gentleman, he said he'd bring his air mattress. Again, no pressure. I'm trying to be cool and yet there is definite chemistry rousing the libido. What if this is my only shot?

Should I waste time? Over-think everything? Dating is so confusing. I don't even know if we are dating yet. Mellow out already. My rebel, bad girl gravitates to him like an irresistible magnetic energy. I've seen the pickins' out there and they are slim to none. This is a real possibility, so saddle up. On that first ride with him, to the Bosque Del Apache National Wildlife Refuge, in San Antonio about sixty miles away, I had such a wild child rise up. Something in my bones, my soul that responded to the rumbling power, the surge of acceleration. Such a rush hearkening back to the drug days.

That evening our conversation struck a deep nerve, "I feel like I've known you all of my life, or maybe in another life. It is so comfortable with you as if we've been connected somewhere, on some plane, it's uncanny."

Ordinarily I would be reserved, even fearful of letting my guard down like that but I trusted him to be safe. Not perfect. Nothing is, but fun, yes, easy, yes, magic, romantic, YES. We crawled into our respective beds, chaste, not ready to make the move, well, I think I would have but was waiting for him. As I laid there I thought, well, I can at least give him a hug. I got up, in the dark, telling him I was coming in for a hug. My foot caught on the bed post splaying me across his body.

"Oh my god, are you okay, Jesus Christ, I'm so sorry. God, what a klutz."

"I'm fine. Fine. You didn't hurt me. It's fine."

He gave me a sweet hug as I attempted to pry myself gracefully off of him which was a joke having about knocked the wind out of him or broken a rib, no less. Sheesh, nice move, Anne!

Having time before my Santa Fe job I followed Frank back to his place. A word of explanation here about our sexual experience. I held out for oh, say two weeks, my usual MO being three months before I slept with a new beau. The most intimidating aspect being naked with this old body, the vulnerability, having another person see it in all its droopy folds, bumps and spots. I do keep in shape but age and gravity are merciless. I say I look okay from the front but no side angles, please. Anyway, this felt so right with him that I waived the waiting period and jumped his bones when we got back to his place. I'm not going to get into all the graphic details except to say he knew his way around a vagina and was a spectacular lover. Generous, gentle, patient, everything this woman needed to respond. He was open to every suggestion wanting to be on the mark, not assuming he knew my preferences, and willing to make necessary adjustments. What else can one ask? Copacetic. I contend, if things work well in the bedroom, one can excuse or forgive so many other annoyances but on the contrary, if it doesn't, it's really difficult to endure all the other sore points and challenges in a relationship! Heart, soul, body, mind… all one in those wondrous seconds. Gotta love it and maybe because it's beyond all reason. I'm attracted to the abnormal, odd. Like me, sometimes dangling on the precipice of sanity, anticipating a plunge, embracing the insouciance. It is hysterically funny trying to figure out this new gift, this magic. Love, at any age, but particularly at this 'maturity' is rare although I contend you are always every age you have ever been so if I act like I'm 20 and gaga, referring to my mental abilities, I'll just chalk it up to being a senior citizen. Now to achieve an equilibrium, balance in this new endeavor well, it's nothing short of a miracle no matter how well suited you are. Devil may care, if you dare.

And this: for yet another unique adventure. He'd told me about his desire to invest in the gold market, Tucson being the largest city for an easy overnight and I thought, this'll be an education. With an envelope of twenty-four thousand cash and a pistol, just in case, we installed Cyrus, his huge German shepherd, in Cammie's back seat heading west on I-10. Across the buckskin desert, saguaros softly nestled into the hills, gorgeous billowing clouds dotted the indigo sky, while boulder mountains precariously piled along the route added spectacular atmosphere to our flowing conversation. I thought to myself, is this for real, you know, too good to be true?

"If we get stopped, the gun is yours, okay, because as a felon I'm prohibited from ownership," Frank informs me.

"Have you actually fired that weapon at anyone?"

"No, I haven't but I'd like to think I could deal with a situation."

"Ya, it seems like you could."

At six feet plus, still with some impressively hefty biceps he appears to be one tough cookie.

"A female could never pull off this kind of escapade," I explain. "Having twenty-four thousand in cash, packing heat. So unrealistic."

I can tell he hasn't given it much thought, the gender inequity. Most guys don't much realize our limitations. At least, that's my understanding. Although, to think of it, I don't know many other guys who'd roll like that either. This one definitely has a flair for the dramatic. And do I like it? Oh yeah!

Frank, having lived in Tucson, was intent on showing me the Saguaro National Park where we could drink in the glorious sunset. Sitting atop a picnic table I leaned back between his legs hearing only the thump of his heart. Such peace and warmth, so tender, enveloped in his arms, I felt myself letting go, bit by bit. After a light dinner and amore, wrapped around each other, I was lulled into the loveliest sleep I'd had in ages.

With morning came a tour of the gold market culminating in the purchase of some almost phony looking gold coins. No shit. They looked like the bags of chocolate coins in the little yellow mesh bag that banks gave out at Christmas in my childhood. Driving home, his home, I'm ad-vising myself to stay guarded, no head over heels bullshit. There's reason to be circumspect, no rush. Something in me wanted to charge ahead, full tilt and at one period in my life I would have, but this was worth prudence.

"Have you ever been to a sweat lodge?"

He was determined to bring me that evening, explaining where it was, how it was advantageous to one's health, a detoxifying process for the mind and body. My prior religious experience made me extremely suspicious of any ritualistic practice and this immediately roiled my defenses. With strangers, in an intimate setting, virtually walled into a steamy enclosure I was feeling a familiar foreboding. I should have trusted my gut but I acquiesced. Pulling up to the scene that evening I was struck by the myriad oddballs assembled for the event. Way too many. The leader gave somewhat of a teaching elucidating the practice, how one would be affected, which only enhanced my trepidation. That place in my soul is kept buried, mostly inaccessible to any and all that I don't know well enough to trust. It was explained that men and women sat on separate sides in the hut immediately sending a ripple of patriarchal dominance up my spine. Legalism, fundamentalism were echoing from some dark place so why I even ventured in...? Several more red flags should have been enough for me to bail but I felt trapped wanting to show Frank my willingness, 'a good sport,' if for nothing else than to have a defense that I did try. We were squashed in, scorching hot rocks shoveled into the center as more instructions were rattled off about each of the four sessions, wherein at ensuing breaks the faint of heart could escape. The flap was closed, heat built so intensely that I literally had to get my face down touching the earth, with a towel over my head, in order to breathe. The instant that flap was opened, in a panic, I clambered over ten sets of legs stammering the password!

Waiting outside on a bench I assumed Frank would follow shortly but he made it through the entire four sessions. By that time I'd retreated to his truck where I sat fuming.

"They're having a feast afterwards. Do you want to go in?"

"Certainly not! I am so done. Seriously, you leave me waiting out here for an hour or whatever the hell it was and now I'm supposed to go in and be all cordial?"

"I don't get why you're so mad. I'll just go in and say goodbye. It'll take a minute."

I was livid but knew he didn't have a clue about my religious phobia and yes, I was acting unreasonably but it hit that sore spot that if you'd never been in a cult, you couldn't understand. Like lava flowing over, spilling out of me.

We let it settle, making nice the next morning as I loaded Cammie for Santa Fe. Obviously, it would take a while to peel back the layers as this relationship developed. Or not. It was a trigger, that caution hurling me back into my fantasyland where Nick and I understood these heart insights, unequivocally.

My Mesa friends were still trying to unpack Sydney's death, as well as Blake's. So enmeshed in each other's lives, the dynamics were a challenge that kept me circumspect trying to be diplomatic, sympathetic and loving. I found myself defending them to each other, being the mediator regarding their hurt, heartbreak and questions. There are no pat answers with suicide but everyone had an opinion. Right or wrong, they were entitled to them. Grief is so damn hard and confusing it brought back reminiscences, all of the confusion after Nick died.

As individual as everyone's relationship with Sydney was, so was the variance in how each one was coping, dealing with the emptiness, the void overflowing with pain. Listening, I offered my insight and experience cognizant of my role as the forerunner in bereavement. Lillie and I were more sympathetic, she with her professional background teaching nursing, having a more clinical understanding. Dylan and Maggie were more angry than anything else. They'd found her, were right there, left with that ghastly imprint. I didn't argue with them but did offer my experience telling them I came close to removing myself from my earthly existence the year after Nick died. It hurt that much and that was the only way I knew it would stop. Mostly, it required kindness, gentleness and faithful patience allowing time to heal the wounds. Time, in my situation, was a miracle, unexplainable, incomprehensible, the only thing that gave me hope.

I do miss him. Frank. Go figure. Wow! I want him here with me but I still have to reign in my feelings. It's too soon to let my heart have its liberty. Not sensible. Not logical.

What does the heart know of these things? I can't just follow my heart, right? Is that safe? Wise? My brain is in a debate with my gut. What if it blows up? Fizzles? Takes a sharp U turn? What if? What if? What if? Why don't you be a little more neurotic or obsessive? Is he thinking this way? Don't come on too strong, don't crowd her, be cool? I need to give space. Chill. Enjoy him when he's with me and let him be unencumbered when he's not. We'll have lots of time apart so I cannot be down, or possessive, or insecure or even unhappy when I go back to life in the Midwest. It is what it is. We're a little over a month old. Jeezuz, is that all?

Driving back the 1,700 miles afforded ample time to reflect on Frank's history or should I say histrionics? We both remembered Mr. Lucky's. Located on Lake Streets and Nicollet, in Minneapolis, opening in '62, it was the only local nightclub devoted exclusively to teenagers. I had been there a few times enjoying the burgeoning Twin Cities music scene with groups such as the Chancellors, the Underbeats, the Accents, Gregory Dee and the Avanties, all building a devoted fan base of teeny boppers. AND this bit of trivia, Frank had begun his drumming career with Gregory back in high school but at that time their band was called Gregory Dee and the Bashers.

We'd all heard about Glen Lake reform school for juvenile delinquents but I had never known anyone who'd done time there. I was a bad girl but never *that* bad or was just lucky enough to not get caught. Frank did actually land there after an attempted robbery. Maybe not such a terrible thing the upside being that he used the opportunity to make up work for his failed senior history subject. He and three buddies held up a pizza delivery guy for the money but the food as well. They'd been drinking beer on a Sunday, driving around

217

Minneapolis, jiving, talking, and came up with the brilliant scheme to run away to New York. He didn't say who first suggested the idea. They were hungry and cash strapped so the addled brains agreed on a fictitious address and called in the order from a pay phone. A plot employed by the hoi polloi, this specific pizza joint had vowed to thwart such antics. As the delivery guy brought the pizza up the walk, Frank and the boys grabbed the pizza demanding the money. Gary stuck his finger in the guy's back. That little maneuver, threatening someone's life, ramped it up to armed robbery. It was a set-up. Boom. Red lights flashed, and just like that, cops were all over the scene. Boxed in, there was no place to run. Shoved into the cars and driven downtown, they were locked up overnight. Parents were told to come the following morning for the hearing, at which time the hoodlums were released. Two weeks later the judge sentenced Frank and another of the guys to ten days on the discipline squad at Glen Lake but the other two, who'd already turned eighteen, took the option of signing up for the army, heading straight to Vietnam. The newspaper headlined cleverly, "Pizza Caper Went Bad: Boys Didn't Get The Dough."

By some inchoate machination, Frank was accepted to the University of Minnesota and with the aid of dexedrine he actually embarked on a course of erudition. His parents having moved to the suburb of Burnsville, ostensibly to escape the stigma of their son's reputation, informed him he could get an apartment on campus or go the fraternity route. Sigma Nu was chosen for multifarious reasons, the most salient, of course, the parties. He didn't last long after 'borrowing' a member's car ending up with a DUI.

What was I getting myself into? Good question. This irascible dude had a most checkered past indeed, however,

218

he'd been clean and sober, lo, these many years. Steady, solid, trustworthy, right? I did realize de facto if he ever started drinking again, it'd be over! I wondered how he ever straightened out enough to head up a thriving and successful masonry contracting business in Santa Fe for most of his adult life!

Note to self: find out.

The following summer, barely squeaking by with his courses, Frank got a job with a railroad crew, all black, except for one other guy named Grant. Good money for a college boy but definitely not his bailiwick. They introduced Frank to marijuana, rolling joints with strips of paper bags. One Friday night the crew invited Grant and Frank to party with them on the rough North side. After a sumptuously greasy home-made fried chicken dinner with Junior, Jigs, Leroy, and Banks they all piled into a huge Cadillac sedan to hit the blues bars. The first joint, the Regal, nicknamed the Bloody Bucket, rightfully earned by the high incidence of fights and shootings, was headlining Mojo Buford. Frank, a decent drummer, having started out with Greg Maland, the lead in the aforementioned Gregory D and the Avantees, of Mr. Lucky's fame, marched himself straight up to the stage and told Mojo, 'I'm a drummer, I'd like to sit in if I could.' They let him play three songs during which gun fire erupted outside the bar. The band didn't miss a beat. Everyone else hit the floor, ducking under tables, scrambling for cover. Mojo got Frank's telephone number calling months later wanting to put together a white band but Frank'd had to sell his drums to pay off another DUI, sadly ending whatever musical aspirations he'd entertained.

There's a light, new beginning as it were, and I'm so grateful. Frank has a lot to do with the transition, obviously.

219

Maybe it's a feeling of completion. Maybe because I feel happy, content. I'm excited and in wonder at how we can and will evolve. Much to determine.

Also, it depends on Aaron. My oldest son now diagnosed with cancer. Thyroid. They tell you it's a good kind to have. What an illogical statement. You must have to be an oncologist to grasp such a notion. It is highly treatable with an outstanding cure rate. Well, that's something. Surgery, radiation and monitoring for ten years afterwards.

Arriving in Minneapolis, Zelda and I tag teamed for the hospital stay. Aaron's neck was sliced from ear to ear with the most ghastly stitches running the length of it. Very Frankensteinish. My heart lurched, I had to mask my shock the first time I walked into his room. Tubes extended from his chest attached to two containers that filled with drainage. Along with the thyroid, thirty-two lymph nodes were removed proving to be malignant.

This mother, the mom so adeptly able to fix (just about) everything. Resolved to comfort, holding it together to give him strength, he reached toward me with care not to disturb a tube, and uttered softly, "Take my hand, Mom."

Suddenly, as if he was still a small child three decades old, sharing his resolve, an epiphany of growth, evolving, grasping a couple of profundities in the process, he whispered, "hang onto love fiercely, and let go of every other invasion attempting to steal your peace."

Lightening the moment he divulged, "I'm going to get a tattoo."

I chuckle. Facing off death will do that to you.

"So I know you won't ever forget this, Aaron. Be mindful of the power you've gained suffering this malignancy.

Remember healing in its time will encompass the body, the psyche, the whole."

I can't trivialize it, and I'm not, because it's huge, heavy but I always say, 'everything happens for a reason' teaching us more about ourselves. It's not up to me to fix any-thing or anyone. Let it be. I will have faith and trust.

With Frank it's apparent I will be with him as much as possible or practicable but it won't be all the time. I don't possess it to give, not owning my life. Gifts are given to us for now, this moment, and the future will reveal its secret in the process of time, of love, if love can be processed, if it is at all describable or definable. Of course, love defies logic and explanation carrying us along the gleaming slippery-slide ride. I'll hang on just like riding on the back of your Road Glide, ever ready to surge, rumbling not unlike the pounding of my heart, quickened in that flutter of sated desire. 'Just here' for as much time as we have. The relationship shuffle: one step forward, two steps back.

To be at arm's length from my son was brutal. Visiting him three weeks after the surgery, Aaron's radiation therapy made him so toxic he couldn't come within three feet of anyone, especially his young daughters. Friends offered their lower level for his quarantine, leaving his meals on the staircase, with paper plates and plastic forks to be thrown away. Aaron related how the nurse came into his room covered in this haz-mat type attire, with tongs handing him the horse pill containing radiation and god knows what all. He had to pick it up with his fingers, put it in his mouth and swallow it. I couldn't believe it. Christ! How he didn't just freak out? My need to wrap him in my arms, always the touchy-feely Mom, not able to kiss him, comfort him was awful. My heart ached. But it pulled our family together on a spiritual plane in such a profound and beautiful way.

On that temperate day Aaron and I were able to sit six feet apart out on the patio. To humor him in my attempt to lighten the mood I brought up the budding romance with Frank, acquainting him with a few lurid stories, knowing he'd convey all of it to his siblings. Regaling Aaron with the juvenile delinquency and especially the bomb making anecdotes it was such a relief to see smiles and even laughter.

"What do you call someone who tells Dad jokes who isn't a Dad?" I mused.

"This is a joke?" Aaron asked.

"Duh."

"I give up."

"A faux pa."

We both groaned.

"I might have made that up but I probably heard it somewhere."

"Thanks for the effort. Anyway, so how did Frank straighten out and ever become a successful contractor?"

"Oh, that's the most far-fetched of all. If it wasn't Frank telling me, I'd think it was made up."

I proceeded to entertain Aaron with Frank's journey into drug dealing. Introduced to dealers on the West Bank, amid a pot dearth, his first foray into the lifestyle was with LSD. That followed on the heels of him having to take four incompletes that quarter of college. His immediate problem was to make those up or the draft would have nabbed him. It was no surprise the following quarter with a full load and four incompletes that he'd derail. Acid gave him a completely altered value system aligning his philosophy with the hippie movement.

A move to Tucson was to facilitate escape or at best, delay the draft. That's where he happened upon a pot connection from Mexico wiring back to friends in Minneapolis to front him money for cheap pounds. Like crazy cheap. Eight dollars a pound. So with a buy of seventy pounds, on foot with packsacks, he and another willing partner, Ken, crossed the border, the distance about a mile. Hiding the packs stateside, they walked back to where the car was parked and drove it through the Nogales border on up to Tucson. The following night they drove back, picked up the stash and proceeded non-stop to Minneapolis, unloading the pounds for a hundred and twenty five dollars each. It was so lucrative and too easy. And then just like that it collapsed. After two more successful runs, the fourth included a crew of four guys bumping the cache up to 300 pounds. Poring over details, setting up time lines, calculating border checks and patrols, attempting to decrease variables, Frank knew lady luck played a more than ample share in his success. And guess what? It ran out. He figured a patrol must have spotted the footprints after the guys made the drop. When they loaded the pot into their van, pulling out onto the road, headlights immediately glared in the rearview mirror. Dumping the bales was futile, but it was instinctive. Pulled over, out of the van with guns aimed and cocked, they were commanded onto the ground, hands above heads. The ensuing destination, Douglas, Arizona County jail. With a lawyer, they made bail after two nights. Frank's arraignment was in front of an aptly named Judge Fry who made no bones about his sentiment, yelling at the lawyer and lecturing about the travesty of such dealings. Frank and Ken decided their best recourse was to jump bail and go underground.

"Are you sure you aren't too tired?" I asked Aaron, seeing his weary posture.

"Naw, I get achy and a little light headed," he said, standing and doing a few hip circles to limber up. "It's gotta be the medication, even the weakness from the whole surgery."

"We can stop any time. I don't want to tax you."

"Well, shit, I've gotta hear the end of this now. I've gotta meet this guy."

"I know. Pretty nuts, right?"

"And you're sticking with this guy? I mean, is this going to last?"

"Fuck if I know."

Another complication with Aaron's surgery had left him with a torn rotator cuff. In the recovery room he'd become extremely agitated in semi-consciousness, flailing about in an attempt to get up off the gurney. One nurse, being tremendously outweighed, tried without success to restrain him, Aaron pulling out his drains and tubes as he lurched around. With extreme effort they got him sedated returning him to the OR to repair the damage. This time they strapped him down so rigorously, restraining all movement that it resulted in a damaged shoulder either by cutting off circulation or just the inordinate pressure. With that added pain and discomfort, recovery was inching along and would possibly require surgery to repair the rotator cuff. It was too soon to tell but it really pissed me off which I did my best to disguise.

As Aaron settled gingerly into his chair I launched into the next chapter. Assuming new identities, securing fake IDs

Frank and Ken traveled up to a friend's farm in northern Minnesota where they hid out. And get this, before heading up north they used every last dime to score another load of pot, first selling in Chicago before dealing the rest in Minneapolis. Brazen, youthful audacity cemented their decision to buy a vehicle, go to Mexico and continue with the smuggling scheme the following winter. How else could they earn money? Passing through Minneapolis Frank contacted his parents learning they'd been questioned by the FBI. Fiercely loyal to their wayward son, they arranged to meet him down by Minnehaha Creek under the Dupont bridge, a few blocks from their residence. Yes, disappointed, yes, scared but still willing to stand by him, to hear him out. He promised to keep them informed not having a clue as to how he'd accomplish that.

From the farm he drove to Montreal where it was rumored hash was in plentiful supply. He and Ken planned to canoe it across from some place along Bear Skin Lake. The buy was two pounds of Red Lebanese, scored from a sultry French woman in Thunder Bay. Fueled by hubris and paddling skill Frank successfully commandeered his canoe and hash across the lake singlehandedly.

Riding on that lucrative wave, convinced his endeavors were obviously charmed, Frank planned another smuggle, a grand finale. That October he and fellow fugitive, Ken, crossed the Mexican border with their fake IDs, destination Playa Azul, Michoacan. With both of them contracting salmonella, so horrible they were shitting blood, after three days they had to break down and go to the Mexican doctor who administered a shot to the ass. It was the biggest needle Frank'd ever seen. Probably meant for a horse. Sent home with syringes and vials the patients kept up the regimen until they recovered. After side jaunts to Zihuantanejo, next Oaxaca, the pair landed on a score of 'Gold' in Acapulco. 400 pounds! So here's the state of Texas crawling with border patrols, these two guys in their early twenties, drug addled, irrational minds, attempting a huge smuggle while on the run! It had to be one of the stupidest scenarios I'd ever heard! They did, indeed, outfox the law, with a bizarre strategy, paying two other guys that they'd met on the beach to drop Frank and Ken off on the Mexico side, with the pot, then driving through the border check. Frank and Ken walked the pot across, back and forth with a hundred pounds at a time, getting picked up stateside stopping in Midland, Texas to get some shut eye. Driving straight through to Minneapolis, riding high, they split up to avoid going down together. Trying to be ever vigilant, Frank spent the better part of his days secluded in an apartment although his notoriety was well known enough to have a song written about his exploits, The Bunde Blues, performed on the West Bank, at the Triangle bar by one of the local musicians. He'd gotten wind of another probe, the FBI questioning his parents, his sister and brother, now even some of their friends. Dogging the leads, the agents showed up at his brother's house a half hour after Frank had been there. Figuring he had to put some distance between them he headed for Chicago and that's where he got popped. Someone happened to see his face on a poster, tipping off police who swooped in. Along with two pounds of pot Frank also had methadone in his possession. After one night in the precinct jail he was transported to an ancient prison built before the Civil War, solely comprised of misdemeanor offenders. They discovered he had a federal detainer and whisked him away to Cook County where he spent eighty-five days. Each and every single day down the hall to the exercise yard they walked him past the room with the electric chair in plain view. Being the only white guy there, somehow, fortunately he didn't have any trouble with the guards or other inmates. Friends from Minneapolis pitched in to get him a cheap 'fresh out of law school' lawyer. When his folks and sister showed up to visit, it cut Frank to the core, awakening his dormant conscience. They truly were exemplar parents, supportive beyond comprehension. Outfitting him with a sport coat and tie they recovered from his pick up, they helped him prepare for his court appearance. Obviously, the guards had not thoroughly checked the coat because the inside pocket contained a Marlboro pack hiding two white crosses and a joint. That night his cellmate, in for murder, and he savored the treasured find. Federal law stipulated that Frank had to be returned to the state he was initially busted in so shackled with leg irons, hands chained in front, two marshals transported him on the slow journey back to Arizona. Pondering his fate, the original sentence carrying five to twenty years, the reality was chilling as he finally had to face the consequences. Terra Haute Penitentiary was the first stop, Frank keeping his cool as rough inmates hollered Jesus at him because of his long hair and beard. Thankfully, it was a one night stand proceeding to Missouri with now two other convicts in the back seat. The process took eight days staying at various prisons along the way as US marshals rotated in and out treating each prisoner like a piece of shit. Leg irons came off only for the overnights. Pima County jail, downtown Tucson, was the final destination. While on the run, fortunately the charges had been reduced from zero to five years. Odd, being that hard-liner Richard Nixon was president. In no uncertain terms he was informed if he didn't

227

plead guilty, he'd be tried on the five to twenty. He complied hoping for a merciful judge, but by some ill wind he ended up standing in front of the very same Judge Fry. The charges were bail jumping and marijuana smuggling. Two years for the pot and three years on the bail charge running concurrently. Consecutive means you have to serve the one sentence before you start the next one but concurrent runs them together. With six others in the court facing sentencing, Frank was the only one that had anything to say, basically pleading that he was a middle class hippie caught up in the movement, now comprehending the error of his ways having been incarcerated. It probably saved him from the five year sentence. Also, on a three year sentence or any sentence, the feds give you one third good time meaning he'd serve two. Having served six months already he had only 18 months to go. *Only*.

14

"That is one hell of a story," Aaron said. "Thanks for the diversion."

"No shit. It's not much different than what anyone else was doing at the time. Your dad and I had dealings with mutual connections, hearing Frank's name, but never actually met him, not that I recall. We definitely could have been in the same boat. It was the times, the mentality. We were swept up in the wave and lived to tell about it."

"Glad of that. And so how did he do in prison? That's gotta be some tough shit. And it begs the question, is he on the straight and narrow now?"

"Right. He's been clean and sober now for ten plus years. He ran a successful business in Santa Fe, had an unblemished career in construction but did have his struggles with addiction along the way."

"I suppose that's another installment, eh?"

"Oh yeah, you'll hear the whole magillah at some point. You know, I can't imagine being that young, facing prison time. But I'm going to leave it for our next visit, another conversation. It goes on and on and I know you need to lie down and I need to get going. God, it's so hard not to hug you," I said, trying to hold back the tears, "I'm so proud of you, your attitude. You know how I wish your dad was here to bear some of this burden. Aaron, I'll forever miss him, never get over him, you know that?"

"Can you say you love this guy, Frank?"

"Well, I guess. So far."

I could see the tenderness in his eyes, his heart clearly moved, as he reached his hand toward me. I extended mine as we pantomimed a clasp, the unfelt grasp.

"I love you, Aaron."

"Love you too."

It was tough leaving him, leaving Minneapolis but my life was full of things to do before the next excursion to New Mexico. Or was it going home? The direction along with my persona definitely blurs. From Mom/Nana morphing into girlfriend, partner, significant other? What or who am I? I'm not a girl and am more than a friend. One of my standard lines is, 'I'm still trying to figure out what I want to be when I grow up' and another favorite from Erma Bombeck, 'Once you're a mom, you're never not.'

My side trip to Santa Fe was again, or should I say always, fraught with emotional baggage mostly or again over Sydney's death. But also, Blake's. I was informed they'd gotten heavily into coke after several decade's hiatus. With a shit ton of inheritance it was easy to become bored with their mundane existence. I'd have thought it'd be just the opposite, traveling, upgrading, remodeling ad infinitum. Blake had overtaxed his heart ignoring warnings, suffering the big one that fateful evening. Maggie thought Sydney was blaming herself, being crushed under the weight of guilt, leading to her 'remedy.' They were still angry with her, thinking it was selfish to take that ignominious way out. And that made *me* angry at them. They hadn't suffered the loss of a life partner to know the agony it bred. You're literally ripped into shreds, destroyed with one deftly crushing blow. I was annoyed with them for not understanding but at the same time trying to give grace and not judge because how *could* they know? If I could have checked out after Nick died … who the hell knows? It is that excruciating. Horrible. Money certainly doesn't solve everything. Much to the contrary. It's no panacea because that's physical, material. What is hurting, the deep spiritual wound, cannot be assuaged by things. That is no cure, much to some peoples' erroneous assumptions. Only love, understanding and patience can bring the possibility of recovery. The scar is forever.

They'd taken her ashes up to the Mesa, where Blake was dispersed. Nick was up there too so I planned a pilgrimage intending to pay my respects, needing that closure. Now, walking the path across the field to the boulder marking their grave, depositing a small stone on the site, I couldn't deny the aura. So powerful, the Jewish gesture of respect, placing the stone, Maggie had told us about the custom when we brought Nick's ashes there. My tears erupted from the depths of my soul releasing so much pent up emotion, taking my liberty knowing it'd be a long time before I'd be back. Meditating with peaceful spans in between the turmoil, I processed what I could, conjuring visions of our life decades earlier, our log cabins, birthing babies, the happiness we enjoyed and suddenly as if sent to restore, acceptance settled my heart and I knew they were somewhere near, holding me with loving energy. At that moment I knew I'd never let go, that they'd always be with me, the undertow of sadness, chrysalis of loss ever at my fingertips, ever buried within my heart's protective shell. But then it literally softens, gently abiding, sensate, the antidote like a rare friend or the love of your life who will never abandon you. No, Sydney remains, entwined in my soul penetrating the bulwark, like skin to bone, sinew to muscle. Golden warmth, inviting rays seemed to metamorphize my psyche to a tranquil center. There is no separation of spirit, no gap, only a wealth of memory and understanding that personifies a character molded through years of effort and toil for the lofty goal of forever love, incomparable affection, pure and unsurpassed to treasure till the final sunset.

Aha! Eight months into the relationship and oh boy, the scales fell away. How can I be responsible for your insecurities, I ask? Will you be for mine? No. How can you? I have to fix myself and you must as well. Isolation is one sentinel against heartbreak. Living in a vacuum? Is that the solution? We hope, expecting to meet such minuscule endeavor with open spirit knowing the jagged scar of the damaged psyche, though holding together, is ever weak and precarious. My visible character cloaking sadness with a tentative mantle may pass for health, portraying well-being but there remains a fog of human frailty and vulnerability that persists with suffocating weight. I let my guard down and you snapped! Such venom! I took the outburst extremely ill. We tried without success to mend, to apologize, placate and put it in its proper perspective but too little sleep, too much togetherness and not enough understanding, I could only sleep with Xanax. Big surprise. "Life is a process of becoming, a combination of states we have to go through." Anais Nin

Frank was with me in Santa Fe dog-sitting for Dylan and Lillie. We'd planned to drive to the Balloon Fiesta in Albuquerque, and even though we'd had a fairly significant blow-out the night before, him losing his temper in a bizarre outburst, we piled into the car and embarked. The whole way

232

there, the entire day and the return to Santa Fe neither of us said one word to the other. You've heard of defensible space, right? In high fire areas of the desert and mountains, residents are encouraged to clear a perimeter of thirty feet, to cut all brush and incendiary materials for security. I envision my arms outstretched thirty feet thwarting access to my soul, my 'dwelling' that remains private, circumspect. My defensible space. And I let him in. Allowed him access and now I had to walk that back. He'd thrown this childish tantrum over the stupidest thing. Rather a news junkie, he religiously, I might say fanatically, watched morning and evening network broadcasts. Me? I limit my exposure, for sanity's sake.

So when he'd finished with one hour and flipped to another station, exasperated I said, "Really? You need to hear the whole shit show again?"

"What the hell difference is it to you? I'll watch whatever I want!"

It wasn't necessarily the words but the velocity. The harsh tone rose up with such force that I was utterly shocked.

"Sorry," I said, in an unrepentant tone, like singsongee saw-reee. Not at all helpful.

"Don't tell me what to do."

"Well, you just watched the exact same thing and now you have to hear it all over again? Or *I* have to hear it?"

I shouldn't have pressed it but was on the defensive. Nothing more productive was exchanged until we returned from Albuquerque and I couldn't take the silent treatment any longer. Pushing the elephant into the center of the room, I asked if we could discuss the issue.

"You talked down to me, made me feel inferior," he stated.

"That is so wrong, so not my intent. You're smart, talented, wonderful, (stroke, stroke, stroke) and you misperceived my

233

comment. You know how sassy, brassy, and in your face I can be."

And that's where I choked up. Dammit. I needed to be mature, logical, not a cry-baby. I didn't deserve his reproach, not in that blow-out way. I knew he had a moodiness but yelling? Unacceptable. Growing up with parents that berated each other with such hostility, I vowed I would never have that kind of relationship. And I didn't. In thirty-one years Nick and I'd had very few fights, in that yelling, vicious sense. Yes, we disagreed but I had a particular method of dealing with any disagreement if it looked like it was going to escalate into 'out of control.' If Nick raised his voice to me, I'd walk away, into another room and if he followed, I'd walk out the door. It was the most effective way to deescalate any argument. It really was quite brilliant and I don't even know how I came up with it.

How much do I compromise, walk on egg shells? I'll suck it up for now— for now, but how much do I adapt for someone to be alright with me? No one's perfect. I have many flaws but what is the limit? What is the balance? Good to figure this shit out before we go to Costa Rica or before I sell my northern digs! We agree to try, to get back up.

We worked through that bout of hurt, anger and missteps to where I feel the disagreement and harsh words were an education. He got a sense of how vulnerable I can be, that I really can't take rough treatment and I got an eye opener into how I come off like a bossy bitch and need to work on my delivery. We avowed our commitment to each other and to growing toward that end. I like to make lists, pro and con in order to reinforce the positive. This was one of those times I needed to weigh the sides. I loved being with him, loved the sensate attraction, his ruggedness that even masks the tender gentleness, the allure and excitement straddling behind him on the Harley, pressing breasts into his back, skootching my twat right up there. You know, the vibratwat. Do I like that he can be vulnerable? Is his insecurity a plus or minus? He certainly becomes Prince Charming slowly and adeptly arousing my ardor, personifying the lyric, 'He's my little lover boy.' With such a strong presence, so centered, aware of who he is, and then Poof! I glimpsed an anomaly reminding me of that song, 'It's so easy to fall in love' by Buddy Holly. That's the easy part and then comes the stark reality of day to day. I wouldn't love him if he were normal, or even much like him. I'm attracted to odd. Look at me! I will choose to look at him as a gift, I mean finding love at this age? Rare. As the scab heals over, falls off leaving a small scar, we will encounter the next hiccup with patience and understanding. Right? The proverbial balancing act. Here's hoping.

Relating some of the month's maladies to Vera on a long-winded phone call, she added, "How 'bout the toilet seat up all the time, or splattery mirror and sink and it drives me crazy the over-all sloppiness. It's disgusting. But I agree, it's a balancing act. On any given day I imagine living alone or why did I get myself into this? But I'm still here."

I made her laugh with this one, "I'm glad my friends think I'm lucky to have him, even if I don't."

"That's one consolation. My single friends always want someone so we *are* lucky, yes?"

"Yes. If you say so."

Christ on a cracker! This is just great! Back to his mountain home, after three days of monsoon rains, finally blessed with brilliant blue skies, we were heading out of his driveway on the bike, destination the Cat Walk, near Glenwood about an hour's ride and we dumped. Oh my god! This is why they're referred to as Harley Fuckin' Davidson. I instinctively put my foot down to try to help him hold it up but got caught under the saddle bag. The bike landed on top of me smashing my leg flat twisting it around as I fell off the opposite way. Gasping for breath, spine tingling screams burst from my mouth in excruciating, white hot pain. Frank got that adrenaline surge lifting the bike off me. I grabbed my leg, holding it up, arms wrapped around under my thigh, trying not to breathe, or move. I'd distinctly heard two breaks, CRACK! CRACK! reverberating through my innards. Was it a shock wave? Were the fractures audible? CRACK. No shit! Barely able to catch my breath I skipped the typical ER waiting room aggravation and was hustled straight through to the examination room where the able staff cut off my shoe and jeans. And I really liked those shoes. The requisite x-ray clearly showed two breaks in the fibula right above the ankle joint. My right leg, driving leg. Yes, it could have been so much worse, yes, everything happens for a reason. Still—Why? Really? I needed this lesson? Can't I be in control of the universe? Mommy fuckin' dammit!

That's one of my family's colloquialisms coined from a three year old nephew. He was in his car seat as his mommy drove him to day care when his pacifier popped out of his mouth landing on the floor. Realizing he couldn't retrieve it, extremely frustrated, he spouted, "Mommy fuckin' dammit!" Mommy determined to clean up her language.

Noooo! A broken leg? After being fit with a temporary cast, crutches, the requisite scrips, instructions, and a blanket to cover my pantsless lower half, Frank drove me home. That night and the next day were a blur of oxycodone, sleep, awkward hobbles to the bathroom and overall agony. As is typical, the pain meds constipated me, doubling me over with horrible gas pains. Whether foggy, zoned or careless, I tripped, arms twisted in the crutches catapulting me face first into the flagstone hearth. Face scrapped, split lip, teeth rattled I finally let loose bawling my head off.

"Frank," I yelled. "Help."

Within hearing distance, immediately present, he sized up my injuries determining I didn't need stitches, "What were you doing? I'm rolling up all of these rugs."

"Easy, gentle," I cautioned as he mopped my upper lip with a paper towel. "I didn't cry the entire trip to the ER and now I can't stop blubbering away."

He held me, comforting, not speaking, just being there. It was the best thing he could have done. Helping me to a chair he got an ice pack for my face. How I didn't break my jaw or knock out my front teeth? I just shake my head. I know he was feeling guilty not being able to save me, for dumping the bike in the first place. Christ! I didn't blame him, stating plainly it was an accident but he was at the helm. He couldn't help feeling responsible.

The following day as I reclined on the couch I ventured to ask, "What the hell happened? How did we lose it?"

"The front tire hit a rock or a dip, I'm not sure which, and spun to the right. If you lose your balance on a Harley, it's going down. I tried to hold it but had to jump off. [And this revelation] "My biggest mistake. I forgot to tell you to keep your feet on the pegs. That would have been a pocket to save your foot and leg. I am truly sorry."

"I know, I know. One of those things, eh?"

I'm lying there with a blown lip, bloody scab and flat, filthy hair, no make-up of course, and he looks at me with those tender eyes and says, "You are so pretty."

"You really do love me, don't you?"

Amazing. Truly. What a man! Followed by thoughts of sadness, in another sense because I'm fairly certain I won't get on a bike again. Ya think?! He gets it, that it's probably over, which I know he'd be fine with. We both make our own choices. It was fun, unique, a few short months. My kids had lost one parent already. I explained to him my reservations. How he'd had twenty plus years' experience in the riding bank to measure this by. In my limited framework this one event took up such a huge percentage leaving me with a predictable conclusion, that is, to never be in that position again, to feel that pain again.

The orthopedic surgeon confirmed the bad break explaining how he'd use a plate and screws to repair the bone, with the added complication of extracting bone fragments. Tomorrow! Two weeks postop for the permanent cast and then the long haul of recovery.

If I had any second thoughts about riding, the surgery dispossessed me of that notion. I awoke in the recovery room throwing up, gasping in torment. My hollering brought the nurse with hypo in hand shooting it into the port. A nerve blocker and morphine brought instant relief while Frank helped me get dressed. Not even an overnight. Hustled right out the door. Twenty-four hours post op I began to feel my toes. Cognizant my attitude could easily derail me, I used all my powers of persuasion in an attempt to stay positive hoping that might help me manage. My mobility was improved with the aid of an office chair, so much easier and safer than crutches. But when all of the nerve blocker wore off the pain was mind numbing. I hadn't considered what it would feel like to have eight screws drilled into my bone. Sonofabitch, that's some hard shit! Mommy fuckin' dammit! I had four babies without anesthesia and this hurt so much worse.

During those interminably boring hours on my back I asked Frank to entertain me with more of his prison drama. He was more than obliging.

With a lovely cup of lemon ginger tea in hand, I was settled into the couch, leg propped, reasonably comfortable.

"Well, after I'd been sentenced, in about a month and a half I was transferred up to Florence, Arizona, a federal detention center for criminals in transit. From there I was transferred to Lompoc in California, a full federal prison. As we neared this huge gray building the US Marshal, a total asshole, said, 'Welcome to gladiator school.' I soon learned guys were getting knifed and shanked almost on a daily basis. Fortunately, I'd been given a parole officer who was kind of a young and idealistic type, sympathetic to my plight. Upon arriving at Lompoc I was able to make a phone call to him relating the dangerous circumstances and in a manner of a few weeks he got me recommended to a minimum security camp in Florence. My closest ally and cellmate was a memorable guy named Gil. With connections to the outside he was able to obtain pot sharing it with me on our daily walks along the fence line telling me 'it turns a black and white day into technicolor.' Regularly a visitor would smuggle it in handing it off while we sat at a picnic table conveniently shrouded by oleander bushes. They didn't watch you that closely giving us a false sense of security. The guards suspected us but weren't quick enough or savvy enough to bust us. Entering back into the building this particular day, walking past the guard, he zeroed in on me with this steely glare taunting, 'You can beat me a thousand times, Bunde, but I only have to beat you once'."

"Jesus Christ, man," I interjected, cringing. "How the hell could you risk it? You had to have known the odds were against you, right? You give new meaning to the phrase, learning the hard way!"

"You can get pretty desperate in there. I know, it does seem crazy *now*, looking back, hearing myself say it but shit. As you can guess, we were busted and I lost minimum custody getting shipped off to Latuna Federal penitentiary on the border of Texas and New Mexico. That put all of my good time, that past year, in limbo. I figured they'd punish me by having me do that whole extra year. I had been just two weeks away from getting out to a half-way house. So, I settled in to do another year, my mind already in that head space. Something in my attitude changed. I think I finally wised up."

I said, "It took long enough, huh? I mean, I don't know how it is, how it was but damn, you were dealt some horse shit cards!"

"Bad luck. Worse choices. Stubborn, thick? I don't know why it took all of that. So I quit smoking, replacing it with chewing."

"Ewww, that is the most disgusting habit. I'll tell you right now, I wouldn't be with you if you were still chewing."

"Ya, don't worry. That's not happening. So along with quitting I got into the kitchen staff working on the salad bar, got on a health kick, started jogging and lifting weights. I took advantage of an occupational program and signed up for a masonry vocational training. VoTech. That's where I realized my subsequent profession, learning how to lay block.

240

About a month later I'm in my class working, and they come in and yell, 'Bunde, bag and baggage. Pack up your stuff, you're being released.' Out of the blue, I was flabbergasted, didn't have a clue what was going on. They issued me clothes to wear home, a ticket to Tucson and a hundred bucks."

"Is that how that usually happened? They'd just show up without warning. Bag and baggage? God, that's quite a system, bizarre right?"

"It was their way of keeping you under their thumb, like you didn't have any right to know anything. You were always aware that you were garbage to them, their puppet, or stooge. Powerless. So there I was on a bus to Tucson, Arizona thinking, my God, I made it. Getting a cab I asked to stop at a liquor store along the way where I picked up a quart of vodka. Hooking up with old friends, I just about downed the whole quart, smoked some hash oil and astral projected above the toilet watching myself puke my guts out. I felt like I wouldn't come back, like I'd die but was okay with all of it because at least I got out. I was free."

"And you didn't die. Sheesh, I think *I* need a drink. And that's when you connected with my old Mesa friends, Dylan, Blake and Sydney, right? But they went to the mountains and you stayed in Tucson. Didn't you say you came up there to see them?"

"Right. Ed and Dom had a party or a dinner with most of the Mesa folks. I don't exactly remember but you were probably there. You and Nick."

"I gotta ask Maggie about that. She always remembers all of those details. It's so interesting to me that we had that thread way back when. Blows my mind. It'd be so fun to locate pictures of that. Someone was always snapping away, documenting our gatherings. Small world, right?"

241

I let out a groan, shifting my weight trying to relieve the pressure on my tailbone. This was going to be such a long haul, such a test of endurance of our commitment. Frustrated, impatient, it's going to take all of my will power. And Frank is such a doll. My gracious man doing everything and anything I ask, not hovering but willing. I'd been holding my emotions in check but that evening with an upset stomach, mounting pain, and even insurance complications I couldn't take it anymore. The dam broke with relieving tears, releasing pressure so that I had a somewhat decent sleep. And I did have the splendid aid of weed, a 'highly' effective and calming pain reliever.

Having never had a broken bone this was all a learning experience. Somewhere I was getting claustrophobic sensations from the cast, the immobility, the same four walls closing in around me. A call to the nurse was somewhat useful, her suggestion to ice my leg through the cast. Surprising and why hadn't they mentioned that remedy prior? That night I had one of the most comforting and vivid dreams ever. I wondered about the combination cocktail of drugs and wine and tokes. Nick, as usual, was the focus.

-the dream-

I was in the basement where I worked- you came to me walking across the floor. You were just the same. So YOU, so kind, so wonderful. I jumped into your arms and just started kissing you, kissing, kissing. You let me but didn't return them until you simply said in a light way, almost with a little chuckle, 'hey, hey,' like that's all, and you gently moved me back from you. There was something left on a heat source in the adjacent room, smoking, ready to ignite. I turned around to find an extinguisher and when I looked again you had put it out. You had poured liquid detergent on it. There was this other guy there in the midst of putting it out. He got smudged so you took the container of hot liquid and poured it on his hand. I screamed, "NO, it's hot!" It was as if you weren't remembering that human flesh burned. I brushed it off him, apparently before he felt it.

We went back to the room we'd been in. A group of Hispanic guys, I think four, walked by us. The last one gave a motion like he would touch you and you didn't let him. To see what would happen I extended my pointer finger to him and he touched it with his, just in passing.

We sat on this old folding lawn chair, you on the middle part, me on the end facing you. I was so desperate to get my questions out, to try to remember what to ask, what I longed to know. You were so gentle and patient. I don't remember most of the responses. One of my questions to you was, 'What happened?' Very easily you said it was about a year. I was shocked, asking, trying to get specifics. 'You knew this was going to occur, you were aware, you felt something'? 'Yes,' you said. 'Why didn't you tell me?' His response, 'Didn't want to worry you.' I started to argue that we could have done something. 'Couldn't we have helped and or'... And suddenly I stopped, I understood, I comprehended fully that it was 'his time' and there was no changing it. There would have been no other outcome. I knew it and he didn't say anything else about it. He knew it, too.

Then I said, 'Where do you live?' He took me out the back door of my building and led me to a red stone wall about chest high. He pointed off, I think it was to the north. When I looked, there was a mass of snow-capped mountains, far enough to be distant but crystal clear. The appearance was bright, majestic, glorious, with an almost shimmery outline, flowing together, in a northern lights vision.

So incredibly beautiful, luminescent. He said, 'That's where I live.' I looked from one end of the horizon to the other and it was right before me in plain sight. As plain as day. He opened my eyes to see his home or dwelling place. Right there, comforting, in that it was not far. There was sky above the outline, but no ground below.

The mountains, though, the mountains, such a sight. I've never beheld anything so spectacular. Words don't suffice. And he just showed me them like—isn't that nice? He wasn't emotional in the sense of humanity. His countenance was so steady, ethereal. He exhibited an almost childlike expression but still with the essence of his manliness. Then I awoke, but the impression of him just observing, just there, is what I'm left with. He was definitely on a different plane ...not of this world.

15

'Every noble work is at first impossible,' written by someone named Carlyle. Springing off of it, I journaled. It was always dichotomous, the tearing in my soul, wanting to be healthy and let go but so comforted by the fantasy world where I am one with him.

Here it is, 4a.m. and I'm documenting as much as I can recall of that latest dream about Nick. Propped up in the downstairs bedroom, Frank's upstairs. I have guilt feelings about not being faithful, not being all in, still living so much in my past. I don't know how to let go. He's too powerful, Nick, heart to heart. Should I try to fight it more? I had therapy that first year trying to keep somewhat sane. And here I am, years later with the same juxtaposition. As if I'm not being entirely honest with Frank, not being present, having too much time to think.

Someone opined "Death is nothing at all." I don't believe it for a second. Death is everything. You can beat your head against eternity's impenetrable wall and all you get is adamant refusal. No, you are not allowed access. It is a fixed chasm between earthly and spirit where all you feel is pain and lonliness. With all of the bargaining and pleading, death will not be deferred, it will not yield. Your number's up. What happens then? Until that moment we have no clue.

It wasn't exactly depression closing in, maybe despair but combined with all of the idle hours to ponder, I was falling into a dark tunnel of loss. I thought, what is this cloak of sorrow, such a weighty blanket of shuttering silence? The abyss, who can fathom, inhaling, exhaling till the last, till we're there, till the last connection to *this* life is past. Still seeing Nick so vividly, eyes dead, foam oozing from his nose, ears as if something exploded in him. The imprint remains horribly indelible.

Closing the journal, lying back I drift off waking to the aroma of coffee wafting from the kitchen where Frank is brewing up our morning quaff, and I think, lovely. I'm lucky. Right then I decide I can't tell him about Nick's visitation, my ruminations during the fitful night. That is not useful. Nick and I made a conscious decision to not dwell on our past liaisons so as not to adulterate our present commitment to each other. Although with his college girlfriend, the three year one, I had to pry, had to know what kind of threat she was. That was my twenty-year-old mindset way back when. Nick confessed they had a less than fulfilling intimate relationship. It gave me the upper hand, totally, because even as young as I was I knew how to make him powerless to my feminine wiles. A good blow job would seal his fate! Hah! Vera's partner, Gabe, quipped, 'there's no such thing as a *bad* blow job.' And we're the weaker sex, right?

Anyway, it seemed like a good tenet to apply to this current union. Not elaborating on past relationships, that is. Let it go. Move forward.

Frank walked in carrying two cups of coffee, smiling, "Good morning, love, how was your night?"

"Oh, God, does that smell wonderful. It was alright. Not a lot of sleep but I'll nap today. Sit down here next to me," as I planted a kiss, careful not to upset our cups. "Sorry about the morning breath. Plug your nose."

246

Into December embarking on the physical therapy regimen, I'm resolved I won't be back up north for Christmas. No kids, no grandkids, friends so far, my despondency is profound. Prior to Frank I relied on my kids to provide way too much. There's that point when children become the adults, the caregivers, and you, due to whatever need, are relegated to the underling. Especially those first two years. Seriously worried about my frame of mind and pervasive isolation, Zelda, desperate for advice had visited my dear friend, Meryl. Since junior high we'd been BFFs.

"She's off the deep end and I'm afraid she won't come back, won't get up." Zelda explained, tears spilling over.

Meryl comforted her with sage wisdom having lost both parents, dealt with two failed marriages, and so many life challenges.

"I believe she will make it. She's tougher than you think and we need to communicate that to her. We can give her our strength right now. We can be her safety net. God, how long have I known her? Been her best friend? Shit, it's probably about forty years."

I never knew about that conversation till a few years afterward and when Zelda told me about it, well, my love for Meryl went even deeper. Partly due to that conversation, Zelda even came to live with me that first winter, her being in a transition phase with work and apartments. It was a godsend. When I reflect on the trajectory she'd had from such an early age, born in the log cabin, attending kindergarten through eleventh grade in the same building, in the tiniest town, a thousand inhabitants basically all from the same Norwegian genetic code. That's what probably gave her the impetus to run as fast as she could and never return. Flashing the middle finger to her senior year she bounded to college after her junior year using it as a launch pad to achieve whatever her heart desired, landing on the Houston Grand Opera and the London Philharmonic. She lit out for Italy, alone, venturing into the unknown, with side jaunts to Paris, Greece, and I can't even remember where else. Still, my baby Mesa Poleo girl hadn't lost her down to earth upbringing as she threw herself into the caregiver role.

For me, the world stopped when Nick died but both Zelda and Aaron, embarking on adult life bolstered me in the most tangible ways. As profound as their loss was it had dissimilar manifestations, even their ages meant they'd bounce back with the resilience of youth. And though Nick was no longer present I loved *seeing* him in his offspring, a gesture, something in the jaw line or smile, the eyes, an inimitable tone in the voice or a way of understanding something. It was uncanny.

All four of them, standing with me at Nick's wake, barely leaving my side, even holding me up at times when my legs got shaky, is still a marvel to me. Their strength and stamina literally kept me alive. As the line to the funeral home stretched down the sidewalk that frigid evening in February, hour after hour Aaron remained by my side, shielding me when necessary against nosy questions, impertinent clods that didn't know enough to be sensitive or discreet. Aaron would tell them to move along. Point blank. We can't talk about it, he'd say to their surprise if they were stupid enough to inquire about details. Everyone should have such a shield, a Hulk, guarding his Father love, Father's love, Fathers' love. I looked like a truck ran over me and I didn't give two shits. Wearing the same outfit for days, probably BO, I could have cared less, going through the motions, the ritual of memorial to facilitate closure. How many days prior Nick and I were

248

lounging on the pristine beach, sipping pina coladas, deciding what we'd have for lunch? Then I was running through the terminal, slicing through crowds of passengers, being escorted to the room, hand on door handle, a piercing wail ascending to the ceiling, permeating walls, corners, stabbing at heaven, cries of 'WHY, HOW, BRING HIM BACK,' from wife, mother, child, daughter-in-law, encircling wolf-pack, Luna's howl, trying to catch our breath, and finally the collective sigh, arms clenching as if to never let go.

"That's some fairly classic PTSD indicators," my therapist informed me when I related that to her. "Medication and various coping mechanisms can be of aid. Time is a major factor when dealing with this type of shock."

Somewhat encouraging, I determined to commit to her mainly for my kids. Chloe and David still in college, they needed a mom who was sane. Remembering the phone calls from Mexico to each of them, destroying our intact family.

Maybe shock is actually a way to keep one's sanity. To block out the horror, to suspend that downward spiral with a state of torpor. It seemed to cloak my psyche enabling me to cope. My therapist was brilliant in helping me sort it out.

I'd grasp each tiny improvement like a life-line, detailing hundreds of quotes in my journal like water to a parched soul. 'For each ecstatic instant we must an anguish pay, in keen and quivering ratio to the ecstasy. For each beloved hour, sharp pittances of years. Bitter contested farthings and coffers heaped with tears.' Emily Dickinson.

The conversation with Vera was so overdue. We hadn't talked in how many weeks? She knew about my calamity, even offering to come and help with my recovery but I declined.

"You wouldn't believe how he waits on me, treats me," I told her. "It gives me such security. Every morning it's like I'm horkin' up a lung with the pollen and dust here, gross hacking, along with post nasal drip, all day mopping snot! And still he dotes on me."

"Well, he better. It's the least he can do."

She was being the protector, taking offense for the injured party. I reassured her he felt horrible adding he didn't need anyone to make him feel worse. No need for scurrilous accusations.

"Thanks for improving my vocabulary," chuckling at my ten dollar word. "I do know what it means. You're not the only one with a thesaurus. You should write a poem about that rhyming with clitoris."

"Oh, that's perfect. I have so much time to write but no incentive or inspiration, and yes, I can see that working," laughing, I drank in Vera's spirit, the camaraderie. "I can always count on you to bring me up. How lucky am I to know you?"

"Back at ya, you've done the same for me, girlfriend."

"Oh and you'll love this. I was talking to my mom yesterday and she told me about her neighbor across the street who is this religious nut, which I know exactly from my holy-roller days. Anyway, when my dad was hauled away in an ambulance, he'd had a stroke, which I won't go into now, but this Carol lady came galloping over grabbing my mom's hands saying she wanted to pray with her before she followed to the hospital. So Carol yammers on and on about Jesus this and God that and wouldn't let go of Mom's hands. They're so insensitive with their ridiculous agenda until finally Mom was able to jerk away. A week later, Carol related to my mom that God had led her and her husband to sell everything and go live in a trailer park in their camper. I blurted to Mom, 'God is always saying shit like that. He's such an asshole!'

Mom cracked up, saying, 'I wish I could think of things that quick to say.'

"That's priceless," Vera said. "I love it. See? That sort of thing tells me you will come around, the way you can still hit the high note, your sense of humor. Just give it time. You'll see and you'll be fine. Let's try not to let so much time go by between our talks, okay?"

"For sure. Have you heard of slacktivism? You don't have to go yet, do you?

"No, I'm fine. I'm sure you're going to educate me."

"It's one of those social media actions that, in my opinion, lets you off the hook of actually doing something about an issue. Say, if you retweet something or *like* something on Facebook, apparently that gives you the sense of being involved or actually caring. But it does not necessarily translate into truly being engaged enough to work toward a cause. So young people in particular bypass hands-on, grass roots endeavors, not donating money or their time but simply signing a petition or some other low risk measure."

"I think the younger generation is too frustrated or exasperated with this whole system. I know my kids don't believe we are doing enough to correct the environmental crisis. And they look at the government as mostly broken. I don't disagree. If I were that young, it would be really hard to have a positive attitude about the future. It is pretty scary."

"Ya, I think about my grandchildren and wonder what the world will be like for them. Will there even be a world, although I have to believe they will have a full and rich life, they will have a planet. Like there are children that will

251

invent solutions that we aren't able to fathom. There has to be a way to fix things, right?"

"Right. That's the spirit. Keep that mentality and do what we can. Cloth grocery bags, energy efficient appliances. I wish I could afford to install solar panels and I know they've come down in price but to undertake the whole change-over isn't in my budget. I'm just trying to keep up with present expenses. God, stuff is always costing more," Vera intoned.

"Oh, yeah, I'm so glad I'm not still buying groceries for a family of six. We'd never make it. And clothes and shoes. I really feel for families. And then there's the one percent. Jesus, don't even get me started on them. With so much wealth don't you wonder how people are starving, uneducated, have no health insurance? Billionaires that could give so much more. How do they not care?"

"It's criminal," Vera agreed. "But I will leave all of that for our next conversation. Or maybe not. It is so discouraging. We need to stay on a more upbeat note, especially while you're convalescing. How's the insurance haggling coming?"

"I think his policy will pay for the medical and PT but just. It's all so goddamn expensive. The drill used to install the screws into my fibula was $700! I said, I've gotta see this drill, and furthermore, I want to keep it. But when I told Aaron about it he said they only use it one time for hygienic reasons. He knew a person who got an infected hip after surgery and had to heal from the inside out, meaning they couldn't close the entire area, having it drain constantly. She was in a wheel chair for close to a year. Can you imagine? Anyway, one insurance lawyer told me if I broke up with Frank, call him. I guess I could go after his assets. Hah!"

"Did you tell him that?"

"Oh yeah. Put a little fear of god in him."

252

"You're terrible."

"I know. And then I came up with this one. What do you call an attorney who fucks you for his fee?"

"Oh, this oughta be good."

"A pro boner."

She chortled, "You didn't tell the insurance adjuster that, did you?"

"No, but you know I wanted to. Like would you barter?"

Reluctantly I had to let her go, she had a life. We set up a phone date for three weeks hence and I went back to my jigsaw puzzle. Aaargh.

One month after the accident we went out to a restaurant, listened to a trio play some music, my mindset being that I could not be imprisoned, totally hindered by my handicap. I needed to go to the limit, determine what that was on a daily basis and reach for the end zone. A push, so to speak and if I overdid it, then I had back off. It was the only way to know. Keeping it within reason, careful, and mindful I was facing my challenge with the intent to get to full speed and force.

Frank told me, "Even if you wanted to ride, I wouldn't let you because I couldn't take it if anything ever happened like this again."

Gotta love it.

It's not always all bleak, but this season has surely gone on long enough already. Frank's been battling bladder tumors for about five years having to undergo cystoscopes every six to nine months. Treatment has been straightforward with surgery to remove the superficial tumors when necessary. Basically, in and out the same day in LasCruces, approximately two hours from Silver City. It's all done through his penis, up the canal with instruments, lasering, catheterizing him, then sending him home where he takes over the process for a week. Dosed with antibiotics and pain killers I became caregiver albeit very slowly and clumsily. Hobbling through the recovery area I almost biffed it with my crutches.

The nurse quipped, "Boy, you two are quite the pair. Can you drive him home with that cast on?"

"I drove him over here, so yes, I'm confident I'll manage," I averred, possibly a bit heavy on the hubris.

Barely twenty miles out of town Frank had me pull into Love's Travel Stop feeling pressure in his lower tract.

"I'll check the bag. It feels like I have to pee but it should just be going into the bag. Something's weird."

"I'll wait here. Good luck."

It seemed forever when he headed toward the car, his face expressing doubt, eyebrows furrowed.

"There's nothing going into the bag. It should have something in it. And I'm feeling definite discomfort even with this anesthesia still in me."

"Let's drive around the back, where the truckers are and we'll both try to figure out what's going on."

I pulled around attempting to find a space not right next to a semi where they could look down and see the whole spectacle. So with pants down, the tube in place, I noticed that the arrows were pointing the wrong way. The nurse had it upside down so of course, nothing could go in. Dipshit! She's the one who thought *I* looked inept on my crutches! We dug through his discharge papers, finding the instructions, both reading as fast as possible. Frank clamped off the tube, unhooked the bag from his leg and turned it around. You do wonder what anyone would have thought walking by. Some kinky ass shit! When he undid the clamp the urine gushed in as Frank's face noticeably relaxed.

"You should call the surgeon and tattle. What if we wouldn't have known how or what to do? That's a pretty basic procedure a nurse should not screw up."

"I might. I'm just glad to get it fixed. I couldn't figure out why I was feeling so much pressure."

"God, I guess there's no more mystery for either of us, what with your dick hanging there, my constipation and gas these past weeks. So much for private bodily functions. Part and parcel of our humanity, however frail," I offered, leaning over to give him a kiss.

I powered on, driving with my left foot, the right casted one propped up on the dashboard until I needed a break. Ordinarily I wouldn't have allowed him to drive under the influence but my tailbone felt like it was poking through my skin.

The cast is off! Relief. Four days early but there were two pressure points that were absolutely killing me so I convinced them to saw it off and have a look. What a freak out that was, watching this guy fire up the blade knowing precisely how much pressure to apply, and not slice my leg. The withered leg now looking like a stick, no definition. Sending me home with an air cast I was instructed to try some light weight bearing and one exercise for an entire month before the actual PT.

A few pounds have crept on, which I hate. I have always, my entire life, struggled with it and am not going to balloon up now. No matter what. But with no walking and mainly sitting on my ass I am having to reduce my intake to bird portions.

255

In my downtime I continued to journal, expressing the phrases and thoughts that intentionally encourage health to grow and take residence in that vacated place. The outlet is a veritable remedy for all that ails me, flowing, releasing, and even teaching the insights I'm searching for. It calls to me, gently prodding me to write, day after day, and when I resist, when I say, 'I'm sick of it,' the inner voice whispers, 'open the folder, see how long it's been since the last entry.' Invariably, it's almost always less than a week. Unquenchable bent.

I already anticipate the necessity of removing the plate as I am acutely aware of sensations if I even brush it putting my sock on. It looks so bizarre. And well, that's the bottom line, right? How it looks! Christ.

The fire was likely started by a car that had pulled onto the shoulder on Highway 90 just outside of town. As a volunteer firefighter, Frank responded to the call but was unprepared for the catastrophe that ensued. In minutes, with sixty-five mile an hour winds propelling it, a grassy field was consumed, the flames jumping right across a paved road into a subdivision. Frank and another crew member were right in the thick of it as fifteen homes burned. He finally arrived home at 1a.m. exhausted and coated with soot. I'd waited up for him, having a mild flashback to tragedy, not losing it, but definitely pondering how to protect the wounded and scarred elements of my psyche. I live under a shadow of an enduring, irrefutable cloud that whispers, 'why didn't I relish and treasure my moments with Nick more?' Remembering the pain, not far below the surface I employ a coping mechanism and a means of survival, making a plan and divorcing myself from the reality. Preparedness for loss. There's a part of me that is always cognizant of him not coming home, of the phone call with tragic news. Love is so complicated and yet I still adhere to the Tennyson belief, 'better to have loved and lost, than never to have loved at all.'

Silver City has traditionally attracted its fair share of nut jobs, eccentrics, and independent mavericks, with its rich Wild West antiquity. Billy the Kid, Pat Garret, and the likes of Madam Millie, the hugely successful purveyor of whore houses from New Mexico to Alaska. Folklore richly abounded throughout its lurid past with tales, however tall, of brazen characters. Frank's old smuggling partner had turned him on to the rural area where he now resided, Ken living less than a mile away. They weren't close friends but had kept in touch over the last decades. We'd been over to his ranch for various gatherings, soirees, as it were. Invariably, Ken would commandeer unfortunate guests with his outlandish ramblings touting conspiracy theories. A few years before I was with Frank, Ken even hired several neighbors to build an underground bunker ostensibly to hide all of them from the impending apocalypse. Frank considered selling out and moving away just to distance himself from the mania. Ken would predictably yammer on about how 9/11 was staged, how all of the stories and reports were fabricated, that there was no way buildings would collapse like they did so explosives had to be detonated from within. If that didn't exasperate you enough he'd insist that our TVs were watching us, keeping track of everything and anything and I do know the technology supports that but I'm not scared of and don't want to live in a paranoid continuum. Nobody ever landed on the moon, and on ad infinitum. I won't allow

257

myself to be sucked into such negativity. Life is reasonably good from where I stand.

Ken's oldest daughter had married Richard, the con man who was the 'brains' behind the bizarre utopian nightmare. Truly dumber than a box of rocks.

One of the lines gullible Ken fell for was that Richard's father was a billionaire. When the world came to an end, if the human population got poisoned, Richard asserted his family was in possession of vials containing an antidote that would save them from any kind of chemical or germ warfare. The scheme included every willing body in the neighborhood to construct an underground bunker, four stories down, on Ken's land which they then would be allowed to inhabit while supposedly keeping it all top-secret. With almost daily updates and alterations to the effort, one of the side-bars Frank heard, sweetening the deal, was that Richard offered to buy Ken's estate for a million dollars. Over the course of several months a total of fifteen deals fell through for one nefarious reason or another. Always some glitch. Frank did his best trying to convince his neighbors not to fall for the bullshit, not to trust a single word from phony Richard or change any life plans because of what Ken was promising. No surprise, Richard disappeared 'borrowing' Ken's Jeep along with one of his guns. Two of the neighbors helped Ken search for three days without success finally deciding to call Search and Rescue. The authorities found him near the Gila River heading toward Lordsburg. He explained that he was depressed over a million dollar deal that'd fallen through in Arizona. Plausible to Ken, the shit show continued.

Following that fairy tale a contingent of the household went to Costa Rica paid for by money Richard had garnered through a, wait for it… successful scam. With no small amount of suspicion someone discovered through an internet search a vast record of Richard's crimes relating to fraud. Richard never returned from Costa, was never seen, or heard from again. All they knew was he'd been thrown in jail for trying to skip out on the hotel bill. That was ultimately the last straw for Ken. He kicked his daughter out, the one that had introduced Richard, in an effort to purge himself of the fiasco, transferring blame to her. She had three young kids and this was winter, twenty five miles from town, and no vehicle. Neighbors saw them trudging through the snow and offered them transport into town. Ken never admitted to any wrongdoing and never apologized.

Ken's lifestyle hadn't changed much in the subsequent years. That's when I met him, experiencing an instant dislike. I noted an uncanny resemblance to Yosemite Sam in a scraggly, skinny, blonde facsimile. Forever living up to his reputation as the braggadocios godfather, he continued the downward spiral with a questionable cleaning person. Brandishing his guns in an attempt to impress Felicity, flashing his gold stash in a failed bid to get laid, he instead guaranteed his pawn status to the purported meth head and her gang. It's difficult to discern what actually happened with the fatal home invasion that took place, Ken being certifiable and well, meth? Exactly.

"Oh shit," I said, hearing a truck pull into Frank's driveway, my aversion for the pop-in obvious. Craning my neck toward the window I recognized Ken's vehicle, *his* early morning impromptu visit especially unwelcome.

"I'll go out and meet him and see if I can fend him off," Frank offered.

I lifted my hands in a prayer position, making an eek face, like Pleeeze. Vigilant, watching the conversation, now they were walking toward the door. Shit. Shit. Put on my tolerant mask. Hopefully, it wouldn't be too long.

"Ken had a break in last night," Frank announced, knowing an explanation was in order post haste in that 'try to be nice, Anne,' tone. "He wants to tell us about it and figure out what to do."

"So you're okay, it looks like," I said, with all the faux grace I could muster.

"Ya, I'm good, but barely."

"Do you want a cup of coffee?" Frank asked.

"I'm fine, thanks."

Sitting across from us, Frank and me on the couch, Ken launched into the drama, "It was about 2a.m. when I heard Serenity screaming."

"That's your daughter? How old is she?"

"Right. Thirteen. And she was downstairs, me upstairs, so I grabbed my gun running down where this guy is standing over her holding an AK47. I see another guy off to the right in the shadow and he's got another AK47. I fire at him hitting him square in the chest and he flies backward but doesn't go down. Neither of them return fire and I continue to shoot. I hit one in the neck and that bullet put him down. The other guy drags him out, they're firing off several rounds as they take off down the driveway. I gotta think they must have had bullet proof vests or that first chest shot would have been fatal. There were a bunch of footprints at the end of the driveway and blood, as they loaded the wounded guy into a vehicle. I found one of the weapons in the weeds right next to the road."

I was fairly certain Ken's daughter would corroborate the story so didn't dismiss it as complete bullshit but at the same time I was sitting there thinking, this man is beyond loony

260

tunes. It was straight out of 'Crimes Gone Wrong' or 'World's Dumbest Criminals.'

"Frank asked, "So now what? You can't let the cops know you had a gun, you're an ex-felon, right, and where's Serenity now?"

"At first light I ran her over to Tucson, to her mom's. Ya, I don't trust the law, don't think they have much crime solving expertise, and ya, there's the gun."

There'd been an incident, more like debacle with the local authorities that made national headlines shaping and cementing our opinion of present law enforcement. The saga began with a man in Deming, about an hour south of Silver City, getting stopped for an illegal right turn. The officer claimed he saw the driver clench his butt cheeks upon exiting the vehicle and dispatched a drug sniffing dog. Determining probable cause the perp was subjected to two cavity searches witnessed by multiple 'observers' after which a court order was obtained for the purpose of performing a colonoscopy to ascertain where the alleged contraband was located. To his credit, the surgeon at the Deming medical facility refused to perform said procedure citing unethical practice. So what did the cops do? They hauled the victim to the county line where Silver City cops met them for transport to Gila Regional Medical Center having ascertained consent from another surgeon having no problem with a forced colonoscopy. Imagine how freaked out you'd have been by then! No drugs were found, a lawsuit ensued, DUH!, and a 1.6 million dollar settlement was awarded. None of the authorities were punished, no charges were brought and the joke we told each other after hearing of it was, 'Well, ya, probably I'd take it up the ass for 1.6 mill.'

Those cops were not who you wanted to call in a clutch! The following day at our neighborhood meeting, six of us, to brainstorm Ken's predicament, I wondered if I should remind them all of the colonoscopy saga. Frank and I didn't seriously believe we were in any danger, concluding that Ken made himself a target by his own stupidity. I found a report online of a man shot to death but the details described it happening in town, one bullet to the neck, no name, no age, no one being charged, the victim pronounced dead in a local address and the body was shipped to Albuquerque for examination. We also heard of a flyer circulating around town soliciting any information with a tip line. All of it extremely sketchy, we tried to assemble the pieces, figuring maybe nothing would come of it. Wrong! Ken ignored the consensus and involved the cops. He had heard a rumor accusing a crooked officer of providing the vests. The mountain literally crawled with police including one of those huge black crime scene lab mobile units, also several black Escalades with the opaque windows. For two weeks every time we went anywhere we'd have some official vehicle tailing close enough to run my out of state license plate. It was all very unnerving. More interesting than some no account meth head being murdered was Ken's background as a felon, living in a palatial estate never having worked a job or paid taxes. 'Splain that one to me.

Much to our relief, the entire drama fizzled, questions remained dangling and our fractured relationship with Ken was likewise fatal. Through all of that craziness I still loved the area, the Gila mountains, and fully believed the neighborhood would settle back into its desert rhythm. Frank and I sat on his north portal watching the shadows color the hillsides, first gray, then deep purple. Seeing all the way to the distant snow-capped Mogollons, I thought, if he ever sells this place he has to advertise it with the tag line 'Million Dollar Views.'

"You know, I sit here thinking," Frank opined. "The mountains don't change, they're not the least bit affected by the tragedy that happened a half mile from here. They're not bothered. There they are."

"I love that. Love you. Here we are. Just here."

We take a deep breath and exhale. Ken sold out and moved to Mexico. End of story. And I think it is. Let's hope so!

I couldn't wait to get back to Dendrobia and carve out some girl time with Vera and Blair. Usually a two and a half day drive, this time I made it in two long ones. Crossing the state line from Missouri into Iowa the sky blackened dramatically, in minutes. Heading north on I-35W through DesMoines the radio was issuing warnings about multiple tornado sightings. Altering my course I turned east keeping a wary eye on my rearview mirror. Ahead it was clear, noticeably brighter and I bumped up my speed concocting a line of defense if I was pulled over. 'But officer, I'm trying to outrun the tornadoes.' The gods were with me, I was spared arriving home safely. After the night's repose in my own bed, with a steaming cup of coffee I sunk into my favorite over-stuffed chair to hear the local morning headlines. The lead story reported a total of seventeen tornadoes that touched down in western Iowa, including an EF4 that utterly flattened a small town but fortunately, no deaths.

Before I left New Mexico I'd insisted Frank see a doctor about his painful trigger finger. It had been bothering him for weeks and honestly, I was tired of hearing the complaints. I think men really do like to whine and gripe garnering sympathy and/or special treatment for the least thing. Oh my god, you'd think it was a broken leg! If the male gender had had babies, our species would have been extinct in one generation. His finger would lock up and when he'd snap it straight it really killed. I guess with me not there anymore to listen to his sniveling, he'd gone to the doctor who ordered an EKG, standard for pre-ops. Apparently the finger required surgery to cut open the restricted section of tendon. His EKG showed some abnormalities, the cardiologist asking about dizziness, fainting or shortness of breath to which Frank denied symptoms. Sending him home with a twenty-four hour monitor, wires were attached to his chest recording every heartbeat. Hearing that, you can imagine how I slept. Not. I kept telling myself he'd be fine, there'd be nothing wrong, he'd live a long life. It wasn't a death sentence. All of my less than kind words evaporated taking a back seat to his currently more serious dilemma. Funny how that happens ... when I'm away, when he may be in jeopardy, my cynical heart melts. I could feel my soul calling to him, longing for the closeness as I searched my memory for every sensory remembrance, the vibrations, his fingers pressing gently into my shoulder blade. I'd trace the creases on his neck, face, soft whiskers, that adorable shock of white hair. And sexy, YES, even brooding at times, the way he seemed to transport himself far away, beyond the temporal, his zone. Just here. I wish I were there. Missing is beautiful, endearing, deliciously enticing, missing those sweet lips, tasting.

Mommy fuckin' dammit! His heart dropped over 200 beats in 24 hours. Two days later I was back there. No shit. We were both in shock. I'd packed my car. Again. Cancelled the plumber, window consult, all of my plans and lit out at dawn.

When I called Vera to explain, she all but hollered, "You're what?"

"Frank needs a pacemaker and he says I don't have to come but I'm going. I have to. No way can I sit up here while he undergoes something like that."

"But how can you manage it? You just got home two days ago. I need to see you. I'm coming over, just for a while, and a hug, okay?"

"Sure. You can help me load up the car."

It might have been better if I hadn't seen her. Like don't know what you're missing. We were tempted to dive in and slam a couple of shots but my inner turmoil kept a lid on it. I had to keep my emotions and tears in check knowing if I let down at all I'd spiral out of control.

A day and a half later I was in Silver City. I really booked but I was freaked. My experience with Nick, the fact that it was Frank's heart, his heart! I didn't even question it. I just went. Along the highway I indulged my classic anxiety, going down the rabbit hole of loss picturing myself alone, bereft, no longer going to New Mexico. Don't die. Please, I prayed, give us more years. Frank reassured me that the doctor told him it was routine and I knew I had to pull it together and buck up before I got there, and I knew I would. With the help of Xanax.

"I'm writing a song," Frank jokes. "Prepare to meet your maker, your pacemaker."

"Very funny. I'm glad you have a good attitude."

"You're the best thing that's ever happened to me," he says, pulling me onto his lap.

I answer, "You're the best thing now."

I have to say it that way. He understands.

Anyway, we're trying to keep it light in a pay it forward mentality. We drove into town and gave away two hundred dollars to homeless people. I've had a decades long custom to give food to the homeless, canned goods, fast food meals but this day we agreed to do the cold, hard cash. We were both trying to keep our minds off the procedure, that gnawing in my innards threatening to pull me down... and back.

He didn't receive general anesthesia, just a local and morphine IV but when they sliced into his chest, he shouted, "Hey, I can feel that."

Craptacular! Another of my family's oxymoronic colloquialisms. Jesus, talk about setting the tone of anxiety. After another shot of local the nurse told him he could watch it on the monitor but one glance and he almost threw up. An anti-anxiety med would have helped, and ear plugs. It seemed reasonable but no one suggested them. I was almost ashamed of my worry and questions, they treated it so nonchalantly. Doing hundreds of pacemaker implantations must produce that kind of ambivalence but *your* loved one, Frank, is the only person I'm concerned with. Don't they get that? Released the very next day, significant pain is worrisome but I'm being a dutiful caregiver. Honest. When it is a bona fide need I can step up and be the best nurse. He didn't have any symptoms prior and afterward he now complains of flutters and other weird things that make him stop short to catch his breath. The doctor reassures him it's fine, normal. The heart simply doesn't like to be messed with.

Slipping outside to take the call, I saw Maggie's number come up on my screen. I didn't want Frank to hear our conversation knowing I needed to vent. Thank God for my girlfriends. I believe there is tremendous value in disclosing your soul to someone dear, like psychotherapy, but free. A listening ear combined with compassion and deep connection can sometimes take the place of medication and certainly benefit far better than social media. That's my personal opinion garnered over decades of treasured relationships. The disconnect I detect from the techie crowd smacks of fringe connections, a single post instead of in-depth communication. Where is the personal, one on one interaction? Conversely, I read about CBT, cognitive behavioral therapy, a form of talking therapy used to help people with mental health issues learn alternative ways of thinking and behaving in order to reduce stress. It's exactly what I employed with my close friends practically my whole life.

"I'm so glad you called," I gushed to Maggie.

"I heard from Lenore about the surgery," she explained, (Frank's ex). "Is he doing alright?"

"It was so bizarre, the whole process, implanting this device, attaching wires to his heart to make it pump at a steady pace. How do they do that shit?"

"Who knows, I'm just glad they have perfected it. I looked it up and it's supposed to be safe and effective, not many complications. Mickey sends his love and wishes for more bike rides."

"Oh, of course he does. The doctor said no motorcycles for eight weeks. You know how Frank is about his riding. We'll see if he lasts that long. Although when we were discussing the procedure prior to the date he was noticeably nervous about the possibility of dying on the table. He must have had some kind of come-to-Jesus moment because he made a statement that he was ready if that were to occur, like if it's his time, so be it. It sort of freaked me out, in that, 'oh shit, is this what I need to prepare for' way?"

"Well, I've known him for so many years, he's maybe somewhat dramatic even a little hypochondriac. He'll be fine. Tell him to think hard if he thinks he's ready, when shedding that birthday suit—don't unzip too soon."

Maggie had that inimitable ability to slice through the bullshit straightening my attitude right out with her humorous rationale. We yakked for a half hour when duty called from the restless ailing denizen.

16

After a week's recuperation and cabin fever, for a
diversion, we drove to the Catwalk about an hour away near
Glenwood. One and the same destination that fateful broken
leg day. We hiked along the sides of a cutout, a vertical rock
wall hewn by an enormous volcano eons ago. Sauntering
along metal walkways anchored into the rock above the
meandering river, it was utterly breathtaking. Carefully, we
navigated a small portion of it, he watching his stamina, me,
my footing. All along the way a yellow and black swallowtail
butterfly floated nearby. I thought it was an omen of serenity
and peace recalling a very similar one the day Nick's ashes
were scattered on the Mesa. Lovely, lilting. Was Nick
watching over? I asked him to make everything okay if it *was*
him. I do not understand but know my faith encompasses a
belief that everything happens for a reason, all tangled
somewhere amidst these recent and prior events. That vast
arc including the broken leg, the pacemaker, even the home
invasion. I kept thinking to myself, 'Please don't die.' Dread,
premonition? It will happen, like the sun rising, like sand
washing out to sea. Is that morbid or pragmatic? I know what
I know, the overpowering undertow. And this; as strong as
their presence was, that's how strong the absence is felt, so
powerful and profound, the depth of grief surpasses,
continuing forever! How I dread it.

And how mind blowing to see the actual pacemaker in his
chest. It's a disk that protrudes maybe an eighth of an inch,

269

about an inch and a half round that I need to watch out for. Like I can't press on it so I have to snuggle into his right shoulder because my head would hurt him on the left. He can't have his cell phone near it, in that chest pocket of his shirt, can't be near a car battery or loud concert speakers. His symptoms will either dissipate or he'll get used to them, but we 'don't have to worry.' Shouldn't worry. Try not to worry. God, I hate this worrisome heart, how it bothers me. Although, in the larger picture, the scope of life, this isn't that bad. We're both fitted with titanium devices now.

Aaron had his check-up today. Crossing fingers for a good report. Please. I know I'll be headed north soon. It's calling to me. Something in the air, a voice in my heart says you're needed elsewhere.

I ask gently, when he calls, "Now what?"

"Some of the lymph nodes look suspicious and one of the levels indicates a problem. At this point I don't know what any of that means. Possibly surgery, radiation..."

His voice trailed off and we let the silence hover. I did not want to hear that, the fearful undertow. It needed processing, more investigation, another opinion. My head was already on the road. The plan was for him to see another specialist, and his surgeon the following week. PLEASE! Give him health.

"Try not to worry," me, adding my sage ism, "worrying is praying for what you don't want. I'm so sorry. I'll be back there soon. I love you."

On the two plus day drive I got a call from my mom. It's a good diversion. Or not. I'm so tired.

"How could you fall for that?"

"You have to promise not to tell anyone," she begged.

She was the victim of the most obvious scam but that's why those poor elders are targeted. The call was supposedly from her grandson, my sister's kid, stating he was in jail in Canada on a trumped up charge and needed a thousand dollars immediately. Mom went directly to Western Union to send it.

"He sounded so sad, he was so upset. I talked to him."

"And you were convinced it was him?"

The Western Union clerk appropriately queried her about her surety and that this was a notorious scam but Mom insisted she was right and she needed to help him. My dad was even with her and somehow couldn't deter her. So the next call demanded three thousand and the next six thousand at which point she finally balked.

Only because said grandson, out of the blue, happened to call her, "Hi Grandma, how are you doing?"

"Jerod? Jerod, is that really you? Are you okay? Are you home now?"

Jerod, of course, totally confused, wondered what the hell Grandma was talking about and after getting the gist of the circumstances was mortified she'd fallen for it.

"But it sounded just like you," she told him.

"Ya, they can copy your voice with all sorts of technology such as voice biometrics, phone phishing, stuff like that but I'm sure you've never heard of any of that. Didn't Grandpa suspect anything?"

"Yes, he did but I was so sure it was you and you needed help. I feel like such an idiot. Don't tell your mom. I am so embarrassed."

"Why didn't you call her to see if I was in trouble?"

"Because you said you felt so ashamed and please don't tell my mom so I just didn't want you to suffer anymore."

She was telling me all of it so that I wouldn't be tempted by anything similar, I guess. I think she wanted sympathy which I gave but, at the same time, I did tell her she should call the paper and publicize it so others wouldn't fall victim of the same scam. She refused, citing humiliation. Damn, thousands of dollars! There's got to be a hell for assholes like that. Right?

Maybe some false positives, different interpretation but the subsequent specialist, endocrinologist had virtually opposite results. Aaron was encouraged by a better report, not a clean bill of health, that would be down the road, but nothing alarming or indicative of more treatment. Phew! I breathed, we all did, a sigh of relief. He'd been profoundly depressed thinking about his two young daughters, life, goals. It felt like we'd been granted a reprieve.

Even with that encouraging prognosis our annual summer family gathering was not without its prickly issues. I told Vera and Blair, 'with four kids someone's always going to be miffed at someone about something.' We'd finally had our reunion/debriefing with dinner at E.T. and the wind-up back home in my yard.

Getting stupidly tipsy, the conversation was now verging on disturbance of the peace well after that ordinance cut off of 10 p.m.

"Why don't we move it inside," I offered. "I'm not ready to let go of you two yet."

"It's so gorgeous out here, though," Vera said. "Let's have one more smoke and then we'll retreat."

"Fine by me," Blair chimed in. "You've touched on your accident, broken leg, and the bizarre home invasion and I want to hear more details. Is Frank safe out there? You said he's keeping a loaded weapon in his nightstand? Doesn't that freak you out?"

Cognizant of neighbors close by I touched my index finger to my lips, "Softer. We don't need to advertise."

We adjusted our chairs into a huddle, toning it down to almost a whisper. I related the saga of Ken's background, his strange and criminal predilection, as well as his off the wall imaginary theories of flat earth and government surveillance.

"I don't fear for Frank. He doesn't either. That's just him. Mr. Self-Assured. Not all the time but concerning that issue I'm impressed with his, ah, balls. You'll see when you meet him, his essence, and it's unassuming which makes him even more desirable. Charisma? Something."

I related the anecdote of him being mistaken for Donald Sutherland that time in Trader Joe's.

"There is a resemblance, definitely but I'd say it was more his spirit. Something. Anyway, very attractive. The whole Silver City area, the town, the mountains have this aura, an element of confidence, the wild west experience. You know they have the concealed carry law and I don't even want to think about all of the armed wackos next to me in the grocery store."

"I'm so blown away at the gun culture here," Blair said. "Look at the destruction in our country, the outrageous number of deaths, the mass shootings, the children's lives cut short. It's the most horrifying thing to imagine your child a victim. It's unconscionable."

"Oh I agree and don't know how one survives that loss. You send your loved ones off and that's what they encounter? How can they even learn anything worrying about whether or not gunfire will erupt in the hallway outside their classroom?"

After another session indoors, obstreperously hashing over particular environmental and political touchstones, waxing philosophical we concluded that the witching hour had arrived.

"Unless we want to embark on a séance or you two want to sleep over I say we call it."

They agreed helping me carry our glasses and empty bottles into the kitchen. This was a record. Three bottles and a fourth opened but unfinished, I doubted Blair's ability to navigate home. Vera was two doors down but we both insisted Blair should remain overnight.

Thankfully, wisely Blair acquiesced, quipping, "Our kids would kill us if we got thrown in jail."

"If they only knew what we got up to!"

Declaring our undying love and devotion, with kisses and hugs, we sappily and slobberingly bid each other buenos nochas.

Have I mentioned Frank likes to camp? I've gone along with the notion showing him what a good sport I can be. Why? I do not know. I've got a magnet on my fridge, with a darling lady dressed in a luxurious peignoir sprawling in lush bedding that reads, 'I love not camping.' The few jaunts have been successful in garnering my resentment of the practice and him but as well a self-disgust for my lack of conviction, feeling friction build into a conspicuous gulf. Is this simply a rough patch or am I contemplating bailing out? We've had some reality checks as of late, not surprising, but I don't want to hassle with anything. Truly, I'd rather be alone. He's shown me his moody side, which is compounded when he's out of his element.

We're in Wisconsin for the summer and the cloudy days bring on a new person. Mosquitoes force him indoors and rain prohibits riding. Hey, it could always be worse, right? My control freak is a bit out of control, by the way. Admitting my complicity isn't difficult but is this what reality looks like? There's definitely a preordained duration, most probably bolstered by chemical brain imbalance, where you refuse to see faults, or if you do, you excuse them, and ignore them. But sanity must prevail, eh? So does that chemical drain out, drip by drip? Familiarity breeding contempt? Uncertainty, hurt, sadness? Pick, pick, pick. Slights to glaring infractions all droning disaster as we side-step the inevitable. Can't you put the goddamn toilet seat down? He admits he misses his place and wants to be back there. What did I want a relationship for? I know I was lonely, wanted the connectedness, the companionship (like I had once) but that was a one-time thing. It's impossible not to compare. I don't fight. I won't. It's never been my practice. I retreat and disengage. And now I find myself pretending it's all okay because I don't know what else to say. I just want peace. I want to be myself. It's the wee hours of the night and I'm wrestling with stay or break up, break our hearts or keep on. It would be a crushing blow and I'd have to be reasonably certain of my choice to be solitary. He was in the shower yesterday, I slid in next to him wanting, needing, desperately desiring a deeper connection. But I was a phony. Water splashing my face, he couldn't see the tears. The words wouldn't come. Those destructive words, "I can't do this."

We talked it out. This growing together, searching, finding compatibility, then losing it, then around we go for another ride. I remember that song, *'is that all there is?'* I love him.

He is adorable and exasperating. Me? Well, I'm a piece of work. Failings, shortcomings all over the place. It's what a mature relationship looks like. He's set to leave anyway, heading for Sturgis, and then home to New Mexico, so I'll have ample time to miss him and morph into a doting paramour. Ah me.

I'm relishing the sufficient time to spend with my girlfriends whom I feel I've neglected this past year mainly due to the boyfriend. I don't want to be that girlfriend. No, I will make a conscious effort to not be her. Because I do love women in all of their oddity, eccentricity, depth, strength, resilience, craziness!, insecurity, and their like-minded individuality. Bodies with variant characteristics; short and frumpy, long and elegant, personalities including morose and flighty, raucous and reserved, my girlfriends inhabiting variant spaces and stages of my life, the longest, Meryl, over fifty years! It's my life blood, what with their intuitive intelligence, artistic and beautifully gracious energy, infusing as well as taking from me, not leaching but using as it were, what they need or require. Despite scars and offenses that date back to junior high, relentless remembrance of rejection taught by catty cliques of competitive cunts, I absolve all of that with true relationships. I warned my sons to watch out for feminine wiles, their frappe of swirling drama. Girlfriends should be a mostly safe endeavor, albeit we're all flawed, evolving with respect, wisdom, experience and of course, deliciously titillating gossip. For the most part, at this age I try to surround myself with people who want the best for me, those I cherish, trust and depend upon. I simply love them. This is also on my fridge, "A friend may well be reckoned the masterpiece of nature." (Emerson) I believe it with all my heart.

276

I know people look at me thinking I have it all going on, that my life is full and fabulous and I can't argue with that especially by comparison to some but why do I feel something's missing? Could be because my parents didn't validate me, forming a core foundational insecurity. When do I say enough? When do I let it go? Rest, be assured, take pride in what I've done? It's a tough one. When I'm gone from here, this home, in a couple of days I just want to get back here. And after a few days at the next place I'm wondering where to go, who to see. I can hear my mother, Edith, "you don't always have to be going somewhere." But I DO, it seems. Is there a point? Ya, that's what I am looking for. I came home from Chloe's in Madison with the intention of having a fabulous dinner for Blair's birthday at Etoile Cuisine and after, oh say an hour, I was ready to bail. The scene was so hip-crowd infecting me with wannabe seeds. Sucks you right in. Oh, oh, here I am with the beautiful people, it's so happening. My misanthropic undertow and at the same time, my desire for popularity or approval compete for expression. The Gemini in me arises with a familiar dichotomy. Can't I find a comfort zone where I can BE? Am I still reckoning with Nick's and my life being short circuited so I'm waiting, trying to find that 'rest' of my journey? The direction it had been on for 31 years plummeted off the cliff into the abyss and here I stand on the edge peering for his hand. Evolved? Healthy? Another magnet on my fridge, depicting those 40s female homemakers, has this caption, 'Medicated and Motivated.' Good advice.

Frank's been to Costa Rica a dozen times and is convinced I'll love it as much as he does. I am trying to get onboard, listen and learn ... patiently. It's the southern border, the foreign country that causes anxiety. I jotted this down with thoughts of letting Frank read it, but who knows?

Don't push. Be respectful of my wishes, especially my grief. Don't bulldoze me, running over my convictions, my positions. Don't frustrate what meager control I cling to. Empower me. Encourage me to take charge of my life, owning my feelings, expressing them firmly, unequivocally, arguing my will, my intent, my belief. Support me when you don't agree and if that's not possible then step aside while I claw my way back. No apologies. I'm too volatile, vulnerable, raw. I'm better but limited, so defined by boundaries too narrow, too constricted by my experience. It is true — what happened to me, a widow whose married life disintegrated, in those few jolting seconds. I am a lot better—honestly, tears not all dried up, not even very far away, but feeling this sense of accomplishment, cautiously upbeat on any given day, being tempered, not knowing what will be, what tomorrow will bring. Who's guaranteed tomorrow? The life force demands preparation to remain, preparation to succeed and bear the valley of the shadow, dealing with trips to Costa Rica, with tomorrows as if we have innumerable, acutely aware the fragility, the vulnerability of what we are. Resisting anti-depressants not wanting an alteration to who I am, I've lost too much. I want to hold onto truth and purity of feelings, my emotions. ME. I'm getting used to it, this life. Time is my friend. Time, my helper, and salvation ... till the moment passes.

I want to tell him all of this but I won't. My deepest feelings and thoughts are sequestered too far down into the buried recesses of my soul. So our trip is planned, set for a

278

week hence and I *am* going with so much apprehension but like I stated, I wish to appear whole.

"It's been so long since I've been there," Frank related, bemoaning how many years have slipped by. "How long's it been since you were to the ocean?"

"You don't want to know."

"Oh, why?"

"Because it was when Nick died," I confessed. "I'm trying not to let it affect me, but it's definitely there. I've been to the east coast, Maine, when Aaron lived there, but I'm absolutely bringing a plentiful supply of meds."

There was no way out. We were on the second leg of the plane ride into Liberia, Costa Rica.

"Oh, you'll be fine," Frank said, in his way, which is why I cannot show him what I wrote because he's being dismissive. He has no clue. And how can he? How can I explain to him my Mexican tragedy, what Nick's dying in my arms on the beach did to me?

Worst case, I'll cut it short and fly home. I will give it a shot, acquit myself judiciously, as Jane Austen put it, but I'm leery. How did I agree to six weeks? What was I thinking? It's too long to be so far away. No, I was thinking I need to do this and *can* do this, face my demons. Jesus, talk about schizophrenic!

By day four I realized I was in serious trouble. Xanax was the only way to hold steady. Sleep was interrupted and erratic more due to dogs and monkeys than my emotional state. If I could just rest I think I could have relaxed but flashbacks freaked me out and I couldn't bring myself to open up to Frank even though I knew I had to. He didn't know what was going on and didn't dare ask.

After two glasses of wine, hand in hand we walked down to the beach to enjoy the sunset, "I know I have to try to explain my quandary to you. It's not you, first of all."

"God, I couldn't figure out what was happening. I tried to think of what I'd done and wanted to give you space but I want to help. You know that, right? You can trust me," Frank offered.

That broke the dam, leaning into him I let it out unloading my heavy heart, "I can't stop seeing Nick on the sand, hearing the sound his body made hitting the ground, it's so vivid. I'm taking Xanax, which does help but..."

He held me speaking softly, gently, "It'll be alright."

That's all. Exactly what I needed. Understanding, comforting wisdom. Not a huge soliloquy.

And then, and this was so profound, he stated, "Nick's spirit is all around here. I sense that. It's why you feel so much."

I was speechless. Perceptive and insightful, it was absolutely true and that Frank had the sensitivity to understand that, well, it was the turning point. Lightened, unburdened, quite altered from the heaviness I was lugging, we watched the sun sink into the ocean with a graceful end to the day. Finally.

One week has elapsed with body surfing, languid swimming, walking to the mercado, eating simple fare, coupled with the reality of constant warfare against sand fleas, stingers, mosquitoes, gnats, and ants. Oh my god, the ants. Lines of them stretching up the wall, across the floor and ceiling. Food is only secure in the fridge or over an open flame. Geckos, lizards and iguanas are everywhere but not invasive like the insects. There is certainly no Shangri la.

I'm bent on seeing the green flash, the phenomenon that occurs when the sun is setting on the horizon directly into the ocean. At the final moment, precisely the last sliver of yellow/red there's a burst of neon green. If you blink, you miss it, barely a second. Also, I have delighted in seeing the efflorescence in waves along the shoreline at night. It's the action of the water breaking with a full moon overhead. As it beams along the top of the wave the light reflects through, shooting something akin to an electric glow along the length of the foam. The multi-colors dance with sparkling movement. I marvel at the natural elements.

There is a flip side. Always. The inequity between the haves and have nots, a mere one block away from the tourist regions, one senses the insecurity fraught with danger, scammers, and thieves. I don't like having to watch my stuff, ever mindful that we have valuables and someone else doesn't. The disparity is immoral, the hovels nearby with half a dozen children, laundry hanging along fences, garbage and junkyards exposing the abrasive class system. We're warned not to leave anything unattended on the beach, not to leave bicycles outside at night. I would never make this trip alone, that is, without a strong male presence. My Spanish is meager, Frank's better so between us we are able to manage and he has the monetary system mastered, so there's that.

The six week sentence/vacation is going to be a stretch, so much so that I'm researching how to change my ticket to adjust the time frame. No surprise, Frank is not amenable to that so I'd have to go it alone. So much for my hero.

On a chat with Chloe, back in Madison, she tells me it's eleven degrees. Sheesh!

"We ate at this sketchy restaurant last night and this morning it blew out as expected. No more mystery, hearing the asshole turn inside out!" I told her.

"Ewww! TMI," Chloe whined.

"Sorry, I am fine now, and lesson learned. Pablito's Revenge. That was the joint. Well, not Revenge. That's my sobriquet. Frank was spared, his iron stomach the victor. He is so easygoing it's maddening. He lolls along like a local, just handling everything. I'm such a baby, although I don't think it's that unreasonable to want basic comforts."

"Well, why did you agree to his suggestions and all?"

"He was the authority, having been here ten plus times, staying in these places, even knowing some of the inhabitants. I trusted his decisions and expertise. But we have very different styles and needs. The discovery phase."

"So come home," Chloe bluntly suggested, getting impatient with my bellyaching.

"Shit, it costs way too much and I have convinced myself that I can tough it out. And then I'll break up with him."

"Seriously?"

"Fuck if I know. Maybe. I'm just being an asshole. It's not his fault. I've got to suck it up and get back up."

I didn't explain to Chloe that I had flashbacks of her dad dying. She didn't need to have that heaped on her. She tended to be the worry wart anyway so why divulge? When I'd visited her in Madison shortly after Nick's death I'd been out for a walk and this was the first time I experienced a meltdown in public. As an ambulance approached, siren blaring, I started hyperventilating, my legs turned to rubber as I sank to the ground. Plugging my ears I closed my eyes and was right there screaming down the highway in Mexico. Out of nowhere, a young man knelt next to me gently miming to put my hands over my mouth.

He said, "Like this."

Relief was almost instant as if a divine intervention. He smiled and went on his way. An angel. I never mentioned that to Chloe either. I recalled how she had these peculiar idioms when she was a tyke. She'd ask if she could 'wear' bare feet when the weather turned balmy, like you put them on. And could she have 'lips on' when she'd observe me putting on lipstick like that is how your lips appeared. Smiling to myself, I vowed to lighten up.

It wasn't Frank's fault. I didn't bring it up with him because I wanted to adapt, wanted to be the woman that had this successful relationship with this man. He helped initially but I could tell he figured now I'd gotten that out of my system so nuff said. PTSD doesn't work that way. It's one step forward, two back, an ongoing condition that runs deep with no cure. With three weeks to go I believe I will put the ocean on my not-to-do list. It's going to take a lot more alcohol.

Our next destination was Tamarindo, driving there in a rental car from Samara.

Breakfast tasted fine but two miles down the road I hollered, "Pull over!"

Jumping out I hurled the whole meal while holding my hair back taking care to miss my shoes,. I'm hunched over in front of the car retching and this family comes walking around the bend just ahead. Mom, Dad, four children, a dog, no, two dogs. I try to finish puking so I can jump back in before they get any closer. It's totally obvious what I'm doing, and I'm thinking, Jesus, God, we have to get out of there before the dogs run up and eat the pile. GAWD! I make it, slamming the door, pulling away. Don't look back. Never look back.

What a relief and a terrific find. Mono Loco had a comfy room, a pool, and a short walk to the beach for the next six nights. Eggs seem to be the culprit, I've deduced, now with a third similar reaction and they aren't refrigerated so I'll cross them off the menu. I've all but ruled out traveling by car though, with roads unequivocally treacherous pitted with rocks, ruts, cave-ins, no signs to give any clue as to where one is. With our language barrier we were lucky to get anywhere. Frank put a sizable dent in the front bumper, I added a few scratches, but actually with the way the locals drove we were fortunate that's all we suffered. Haysus Kristos! Our adventure to Monteverde and San Alena (Arenal Volcano) had its challenges but the rain forest, butterfly garden and waterfall were gloriously rewarding. The stairway down to the bottom was fashioned into a rock wall, no hand rail with one foot rises on a lot of the steps, making it extremely dangerous requiring all of one's concentrated caution with every move. Don't fall, my intoned mantra, the entire descent. Almost as perilous, the drive back down from Monteverde on a switchback dirt/rock road conjured images every second of tumbling over the bank into the gorge. To add to the drama we got lost traversing the same route three times before we discovered the way out. Frank regaled me with an account of one unfortunate trip on that very same road where TWO of his tires were punctured on the jagged rocks. He left his wife and another couple behind as he hoofed several miles for assistance.

The last leg of our journey was spent back in Samara at a cabina just feet from the ocean. On our afternoon beach walk we'd noticed a for rent sign in front of the cabina. A fascinating man, Jaime Koss, a local artist in his seventies, was outside gathering inspiration, setting up his paints for the day. Striking a deal for the final week it proved to be a beautiful note to end on. We celebrated our anniversary that first night purchasing lobster from the day's fresh catch. Fishing boats would dock on the beach after diving all day, offering delectable fare for a few colones. If I'd known about Jaime initially, I would have opted to spend the bulk of our time there. We appreciated his company, sharing lunch, conversing as he stood filling the canvasses with idyllic scenes. Around two he'd knock off taking a siesta till evening. Jaime doled out tidbits of wisdom from his vast experience including teaching at Stanford, showing his work in Santa Fe and living in San Francisco until Costa Rica beckoned him home.

Over lunch the next day Jaime mentioned that his town had a reputation for harboring fugitives, some personal compadres of his.

"So is this generally a safe place or not?" I queried.

"Well, I guess, in some ways but you have to consider crocodiles, dengue mosquitoes, venomous vipers and driving."

"Right, we've come unbelievably close to countless head-ons, swerving out of the way around blind curves. What is with the drivers?"

"Oh, they're completely wild and crazy. I don't own a car, either I walk or bike. And never, ever drive at night. You can't tell where there might be a sink hole or pot hole and if you do break down or have an accident a lot of times banditos purposely use something like that to rob you. They'll cause an accident and then shake you down."

"Jesus, if I'd known all that I think we'd have opted

out of a rental car."

"And you've heard about all of the kidnapping?"

"Only when I googled hazards in Costa Rica prior to coming here. Is it rampant?"

I could see Frank was not enjoying this conversation one bit.

As if I was. He deliberately stayed mute through the entire exchange, me thinking, if I'd only known!

It seemed to trigger Frank's long buried memories of his own checkered past plus he was obviously intent on changing the subject as he launched into a bygone era elucidating our interested neighbor.

Frank had a singular style, running his construction company true to old habits, making it routine to knock off at the end of the day with happy hour, calling it beer thirty. All of the guys would gather around their trucks and drink a six pack apiece. From there they'd often make another trip to the liquor store or head to the bar before going home. Designated drivers? Hah, not so much. That developed into official (and infamous) crew parties up at the Santa Fe ski basin involving the entire weekend with a diet of mushrooms, cocaine, and a ton of drinking. The families were included albeit with enough responsibility to segregate the debauchery from the children, sometimes feebly. At least, the kids weren't allowed to use! After four increasingly wild blow-outs Frank had the foresight to end the practice before someone got maimed or killed, but not before he, himself, had the infamous tour de force coining the 'fire roll.' He'd stumbled, unable to avoid the fire pit, and deftly flipped right through the flames. Not surprisingly, his move became a daring game among the wastoids known as, you guessed it, the 'fire roll.'

I understood Frank had had a serious addiction to heroin but was reluctant to know the particulars. Some things you just can't unhear. It came out the following evening after dinner with Jaime.

"I'm interested in your story, Frank, and where you went with your company. How could you keep on, working hard, managing so much along with drug and alcohol abuse?" Jaime asked.

Frank responded, "Let's clear all of these dishes away first. I want to make a cup of tea. Anyone else? Jaime?"

"Sure," Jaime answered. "Do you have ginger?"

"I'll look. Honey or sweetener?"

"No thanks."

I slipped into the kitchen and poured myself another glass of wine. The evening was perfection with enough of a breeze to ward off flying pests. We sat on the picnic table in front of our casita, a mere thirty feet from the ocean being lulled by the softly roiling surf. These were the moments and experiences that saved me. I was going to survive. Yay me!

Settling back into our intimate retinue Frank unfolded the next installment.

"My addictions hadn't deserted me, those unrelenting demons and with the independence of an overseer, I fell into a pattern of laissez-faire floating from job to job, operating and coping in a drunken, drugged cycle, sometimes not ever appearing at a job trusting in my supervisor and foreman to keep the progress on track. The responsibility, the pressure weren't going to stop *me* from having fun. Referred to as the 'Phantom Mason' I kept my crew satisfied with good pay and continual work."

"But my body was breaking down. Aches and pains, muscles, vertebrae always something reminding me of the aging process. It was hard to face. I couldn't admit it or deal with it. I indulged and medicated with a shitload of coke. I finally hit the skids. After decades of over-indulgence, still raking in substantial paydays, blowing equal amounts up my nose, I experienced personal life failures, separating from my wife, and then, just like that, one day this guy gave me the solution. The single introduction to heroin altered everything in my life. The very first time with every pain dissolved, experiencing the unparalleled high, my craving was immediate."

I interjected, "I'd always heard that about heroin, back in my hippie days, vowing never to try it because I *knew*, somehow knew, it would kill me. It had that cache that most probably one time would be enough to ensnare you. I had two good friends back in high school that had that same thing happen. Exactly like you. One time and bam! One of them hung himself and the other one is clean and a substance abuse counselor."

Frank seemed to be on a roll, maybe this was a trial of sorts, for me, if I could be sympathetic, if it would be a turn-off. I didn't know, but he was intent on baring his soul, however ugly. Or maybe he knew he'd never see Jaime again so it was basically anonymous.

In the ozone for months, then years, the harsh eye-opener struck when Frank lost his connection. Up until then he hadn't realized it had taken over his existence. No longer boss, he was taking orders from the smack. And he needed his fix. Flu symptoms, runny nose, diarrhea attacked. He was a closet junkie, hiding it from this crew, his friends, family, maintaining his business, even able to lay block like the young punks. Better living through chemistry, as the saying goes. Once or twice a week at first, then five times a week

288

until it was four times a day. It started out with $25. a day then $50. That ran him $350. a week but his body screamed for more until it was $100. a day. $35,000. a year for the final two years. He began to say, 'come Monday, I'm done,' resolving to kick it. Every junkie's illusion. But you don't have a choice. That went on those two years with Frank abstaining no longer than a few hours before he caved.

Frank's voice faltered, "Sinking lower, unable to make any headway, I finally surrendered to a detox center in Taos. Too ashamed to admit my failings, I told my crew I was going on an extended motorcycle run."

"I didn't sleep almost the entire first week of pure hell. Wide awake all night, nerves shot, unable to relax, skin crawling, diarrhea, runny nose. Through a rehabilitation program called Amistad, out of Espanola, New Mexico, I was one of the miniscule percentage that succeed. Clean for five months, I had to try it one more time. It didn't produce the desired, anticipated effect, even causing me to throw up which must have been the universe stepping in for an assist."

"That was the end of it," Frank stated. "I realized this was my last chance. Now or never. Clean and sober, I scaled back my business to the point where I had to pick up my tools again and join the laborers. And if you don't think that was a downer. Bricklaying is a young man's job and that was not me. At that time though, the whole industry was winding down, the boom was over and I was totally disenchanted with Santa Fe. I'd passed through Silver City on a bike run and now it seemed like the right move to retire there."

"Does it make you feel special, in some way?" Jaime asked.

"Yes, that I survived and made a good living, being able to pay for my kids' college, but also, I will always be grateful and humbled and try to give back. I'm committed to the 'program,' I do an outreach to the local detention center and know it's one day at a time. Forever."

"Costa Rica has a huge drug problem with poverty and corruption fueling the industry," Jaime offered, "drivers are paid off regularly succumbing to the lure of big money. Workers within the customs agencies are bought off so that the certified seals on containers can be replaced after traffickers load them with cocaine. It's well known and rampant practice for corrupt insiders to pass information about container movements and also the specific seal numbers to pass through inspections. I don't know how we're ever going to stop or even slow the flow with such high demand."

I said, "It makes me wonder about the local saying, 'pura vida,' like maybe they should think up something more apt. I haven't seen much evidence of pure life in the time we've been here."

We packed so much into the six weeks, to negate or ignore the growth, to diminish the hardships would be a failure of missed education. I know I needed some time to gain perspective and assess what had truly transpired. Life is for learning, every day stretching. I confess, part of me wanted to stay there, away from the demands of home, being spared the news, mail, phone, responsibility, finances and taxes. Yes, this country has been complicated, the heat up to one hundred and five at times but we made it. Sort of. When we returned the rental car they passed us through without a hitch.

"I thought for sure we'd get charged for the damage. How could they have missed that?"

Frank quipped, "Dumb luck. Let's get the hell out of here before someone notices."

As the Liberia airport came into view, in the time we'd been there, they'd completed this humongous 21st century facility. When we'd arrived at the old airport I wondered if they actually had electricity. No shit! We'd deplaned onto the tarmac walking across a darkened span about fifty feet to a pole shed. It was like receding about fifty years. Anyway, I kept looking over my shoulder expecting the rental guys to be gunning for us. Dodged the bullet on that one.

"Happy homecoming and happy fuckin' Valentine's day to me, eh?" I chortled to Vera, debriefing after the extended absence. "I could give a shit. It's better than a broken leg, or what does Frank like to say? Better than a poke in the eye with a sharp stick. That's what I think about Costa Rica."

She asked, "Are you and Frank going to last?"

My pat answer, "Fuck if I know. I've asked him for flowers several times and decided it's useless. How lame is it to beg for a romantic gesture? I got him too late," I say, with humor not rancor, "He really is one of the good ones. All told. There's times when you know something is right, when you know it's going to work, like with Nick, the decades in which we developed and melded into one heart, mind and purpose."

Vera wisely offered, "And then there are others where you go back and forth for a long time, possibly all the years you're together but whichever you may find yourself living in, you give it your best shot and try to make it work. I can't say why, but I do believe in the end, it's worth it."

"I agree. Well, for now, at least. Today. I do know six weeks of continual togetherness is way too much. If we ever do live under the same roof it will have to have two separate

291

wings and a common kitchen area so we can safeguard our privacy, independence and personal interests. He says you have to build something that way. I say a construction project like that would definitely end with one or both of us in body bags. I tell him I won't murder him. He says, he *probably* won't."

"Let's end on that humorous note," Vera said. "I bet we'll end up living together, in our senior, senile years."

"Vera, it is one of my wishes, to outlive all of our men and live in a condo complex with my favorite girlfriends. God, I only hope!"

Life is a gift I relish and treasure and I intend to die young, no matter how many years I am on this earth.

Full Circle: **STILL . . .**

Still so much fragility in me,
          hidden by bravado.

The tears pour over a welling
          of my lower lid
          to cheeks
          that anticipate anointing.
I lick my lip and it's salty,
          and I miss the taste of my sweet love.

Sitting on this faded plum, nylon chair
          you bought,
          I don't remember where or when,
but you scoured the back roads along the Mississippi
          before you discovered it,
          paying twenty dollars.

          Better than that was the wrong turn onto gravel,
"I found this clearing enclosed by walnuts and red oak,"
you'd tell me,
          knowing I'd fix a picnic basket
          and we'd spend a sun-bathed fall afternoon there
          immersed in the nature
          of each other.

          I can still close my eyes
                    and feel your soft breath
                    in my ear
                    six years after the ocean
                    called your name.

ACKNOWLEDGMENTS

First I would like to express appreciation to my initial readers urging and guiding me in the pursuit of excellence :
Leonore Hildebrandt, Alethea Eason, John Kjome, Kate Towle, Annie Kile, and Deb Snider.

I am extremely grateful to Scott, Val, and Terri for being willing characters, compatriots in my complicated life.

My gratitude extends to the entire writing community in my radius that has given me a place of expression and belonging.

Praise for *Get Back Up (once more)*

In *Get Back Up (once more)* Lynne Zotalis invites us to accompany her on a raw and deeply personal journey. It is with her, on this rocky, challenging road that she courageously illustrates the tragedy of loss and it's steady and dark influence. "...trying to find that 'rest' of my journey...the direction it had been on for 31 years plummeted off the cliff into the abyss and here I stand on the edge peering for his hand."

In some ways, Lynne reels through this loss, and through her grief, experiences more of the same. Losing friends, experiencing the disrespect of heartless passers-by. "According to the laws of conservation and energy, not one whit of you is gone, you're just in a different state." Life is not impatient, nor is it impartial. Lynne describes her repeated challenges as a means for catharsis, a path to some level of healing. Anger, frustration, disbelief are all on the canvas of her experiences. "I dread the next loss, but I don't live there." These are the details where darkness, personal strength and will are shared with us. Lynne has not only taken off her clothes, she has torn away her skin, exposing her wounds and her determination to engage in this life we all are gifted.

Get Back Up (once more) takes us down one of life's more difficult pathways. It also reminds us of our inner strengths, the value of those individuals that appear in our lives only for the purpose of making us better humans. This story leaves us with a lovely message at the end of this incredible ride: "Life is a gift I relish and treasure and I intend to die young, no matter how many years I am on this earth."

--- Hank Blackwell, author of *Closer to the Door: Poems on Aging*

Get Back Up (once more) is a pleasure to read. I found it funny, poignant, and full of all that messy stuff that makes life worth living.

> --- JJ Amaworo Wilson, author of *Nazaré*

Lynne Zotalis has lived a rich life, with her arms wide open and her heart full. She has experienced extraordinary love and profound sorrow. Her books tell of a life well-lived, fierce and bold in every chapter, unapologetically embracing whatever may come. Her honesty and authenticity vibrate on every page. It is a privilege that she trusts us with her story. Thank you, Lynne.

> --- Deb Snider, BA, MA, MFA, Artist, Lover of words

Lynne Zotalis's acclimation to her new life is both vivid and colorful. At times, it's as if she's operating in a dream, at a carnival in a house of mirrors. Finding a glimpse of normalcy or grounding to launch a new version of herself is the treasure she seeks amid post-loss fogginess. With resilience and humor Lynne is sustained with a powerful presence to muddle through an unmooring time and set of dynamics. I do so value the sense of wonder and poetic skill throughout *Get Back Up (once more)*.

> --- Kate Towle author of *Sweet Burden of Crossing*

In *Get Back Up (once more)*, Lynne Zotalis picks up where her memoir *Hippie at Heart* left off, but this sequel also stands perfectly on its own. In vivid and frank language, Zotalis takes the reader along her path of mourning and her search for healing, for new friendships and love. Deftly, she lets us meet memorable people and takes us on bizarre adventures. Through it all runs Zotalis' wonderful sense of humor and a wit that simply uplifts.

> --- Leonore Hildebrandt author of *Where You Happen to Be*

In *Get Back Up (once more)*, Lynne Zotalis rips apart any assumptions about what it means to be a woman of a certain age in 21st Century America. Bawdy, irreverent, hilarious, this book is also exquisitely poignant as it captures the reality of losing those we love the most and the courage it takes to live a full life in the wake of grief.

> --- Alethea Eason, author of *Charlotte and the Demons* and *Whispers of the Old Ones*

Ms. Zotalis' protagonist navigates the life of widowhood in a tale etched with pathos, chaos and rollicking humor. This isn't a work directed solely toward women but a story that will resonate with all who have lost a loved one.

> ---Mark Fleisher, author of *Knowing When* and other books of poetry.

Made in the USA
Monee, IL
24 February 2025

12694808R00168